DATE DUE

HARVARD STUDIES
IN COMPARATIVE LITERATURE

Harvard Studies
in Comparative Literature
Founded by William Henry Schofield

2 I

VISSARION BELINSKI

(1811–1848)

A Study in the Origins of Social Criticism in Russia

Vissarion Belinski 1811–1848

A Study in the Origins of
Social Criticism in Russia

HERBERT E. BOWMAN

HARVARD UNIVERSITY PRESS

Cambridge, Massachusetts

1954

F Preface

or all but the specialist in the literary and intellectual history of Russia this book will serve, if it serves in any way, as an introduction to Belinski. So far only one other volume in English has been published about this major Russian critic: the Soviet translation of a Soviet anthology, entitled *V. G. Belinsky: Selected Philosophical Works.** Unfortunately, the selection that is there made from Belinski's writings is only partly representative of his whole development. In any case such a book, even if it were without faults, is no rival of mine, since it has been my interest to do something quite different: namely, to present a critical analysis of Belinski's intellectual career. To this end I have concentrated upon the main lines of his evolution, trying to make sense of it and to discover whatever unity it may possess. Belinski's published articles, written on a wide diversity of authors and works, fill a dozen sizeable volumes. It is obvious that a book like mine could not be expected to present the total Belinski in this sense. Instead, I have aimed to present the total Belinski in another sense: to give here all that one needs to know in order to understand him. Necessary to this design is, of course, a discussion of all his major articles, as well as of his most important personal correspondence (which alone fills three volumes). All translations, of numerous prose passages and occasional lines of verse, are my own.

In pursuit of my subject I have undertaken to give the non-specialist reader some introduction to the intellectual and cultural situation in which Belinski lived and wrote. That situation is of interest not only because it helps to explain Belinski himself, but also because those times constitute, as it were, the adolescence of

* Foreign Languages Publishing House, Moscow, 1948. 552 pages.

the Russia with which we coexist today. Certain dominant attitudes, certain ways of conceiving the problems of Russian culture, were shaped in those years. I do not mean to contend that Russian history began in 1811, with the birth of Belinski. But it is a distinctive feature of modern Russian history that the early decades of the last century were extremely decisive for the subsequent direction of the national life.

Among the fundamental problems of cultural life which were formulated during the first half of the nineteenth century in Russia is the problem of literature. Nowhere else at this time is it possible to find such anxiety in the asking of questions about literature: What direction should it take? What is its function? What relation does it bear to the national life? Since, among the many Russian intellectuals who concerned themselves with such questions, it is Belinski who first tried to arrive at a comprehensive and systematic statement, any study of Belinski is obliged to become a study in the relation between literature and society. This is what the following essay was originally designed to be.

Just as my interests in this essay have included both the study of literature and the study of Russian intellectual history, so I have a main obligation appropriate to each interest to acknowledge: to the Department of Comparative Literature and to the Russian Research Center of Harvard University. The basic pattern of the present book was first worked out in the form of a doctoral dissertation for the Department of Comparative Literature. Professors Harry Levin and Renato Poggioli of that department have both given me support of many kinds. Although the Russian Research Center did not sponsor the present study, I have it to thank for a research fellowship which allowed me to continue my study of the Russian intelligentsia. Professor Michael Karpovich of Harvard University and Professor René Wellek of Yale University have given me valuable advice and even more valuable encouragement. Finally, I wish to thank the Committee for the Promotion of Advanced Slavic Cultural Studies for its financial help in the publication of this book. Since such acknowledgment as this is my only way of repaying these debts, I am glad of this chance to make it.

                                                    HERBERT E. BOWMAN

CONTENTS

VISSARION BELINSKI
(1811–1848)

CHAPTER ONE

Introductory: Literature and Society

The Problem

An *interest* in the interrelation between literature and society leads not into one study but into a field of study. The history of the subject follows not so much the evolution of an answer to a single question as the unrolling of a series of episodes. The intellectual curiosity or moral concern of the time must decide into what momentary form the continuing theme is to be arranged. The poet's membership in the republic; the fitness of vernacular language for poetry; the claims of inspiration against established canons of taste; the artist's revelation of the spirit of his age — each formulation of the larger problem may suggest a wholly new and independent range of speculation.

Out of the many possible directions into which a study of the relation between literature and society can lead, modern criticism often takes a special interest in devising a sociology of literature. And it is true that of all artistic creation literature may seem the most easily accessible to the social philosopher, since it is expressed in the social medium of language and is always to some extent engaged in the portrayal of social relationships. Yet the chance is also great that social theory will be often frustrated in the effort to account for the work of art, which by its nature displays all the ambiguities of an incorrigible individuality. To admit, as at least one Marxist critic is willing to do, that art is the Achilles' heel of historical materialism [1] is only to admit that all spontaneous self-expression bristles with problems for generalized social theory.

Confidence in a social interpretation of literary creation may take support from a readiness in the contemporary artist himself to abandon claim to special authority as prophet or as legislator, acknowledged or unacknowledged. A disorderly modern world tempts the artist to make an aesthetic or pious or sophisticated or scholarly withdrawal from the traffic of an acquisitive society and to assert his private claim of independent vision in estrangement or aloofness from the world of affairs. Retired as lawmaker for his society, the artist comes to be defined as its creature.

Meanwhile the isolation of the artist becomes one of the targets against which a social interpretation is aimed. To the solitary artist is refused the privilege of seeing in his works no more than a creation of private fancy. Such a refusal may tend to violate the nonchalant spontaneity of the creative passion, but at least it works to dignify the activity of the artist. Too deliberate an effort to see how "from literature it is possible to reconstruct the entire social, political, and economic life of a people" [2] may bring on temporary blindness to the permanent condition of art, but at least the fault of such a view consists in the exaggeration of the virtue of taking the artist seriously.

Recognition of a relationship between literature and society may find its basis either in the proposition that literature is the unconscious expression of social institutions or in the quite different contention that the literary artist should consciously dedicate his work to the elaboration of social themes. These two positions are not only different, but they may appear to be mutually exclusive. Yet historically — and psychologically — the first proposition has had a way of bringing the second into being: from seeing literature as an expression of social life, the theorist goes on to argue that the best art is that which most clearly and fully reflects social conditions.

The effort to interpret the work of literary art as an expression of social institutions may begin far from any attempt to make art tendentious. The long history of systematic speculation upon the sociology of art, distinguished by such names as Vico, Montesquieu, Herder, Hegel, Taine, takes its origin from an interest in a philosophy of culture more or less free from the formulation of dogma. But even the objective recognition of an interdependence between art and society always provides a basis from which orders may sooner or later go forth, that the artist consciously portray his social milieu. J.-M. Guyau's study, *L'Art au point de vue sociologique*, provides one eminent example of how the disinterested consideration of "art from the sociological point of view" is quickly transformed into an eagerness to rule that "le but le plus haut de l'art est de produire une émotion esthétique d'un caractère social." [3] The ease with which Madame de Staël could move from a study of literature in its relations with social institutions (*De la littérature considérée dans ses rapports avec les institutions sociales*, 1800) to the formulation of a program for French literature (*De l'Allemagne*, 1810) is only one historic illustration of the proximity of literary theory to literary policy. Every systematic statement of what art is offers the materials for a systematic statement of what art should be.

The requirement that art become conscious social criticism need not in itself, however, endanger the artist's spontaneity by requiring that art be held to a propaganda service. Precisely in the interest of making literature into valid social criticism, the author, it may be argued, must remain free, in an unhampered and undirected judgment upon actual life. In other words, the exponent of the artist's dependence upon his society may still argue for the freedom of art. Thus G. V. Plekhanov's insistence upon the artist's obligation to his society still allows him to hold that if a writer works merely to illustrate an accepted argument, he is then no longer an artist but a publicist, regardless of the form in which he works.[4] Even a revolutionary as active as Trotski can disparage the attempt to crystallize a "proletarian literature," recognizing that so long as literature remains creative it will transcend a given historical stage of social development.[5]

The peril for the artist which hides in his employment as a public servant must inevitably appear, however, whenever the struggles over social policy become intensified. Only temporary safety can then be found in the compromises which may be offered: as in Trotski's readiness to allow art to "make its own way by its own means" — since "the domain of art" is not one "in which the Party is called upon to command" — and at the same time to impose a sentence of death upon whatever in the free domain of art appears harmful or inexpedient for the social program, since "the artists who are created by the Revolution cannot but want to speak of the Revolution." [6]

The eagerness of the social reformer to use the artist to his own purposes is only one expression of inherent competition between artist and reformer. Art engages energies which any program of social reform seeks to monopolize. Such alienation of affections may turn vigorous art of any school into the enemy of the political operator who divines in the activity of the artist a pole of attraction lying outside his own field of influence. Not only does the perspective of the artist tend to overlay that of the social and political activist, but the very objectivity of art threatens to disintegrate the purposiveness of social reform. However willing the reformer may initially show himself toward the artist's demand for independence, he is continuously liable to see in that demand a counterclaim to which he cannot allow completely free assertion. The defense of a free literature which was so passionately made by nineteenth-century Russian liberals came to its collapse after the Revolution at the hands of their descendants.

The inclination of the political reformer to bend art to his plan parallels in the world of practical affairs the systematic effort of "totalitarian" social theory to exclude whatever it cannot interpret in its terms. Here perhaps the most conspicuous illustration is Marxist literary criticism.

Marxist philosophies of art claim to reëstablish the dignity of the work of art against its prostitution within an economy of private profit. For although, by the tenets of historical materialism, artistic activity is assigned to an ideological superstructure, yet, one Marxist argues, "it does not follow that art plays merely a secondary role (as Pisarev would have it, putting a shoemaker above Raphael); on the contrary, it is the idealistic exaltation of art over material reality which results in the ascetic debasement of art to the level of its more sensuous relationship to life." [7] Capitalist economy, in Marx's own view, by its dominant concern for exchange value and corresponding disregard for the intrinsic value of the objects of exchange, provides no effective motivation for appreciating the work of art as an end in itself; "capitalist production is hostile to certain branches of spiritual production, such as art and poetry." [8] "Viewed from the standpoint of the objective relations of capitalist society, the greatest work of art is equal to a certain quantity of manure." [9]

But the theoretical requirement of Marxist theory to place artistic creation in a dependent position contradicts whatever claim it can make to having dignified the work of art. Historical materialism must ultimately attack the authority of the work of art by reducing it to a reflection of a "material" reality which is alone autonomous. The theoretical difficulties created by such relativism appear nowhere more dramatically than in the province of art. For if art is the creation of a psychology determined by a specific context of socioeconomic relationships, how can the art of a particular time and place continue to make its appeal to other times and places? A fully consistent materialism would seem to destroy the validity of any such continuing appeal. Marx himself could not be taken as a model of consistency in this detail. He was willing to announce a private admiration for the art of Greece despite his own cultural distance from Greek society. He even ventured to suggest that Greek art can provide a norm for all succeeding generations, who can hardly hope to surpass the artistic excellence of the ancient Greeks.[10]

Can this inconsistency be resolved within the Marxist system? Apparently not by Marx himself, who escaped into an *ad hoc* explanation of the continuing attraction in Greek art as the appeal of "normal children" to a modern world in its complex maturity.[11] Such an interpretation, however respectable, remains a digression from the main theory out of which an aesthetic was to be fashioned. It suggests the unsystematic and unsatisfactory conclusion that a separate account must be made for each work of the past which the critic happens to admire. Such a requirement ceases to be a test of an aesthetic theory and becomes instead a test of critical ingenuity.

It may be noted in defense of Marx that he did not proceed to deny his private preference when it appeared to erect a stumbling block for his theory. The obvious alternative is to deny value, except documentary, to all works of the past — of yesterday, almost literally. Such thorough denial of the past in art can force the creative impulse into only one possible avenue of expression:

a fanatical utopianism which leads directly away from the present concrete reality which all true art portrays. In conformity with a theoretical refusal to validate any experience which is felt to transcend time and place, the critic with a completely relativistic aesthetic must deny the experience in order to preserve the theory. In such an extremity the aesthetic is emptied of all content by becoming a system of generalization about experiences which no longer take place.

The bankruptcy to which a closed system of relativistic aesthetics is ultimately brought threatens every effort to explain the work of art by an analysis of social institutions. Perhaps the temporary salvation of every sociological aesthetic lies precisely in its failure to achieve a closed system of interpretation. The intellectual kinship between the explanation of art as the expression of national and social institutions and "the identification of the artist's individuality with a definite political principle," as the Marxist recommends,[12] may not be immediate, but it remains potential.

The Bias of the Russian Intelligentsia

The hazards of a conscious insistence upon the interdependence of art and society are perhaps nowhere more available to observation than in the literary history of modern Russia. Main currents in Russian cultural life during the nineteenth and twentieth centuries have constantly worked to direct Russian critical thought toward a sharp awareness of the social role of literature. In the first place, the intellectual elite in modern Russia has traditionally performed the combined tasks of social philosopher and literary critic. In important cases the two spheres of activity become identical. This feature of Russian intellectual life expresses a peculiar cultural situation, which crystallized with the emergence of a well-defined and publicly active "intelligentsia" in the first half of the nineteenth century.

It became the function of the Russian intelligentsia to maintain constant surveillance over national affairs generally by passing critical judgment — artistic, philosophical, political — upon the whole state of Russian social and cultural life. Collaboration in this critical function constituted the major criterion of membership in the intelligentsia, for in every other respect its members remained free to assume differing or antagonistic positions. The common cause remained the cause of Russia: her enlightenment, her general welfare. All workers in that cause belonged to a single spiritual community, in which the accidental differences of social origin and private life became irrelevant: whether their class alignments were aristocratic, plebeian, or mixed; whether they lived together as friends or enemies or in merely casual awareness of one another; whatever the differences in their formal education, intellectual competence, or moral character; indeed, whether or not they agreed in any important principle in the philosophies by which they passed judgment upon Russian national life or in their conceptions of the best methods to be employed in giving any social or political philosophy a practical expression.

The degree to which the attitudes of the intelligentsia tended to be radical is partly a measure of official oppression and social isolation. Precisely because they set themselves up as critics of the existing order, these self-appointed tribunes, whatever the character of their thought, were certain to embarrass the authorities, by whose lights the very attitude of criticism or freethinking was condemnation enough. The government's stupidity and ruthlessness in suppressing free thought naturally became in its turn an object of critical censure to its victims. By such a tragic or ridiculous evolution even the most harmless opinion could give a start to a career of radicalism. But even more important than official censure in making for radicalism among the intelligentsia is the fact that its members constituted an exceedingly small contingent within a multitude of inert or hostile humanity — a few bright candles in a dark night of popular ignorance or indifference. A sense of being few against desperately great odds helped in itself to cultivate the spirit of a militant minority predisposed toward extreme positions and extreme measures. Looking up to see an insensitive, arbitrary officialdom; looking down to see a vast herd of characterless subjects of the realm aimlessly at large; looking across at each other to see disagreement and disunity among a handful of potential collaborators — the members of the intelligentsia were from any point of view certain to be impressed by

the hopelessness of their isolation and, as an inevitable consequence, to develop the moral and intellectual belligerence that
inspired radical philosophic and political attitudes.

Inspired or irritated by his assignment to an almost single-
handed critical attack against the total structure of Russian national life, the member of the intelligentsia was stimulated to
direct his criticism against the entire foundation of Russian cultural existence. He thus inclined toward "radicalism" in the sense
that he busied himself not merely with pruning the dead leaves of
national culture but with a deliberate probing at its roots; not
merely with specialization upon a selected pathological detail but
with an examination of the total organism. Consciousness of an un-
resolvable social problem in national dimensions has constantly
weighed upon the spirit of the Russian intellectual. Hardly elsewhere in the modern world has so much intellectual energy been
expended in efforts to define the role, the mission, the needs, the
destiny, of the national life. With whatever justification, this preoccupation with crisis in Russia has given continuing stimulation
to the mentality of radicalism.

Thus reinforced by historical events, the tendency to take a
critical attitude toward the national culture in its entirety led,
among other consequences, to an inclusion of all cultural activities
under a single judgment: to a sharpening of the sense that no
single organ of the national life would function regularly until the
total organism was regulated. Particularly in its origins in the
nineteenth century, modern Russian literary criticism, carried
forward at first by an intelligentsia of such "radical" or "totalitarian" mentality, moved toward a social criticism which judged
any particular literary work or current at least partly by its contribution to Russian cultural identity and enlightenment, as the
expression of the national society and also as the vehicle of cultural advance. To be sure, major currents in modern Russian literature run counter to this utilitarianism. Indeed, part of the inspiration of such important movements as Russian Decadence, Symbolism, Acmeism, Formalism, can be found in their reaction against
the confinements and distortions of the social interpretation of
literature, and in their exuberant desire to restore to literary art
its full freedom. But even such major attacks as these upon the

"civic" conception of art did not work toward an absolution of the Russian artist from the responsibility of performing a civic function. Rather the broadening of the confines of art made for a broadening of the artist's responsibility. An eminent example is Alexander Blok (1880–1921), probably the foremost Russian poet of the twentieth century, whose sense of vocation as a voice of national prophecy was acute and tragic.

The tendency to take literature "seriously" finds its most deliberate expression, of course, among the critics. The gravity of his assumed obligations to his public so weighed upon the Russian critic that he typically adopted not only a grim but often also a grandiose sense of mission. A Russian literary historian has defined this moral duty of the critic in explicit terms: "The critic who is without a leading principle which has been rigorously thought out and which is religiously adhered to, is a negative quantity rather than a positive asset to any . . . literature. Over against the world of external reality, he should represent a rich inner world of personal morality, a soul of unbounded receptivity, and a mind occupied by serious reflection. Every fact should find in him an answering echo; both the trivial and the important phenomena of life should stimulate in him the activity of disinterested thought, concerned only with truth and justice." [13] Such a heavy pressure of obligation was bound to shape the very definition of literary criticism — which, in its more extreme "utilitarian" or "civic" forms, came to be primarily concerned with the public to which it was addressed and which it proposed to "enlighten" by means of the interpretation of literary works. This insistence that literary art perform a work of national enlightenment is by no means confined in Russia to the critic. The names of Gogol, Dostoevski, and Tolstoi alone may serve as dramatic reminders of the Russian artist's preoccupation with his moral mission within Russian society. Only in rare cases, however, did the Russian literary artist show himself ready to impose upon art the moral and ideological demands which leading Russian critics of the nineteenth century commonly made.

The conception of literature as an expression and guide of the national cultural life made a particularly effective appeal to the intelligentsia of the second quarter of the nineteenth century —

a period marked by the conscious effort of a great nation to come of age. The dominant problem of the period is nothing less than to determine and to articulate a cultural identity. "All men the least bit wakened to thought set out around this time to seek, with the fervor and greediness of hungry minds, the foundations of a conscious rational existence in Russia." [14] It would not be easy to find another example in similar dimensions of an entire national community turning in upon itself to resolve the riddle of its existence. The student of the period is sure to be impressed or amused by the gravity and extent of its deliberations. But the age is by no means a time of merely dilettante philosophizing about grandiose theoretical propositions. Not less notable than the extensiveness of the philosophic effort is the "fervor and greediness" with which it is made. Questions which strike us today as almost hopeless in their sweep stand at this time as the urgent problems of a vigorous national life. It is this uncommon combination of largeness and urgency in the philosophic quest which gives the period its tremendous adolescent overflow of intellectual intensity.

This age, which might be called "the Age of Belinski," is conspicuous and perhaps unique in its preference for phrasing the contemporary cultural problem in the form of a question about the relation between literature and society. Such a formulation has, of course, a genuine appropriateness. The relationship between the literary artist and his milieu does indeed incorporate the whole relationship between the individual and society. And it is characteristic of Belinski and his contemporaries to have insisted that a conception of aesthetics requires first of all a conception of culture. "What should our literature be like? What should it express?" was a specific way of asking, "How shall we feel about our world? What kind of reproduction shall we make of it?"

The intellectual concern of the period might thus be called "aesthetic" in the largest sense; it is so at the same time in a more restricted sense. For the period of Belinski's lifetime it is difficult to exaggerate the seriousness of the attention paid to literary creation, at least by an enlightened minority. Belinski himself remarked frequently upon this characteristic of his age, as when he wrote: "It might still be said without exaggeration that only in art and literature, and consequently in aesthetic and literary criticism, does the intellectual consciousness of our society find expression." [15] One obvious reason for this fact is the official censorship to which the expression of political and social opinion was subject throughout the reign of Nicholas I (1825–1855), so that literary forms came to be employed as camouflage for rebellious ideas. But such an explanation is only partial. Also important is the paramount influence of Western literary and philosophical theory during the first half of the nineteenth century: of European romanticism generally and of German romantic thought particularly. German romanticism not only shared the high regard for the poet and his work which characterizes nineteenth-century romanticism generally, but it was distinguished by the degree to which it made that emphasis a subject of serious and technical philosophical elaboration — notably in the systems of Schelling and Hegel, which constituted dominant intellectual influences upon Russia of the twenties, thirties, and forties.

In their awareness of the problem of Russian literature and Russian society, perceptive critics like Prince P. A. Viazemski and Prince A. I. Odoevski realized already in the twenties that until Russia atttained a higher degree of cultural self-determination, its literature would be doomed to vacillate between extremes of imitation of foreign models at one pole, and a narrow provincialism at the other. Too free an adoption of the civilization of the West could expose Russia to the danger of national formlessness; by the triumph of a narrow nationalism, on the other hand, Russia was put in danger of being reduced to a meager cultural content. Such are the very simplest terms of the complex and sustained debate between Westerner and Slavophile.

Belinski as Representative of the Intelligentsia

The foregoing outline may be enough to suggest the nature of the intellectual battle which raged for half a century among a maturing Russian intelligentsia. The foremost representative of this decisive era was Belinski. He has often been acknowledged as the central figure of his age: for example, by the novelist, Ivan Turgenev; and by the critic, Nicholas Chernyshevski.[16] Issues which seem irritatingly abstract find their incarnation in his emotional and intellectual existence: in his private happiness and unhappiness, his relations with friends and enemies, his journalistic career. The entire philosophic development of an age, from the idealism of the thirties to the socialism of the forties, is worked out in the battle of his personal development. The quest of his life, as of his time, is a philosophical quest, primarily in pursuit of the nature of social and cultural reality in Russia. To this exclusive interest all his critical judgments are subordinated, often at the peril of his criticism. He bears no mark of the eclectic or aesthete. If his intellectual career seems almost a patchwork of borrowed ideas; if the voracity with which he attacked available intellectual nutriment, often badly prepared and painfully digested, becomes at times pathetic or ridiculous; nevertheless the purpose which animates his shifting thought remains single and constant. Throughout his critical activity, in all its zigzag perambulations, moves the continuing tension between an unacceptable reality and a relentless effort to find its justification; between an imperfect culture and its fulfillment in art.

Belinski's job as critic required him not only to formulate general propositions but to handle the tangible data of artistic works and tendencies. While he may be privately busy fighting cold sweats and hot fevers in changing metaphysical atmospheres, he must make some kind of public reckoning with the books and authors of a growing literature. Perhaps that activity and the zeal which he brought to it compensates for the bad philosophy and worse composition which he frequently inflicts. Yet with all his faults he is perhaps more useful for an understanding of his age and its concerns than would be, for example, the purely speculative philosopher, even of the greatest intellectual finesse. For in Belinski the theory of the interrelation between Russian literature and Russian society continued to depend equally upon an evolving national literature and a changing social philosophy. To the question of the relation between literature and society Belinski's career provides a response in which the most urgent demands of a speculative age as well as the most spirited inquiry of an earnest critical mind find their voice.

Finally, Belinski still stands today as the major progenitor of the Russian tradition of social criticism. Modern Russian criticism has not always followed his commands — has, indeed, on occasion deliberately flouted them. But succeeding critics have always recognized their filiation with him, even if only to lament it. Iuli Aikhenvald (1872–1928), one of Belinski's chief opponents, has argued that Belinski's authority is based on a personal "legend" rather than upon an actual achievement; but the critic who so argues then proceeds to make a more sweeping claim for Belinski's influence than even the firmest personal legend could support: "It is precisely Belinski who in large degree is to blame for the fact that the Russian cultural tradition lacks stability." [17]

Belinski's immediate followers, the "Men of the Sixties," insisted that they were his disciples even as they forced his ideas to march toward extreme positions which he never defended and which he would have considered indefensible. This is what Dmitri Pisarev (1840–1868) called completing the ideas of Belinski.

Wherever important Russian literary movements, such as Symbolism or Formalism, have arisen in defence of the integrity of the work of art against "civic" exploitation, Belinski has been condemned. Thus his enemies have paid their respects to him. Meanwhile the tradition of civic or social or utilitarian criticism, which Belinski did so much to set in motion, has emerged dominant in Russia. Indeed, it has carried all before it in contemporary Russia; so that in the present Soviet world Russian literature has become a perfectly faithful servant of the State. It could be wisely argued, to be sure, that Soviet criticism, far from continuing the older "civic" tradition, has violated and destroyed it, by forcing literature to become the flunky of a particular political regime. But the fact still remains that Soviet critics continue to draw strength from a critical tradition which, as molded by Belinski and his followers, does effectively place over the literary work a fundamentally nonliterary judgment. If official Soviet criticism has subjected that principle to a degenerate interpretation, it must at least be admitted that the original principle lent itself easily to the change.

The tradition of social criticism is no chance occurrence in Russian intellectual life. Belinski, who has been blamed for establishing it, was in fact only its spokesman. Its roots lie deep in the cultural soil of modern Russia. Its hold is reinforced by the same

strength which helped to vitalize the masterpieces of the nineteenth-century Russian novel: namely, an insistence that the work
of art consider man in his wholeness; that the artist be first of all
a complete human being and a responsible member of his society,
a "citizen"; that art never be permitted to become an esoteric or
dilettante or professional function. This moral passion which
dominates the life of a Gogol, a Dostoevski, or a Tolstoi rises
almost to the pitch of hysteria in Belinski.

Belinski's greatness, indeed, rests almost more upon his powers
of righteous feeling than upon his critical acumen. He provided
an emerging critical tradition with a passionate and resounding
statement of principle. It was not a systematic statement; without
doubt one important reason for Belinski's perennial usefulness is
that critics of a variety of persuasions can quote him to their
purpose. Into a major phase of Russian literary and cultural development, he came not so much as its systematic analyst, but rather
as its evangelist. His contribution to Russian criticism was less a
gift of mind than a gift of soul.

Thus it turns out that Belinski has been most sharply attacked
precisely for those features of his criticism which constitute its
historic significance. Aikhenvald, in the famous indictment referred to above, charges Belinski with the capital crime of incoherence and vacillation, so that "it is impossible ever to come
to rest on any valuation or judgment which he makes, for in the
next year of his life or even before that, you are given a completely different, often exactly opposite judgment." He is "a critic
without a system of criticism" ("kritik bez kritiki"), who "began
well and ended badly," arriving at the close of his career at "the
enslavement of art," so that "Paul reverted to Saul."

Yet, as Aikhenvald partly admits, these very faults are characteristic of a legend which has played an important part in Russian
intellectual life. By his very vacillation and lack of system, Belinski
proved his earnestness. And it was by earnestness, by personal
conviction, almost more than by reasoned argument or critical
illustration, that Belinski defended his major thesis: that Russian
literature is and must be the free conscience of Russian society.

CHAPTER TWO

Russian Reality and German Idealism

L*iterature* should be the expression of the character and opinions of a people. Judging by the books which are printed in our country, one might conclude either that we have no literature or that we have neither character nor opinions." [1] In these lines Prince Viazemski sounded in 1823 the keynote of Russian critical thought as it was to proceed for several decades. The two major propositions of his statement continued to serve as first principles throughout the decisive era just ahead: the theory that literature should be the expression of a people, and the accompanying admission that Russian literature failed to meet that requirement. This brief description of Russia's cultural situation having been made, a radical diagnosis is suggested: perhaps Russian literature has failed to express Russian character and opinions for the melancholy reason that an independent Russian character and a clearly-defined public opinion do not exist.

The stimulus for some of the most trenchant critical thought of the twenties and thirties continued to be an unhappy realization of the emptiness of Russian cultural life. Perhaps the most effective elegy upon this Russian death-in-life is Peter Chaadaev's (1793–1856) famous first "Letter on the Philosophy of History," which in its Russian translation from the French carried enough force in 1836 to knock out of existence the journal, Nicholas Nadezhdin's *Telescope*, in which it was published. To his compatriots Chaadaev cried: "Look around you. Is not everyone standing with one foot in the air? We all seem to be on a journey somewhere. . . Even in our homes we seem to be in an encampment; within our families we act like strangers. . . There are lost souls in all countries; with us, this is the general condition. . . Alone in the world, we have given nothing to the world, taught it nothing." [2] In so declaring in the mid-thirties, Chaadaev distinguished himself mainly by the incisiveness with which he put into words a feeling common among his contemporaries for more than a decade: the sense of "one foot in the air." The Russian lack of method in the conduct of life, of logic in thought, the weakness of any tie with a past or a future — these charges merely repeated a familiar indictment.

The absence of clear direction in Russian cultural life about which the critics of the twenties and thirties complained had been created by a tangled set of conditions: on the one hand, an increasingly energetic repudiation of Russian imitativeness; and, on the other hand, an obvious failure to find adequate intellectual sustenance in native sources. So perplexing was this combination of circumstances that the Russian critic stood continually exposed to the famous paradox advanced by Madame de Staël: imitate a foreign model in order to become original.[3] Out of the battle with that paradox the opposing forces of Slavophiles and Westerners were ultimately to emerge. In the twenties and thirties, however, those two currents could still intermingle within a single critical stream. Thus in 1830 Ivan Kireevski could argue for the study of German philosophy in Russia precisely to the end of establishing a philosophic basis for Russia's own individuality: "We *need* philosophy; the whole development of our mind requires it. Only through it does our poetry live and breathe; it alone can give spirit and coherence to our immature sciences, and perhaps our very life will borrow from it the beauty of harmony. But whence will it come? Where shall we seek it? Of course, our first move toward it should be a knowledge of the intellectual riches of that nation which has surpassed all others in philosophic speculation. But the ideas of others are useful only if they develop one's own. German philosophy cannot take root in our country. *Our* philosophy must develop out of *our* life, out of the current questions and dominant interests of *our* national and private existence. When and how, time will tell; but the interest in

German philosophy which is beginning to spread among us is an important step toward this goal." [4]

The poet Dmitri Venevitinov (1805–1827), in an article written during the latter twenties, joined his contemporaries in decrying the imitativeness of Russian culture: "Russia has received everything from without . . . hence the complete absence of freedom and genuine achievement. The origin and cause of the slowness of our success in the field of enlightenment has been the very speed with which Russia assumed an external form of culture and erected a false structure of literature without any foundation, without any exertion of native strength. . . Our position in the literary world is a completely negative one." [5] But his charge of imitativeness is immediately followed by a proposal to undertake a study which could have only one contemporary source: the foreign body of German philosophy. "Philosophy and the application of philosophy . . . these are the subjects which deserve our special attention; subjects all the more necessary for Russia since she still lacks a firm foundation for an aesthetic and since she will find that foundation, that guarantee of her independence and hence of her moral freedom in literature, only in philosophy." [6]

The prevailing uncertainty of intellectual direction may be accounted for at least partially by the relative poverty of native scientific and intellectual achievement. Both stimulated and thwarted by dependence on the West, intellectual life in Russia at the beginning of the reign (1825–1855) of Nicholas I made a forceful effort to abandon outworn imitations of the West and to turn to the building of a more truly national culture. It is that effort which was chiefly responsible for plunging the young intelligentsia of the time into an endless search for new directions. If youthful critical minds display at this time a force which seems to explode in all directions at once, it is primarily because they stand "between two worlds, one dead, the other powerless to be born."

One important cause of this contemporary intellectual perplexity is well illustrated by the fate of romanticism in Russia. The "romantic" revolt against "classicism" in Russia was losing its force already in the twenties. The fact that romanticism in Russia could be only a superficial importation from the indigenous evolution of other people's literary traditions inevitably made precarious the existence of Russian romanticism. A borrowed romanticism is no romanticism at all. The very readiness to accept loans from foreign literary cultures violated in Russia precisely that cultural self-reliance which had become one of the rallying cries of romanticism in the West. The Russian traditionalist thus stood closer to a genuinely romantic philosophy of culture than did the imitator of the West who thought of himself as a romantic. This fundamental incoherence in Russian romanticism limited its creativeness and no doubt shortened its life. Already in the mid-twenties Kondrati Ryleev (1795–1826) decried the artificiality of continuing in Russia a quarrel between classic and romantic which made sense only in Europe.[7] He wisely recommended that the sham battle over words and definitions be abandoned in an effort to return to the cultivation of poetry itself, since there was only one true poetry. It is to this argument of Ryleev's that the future of Russian critical thought belongs. The major effort of the years ahead was to be the formulation of a native tradition of creativity untrammeled by the definitions of foreign schools of thought.

As Belinski was to point out in 1834, the watchword of the thirties was "national character" (*narodnost*) in literature.[8] That major concept has a wide scope of meaning and connotation; but before all else it is a reminder of the fact that the emphasis in Russian literary thought had come to be placed almost exclusively upon the creation of a literature which should grow from native roots. The term "national character" merely phrases the problem of a national literature; in attacking the problem so phrased, all the rival forces in Russian intellectual life came forth with their favored solutions.

This quest for national self-expression was motivated in Russia partly by nationalistic sentiment. Even the most acid criticisms of Russian culture carried with them a statement of belief in Russia's potential powers or destiny or present greatness. Thus Nadezhdin, after a critique of Russian imitativeness, takes a respectful look at the grandeur of the Russian state and prophesies the future glory of "holy Mother Russia."[9] Even if such patriotic outbursts can be set down as only a proof of Nadezhdin's opportunism, yet at least they show that the exaltation of national feeling was not considered out of keeping with a critical analysis of national life. Kireevski, whose motives may have been purer, similarly closes his critical "View of Russian Literature for 1829" on a note of "hope and faith in the glorious destiny of our native land," who, like the youngest daughter in a large family, is already rich, before her entry into the world, with the experience of her elder sisters.[10]

The literary expression of patriotic feeling remains, however, beside the main point of the new "nationality." Literary patriotism in modern Russia was at least as old as Nicholas Karamzin (1766– 1826) and journals such as *Son of the Fatherland* (*Syn Oteche- stva*) and *Russian Messenger* (*Russki Vestnik*) had already been established in dedication to the glorification of Russian life. It is true that the interpretation of *narodnost* as simply patriotism would continue to be made by a faction led in the thirties by Nicholas Grech, Thaddeus Bulgarin, and Osip Senkovski, sup- porters of "official *narodnost.*" But the interpretation of the term which confined it to its place in the official slogan of "Autocracy, Orthodoxy, and Nationalism" played only a negative and re- actionary role in the literary renaissance that was to take its origin in the term *narodnost.* In any case, the real problem of the thirties and forties was not that of creating patriotic sentiment but of establishing a philosophy of Russian life which could give shape and direction to a patriotic enthusiasm universally shared.

As with all words effective as slogans, the term "national char- acter" drew part of its appeal from its very ambiguity, which allowed it to mean all things to all men. But ambiguity is also a sign of uncertainty, and uncertainty marked the debate over the definition of the term because it marked every literary and aesthetic argument out of which a satisfactory definition could come. As it was employed in the literary discussions of the second quarter of the nineteenth century in Russia, "national character" in literature meant essentially a quality of artistic work which is achieved when the national individuality has been expressed. The "national" (*narodny*) poet is the poet who is capable of achieving that quality of expression. "National character" thus might characterize with equal pertinence a ballad upon a folk theme or a novel about the educated classes. The danger for Russian literature lay, as Belinski was to argue, in seeing "national character" only in the most obvious portrayals of the superficially distinctive features of Russian life.

During an age which Belinski characterized as the Age of "National Character," that concept naturally became the hub around which revolved the most timely debates over literary theory, for into the interpretation of that concept went all the current zeal for creating an independent literature. The definition of terms remained debatable so long as the definition of Russia's cultural identity remained debatable. About the desirability of "national character," however defined, there could be, of course, no effective argument. A generation engaged in establishing a national literature was certain to employ "national" as its highest compliment for poets and authors and to require that they draw close to the national life of the people. In the words of Ivan Kireevski: "To be *narodny*, it is . . . necessary to be bred, so to speak, at the center of the life of one's people, to share the hopes of one's native land, its efforts and failures; in a word, to live its life and to express that life unconsciously in the process of self-expression." [11] By this going to the people, Russian literature could be freed from the imitativeness to which it had been so long in bondage and could be transformed into a Russian expression of Russian reality. In this transformation, which partly implied a struggle against the romanticism of the West, Russian literature could achieve its own native brand of romanticism.

But the literary ideal of "national character" constituted only an intention. Some substance for the ideal had yet to be established in the actualities of Russian life. It was necessary to form some systematic conception of Russian life before Russian life could be given its expression in literature. It was this problem which turned the young Russian intelligentsia of the twenties and thirties into philosophers and so into students of the master philosophers of contemporary Germany.

So long as the dominant concern of the intelligentsia remained more philosophical than social, more metaphysical than political, its members were naturally susceptible to the prestige of German philosophical thought. They brought their questions to the teacher

most likely to know the answers. Such is at least a partial explanation of the influence of German philosophy upon Russian thought
during the twenties and thirties. It also happened that Germany
at this time led the world in the field of metaphysics. This accident
of history had intellectual consequences for Russia, for partly on
the strength of her new prestige Germany succeeded in fixing
upon Russia a whole intellectual orientation. German romantic
thought gave Russia not only the answers to problems in cultural
philosophy but also a new awareness of the problems.

Perhaps it is idle to conjecture whether German influence upon
Russian thought at this time was fortunate or not. But it is with
some misgiving that one observes intellectual energies being expended in Russia over problems of an impregnable abstruseness,
encouraged by German thought. Perhaps minds like Nicholas
Stankevich's which might have been productive were lost in the
fastnesses of German forests. More to the point, however, is the
fact that the minimal existence of Russian political and scientific
life led Russian thought toward the problems of art, culture, and
history; and these were among the primary problems of German
philosophy. Thus German speculation carried a specific appeal
for young Russian philosophers after 1825 who were seeking a key
to the puzzle of the Russian universe. Not only the cosmic sweep
of romantic thought, but its very lapses into arbitrary and deliberate vagueness, far from hampering the spread of German thought,
helped to make it exciting. The riddle of Russian nationhood called
for an intellectual attitude of tolerance toward riddles. Such a
contemporary intellectual mood as was signalized by the poet
Venevitinov, who envisioned sculpture, painting, and music as
three divine virgins reigning over the earth (in his 1825 essay entitled "Sculpture, Painting, and Music") and the four parts of the
day as an allegory of the four stages of human evolution (in his
1827 essay entitled "Morning, Noon, Evening, and Night") —
such a mood was hardly likely to find a philosophic home in
rationalism or empiricism. Prince Vladimir F. Odoevski (1803–
1869) has described the climate of these years:

My youth was a time when metaphysics permeated the atmosphere
just as do the political sciences today. We believed in the possibility
of an absolute theory by means of which it would be possible to inter-

pret (we said "construe") all the phenomena of nature, just as there is
now a belief in the possibility of a social order through which all
human needs might be satisfied. . . All nature, all human life seemed
quite clear to us, and we took a somewhat superior view of physicists,
of chemists, of utilitarians who burrowed in *crude matter*.[12]

For good or ill, during the late twenties and throughout the
thirties, a Germanic bias in favor of metaphysical interests marked
the main direction of Russian intellectual life. All the questions of
human existence came to be thrown into the air of overheated
conversations. Such a probing of profundities is always liable to
the charge of naïveté, and there is certainly ample evidence here
to support that charge. But in judging the charge of naïveté, one
must not overlook the extreme youth of this early generation of
"young Russia." Examples from among the authors of writings
composed in the twenties — some of which have been referred to
in the preceding pages — are the poet Venevitinov, who died in
1827 at the age of twenty-two; Ivan Kireevski, who in 1830 was
only twenty-four years of age; and Prince V. F. Odoevski, who in
the same year was only twenty-seven. A similar youthfulness
characterizes the leading spirits of the thirties, many of whom
lived to become "the Men of the Forties." Thus the influential
Nicholas Stankevich was twenty-four when his career of immediate influence was ended by his departure from Russia in 1837.
Michael Katkov, who played a part in bringing Hegel to Belinski,
was hardly twenty years of age at the time. Michael Bakunin's
important influence upon Belinski was already passing by the time
Bakunin was twenty-four. Belinski, it might be added, terminated
the lively Moscow period of his career at the age of twenty-eight.
    Chronological age is, moreover, less important here than the
fact that these young minds, occupied with problems which could
test the ingenuity of the most sophisticated philosophical systems,
worked on under their own power without benefit of any richness
of native philosophical tradition to give sustenance to their
thought. Bereft of the support of a mature philosophical culture,
they were forced by the intellectual circumstances of their age to
work at constructing a coherent set of principles by which their
world could be interpreted and their own function in it defined.
No wonder the age has been compared to the pre-Socratic era in

Greek philosophy. Perhaps the earnestness of the speculation which marked the decades after 1825 is thus partly a measure of the philosophical immaturity of the speculators. In any case the earnestness is real. Philosophy had become the definition of a way of life.

An exaggerated confidence in the study of philosophy carried inevitable penalties. By inability or refusal to master the basic skills and to possess the intellectual traditions of disinterested, systematic philosophical inquiry, youthful Russian philosophers failed to gauge the limitations of philosophy and were finally brought to abandon it altogether.[13] This pattern of faulty understanding leading to rejection is clearly discernible in Belinski's struggle with Hegelianism. But despite his lapses as a student of philosophy, Belinski from the beginning displayed a sociological insight into Russia's cultural situation which never permitted him the naïve hope of a Venevitinov, that by the art or science of philosophy, implemented by the right kind of journal, coherence could be introduced into Russian cultural life.[14]

Whether naïve or not, the hope with which young Russian philosophers turned to German romantic philosophy found support there in a philosophic tradition well suited to their intellectual interests. Two lessons in particular which Germany was qualified to teach made young Russia her willing pupil: first, a philosophy of nationhood; and second, a philosophy of art. The search in Russia for a national cultural identity finds its closest parallel in the intellectual history of Germany. In both countries there occurred an awakening to the necessity of self-definition and of self-assertion against dominant foreign traditions. Both countries passed through a similar period of self-examination and self-reproach. One principal difference is that Germany preceded Russia in time and had achieved a lengthy and systematic elaboration of the problem of nationhood before Russia had fully realized the terms of the problem. By this previous search for its national identity (*Eigensein*), Germany was qualified to become Russia's teacher in the achievement of its own identity (*samobytnost*).

After reading Chaadaev or Kireevski on the formlessness of Russian life, one feels the shock of recognition in a mid-eighteenth-century German appeal to *Nationalgeist*:

For centuries we have been an enigma in our political organization, spoil for our neighbors but an object of their ridicule; distinguished in the history of the world but divided among ourselves and powerless because of our division; strong enough to damage ourselves but powerless to save ourselves; insensitive to the honor of our name and indifferent to the dignity of law; jealous of our leadership and suspicious of each other; in disagreement over first principles and violent in their application; a great but also a despised people, fortunate in its potentialities but most pitiable in its achievement.[15]

Against this sense of national insignificance there was to be fabricated in Germany a *mystique* of the nation which in half a century raised the *Volk* to "an individual expression of the divine," "the bearer and guarantee of the eternal in this world." [16] The special genius of German nationalist theory, as it was to develop, was precisely this combination of a sense of the national life as a coherent organism along with a doctrine of the individual nation as a particularization of universal humanity. By that combination, national existence was endowed simultaneously with organic vitality and moral justification. Although the ideal of humanity was not the national but the universal, it was only through the national that the ideal could be concretely pursued.

The tradition in German thought from Herder to Hegel which underlay the German philosophy of nationhood elaborated a conception of the nation as the individual part of a universal whole. *Vox populi vox Dei.* By such justification of national difference, German nationalist philosophy provided a systematic basis upon which any particular ethnic group could establish its own cultural identity. It is this generalizing, philosophical character of German romantic speculation upon the problem of nationalism that allowed it to bring intellectual assistance to Russian nationalist thought. Of Russian patriotic sentiment there was an ample supply; what native sources could not provide was the theoretical framework upon which native zeal for self-determination could erect an organized structure of national autonomy.

Within the problem of nationhood German philosophy incorporated the problem of creativity, and of artistic creation in particular. This insistence in German thought upon seeing the aesthetic problem in a larger speculative context made a special appeal to young Russia. The starting point of aesthetic theory from Kant to Hegel remained the problem of epistemology, of the relation of "mind" to "nature," of individual consciousness to external reality; and behind the philosophical search carried on by the emerging Russian intelligentsia lay this same fundamental concern with the relation of the self to reality — a particularly lively concern in the Russian world, where the individual critical mind was liable to feel a yawning distance between itself and the world without.

The search within German philosophy for a systematic formulation of the relation between mind and nature had been given its main impetus in the work of Immanuel Kant. It is one of Kant's eminent successors, F. W. J. Schelling (1775–1854), who, in carrying on this same philosophical analysis, was to exert a major attraction upon young Russian minds after 1825. The reader of the later Schelling knows to his dismay the vagueness in which the philosophy of identity becomes lost in the effort to envision a harmony of self and non-self in the dark night of the "Absolute." The attempt at reconciliation is momentous, however, for it established, on a foundation of more or less systematic statement, the conception of artistic creation as the act by which freedom and necessity, spirit and nature, are joined.

Schelling's lectures on the philosophy of art, delivered first at Jena (1802–03) and later, with alterations, at Wurzburg (1804–05), had already marked a movement in Schelling's thought from the transcendental idealism of 1800 to a pursuit of philosophical objectivism. But even by 1807 the essay "On the Relation of the Plastic Arts to Nature" ("Über das Verhältniss der bildenden Künste zu der Natur") still betrays a strongly subjective bias: "If [the artist] were deliberately to try to subordinate himself to reality and with a slavish fidelity to reproduce things as they are, he would produce only empty masks, and not works of art. Thus he must remove himself from the creature, but only in order that he may elevate himself to the force which creates and spiritually seize upon that. He thereby makes his way into the realm of pure ideas; he abandons the creature in order that he may win it back again with thousandfold interest." [17]

A full-fledged subjectivism which yet could make philosophical claim to have embraced the world of self and non-self was precisely the speculative position which could most effectively appeal to young Russian intellectuals who stood in critical withdrawal from Russian actuality and yet who sought to comprehend that actuality in a conceptual embrace. In short, the philosophy of Schelling offered an impressive apologia for the subjective idealism toward which an estranged and isolated intelligentsia easily moved.

To a generation of young Russian metaphysicians seeking a rationale by which they might justify the idealism of their own individualized and self-centered existence and which should include at the same time a philosophy of the national art that they hoped to see created in Russia, Schelling's speculative system was able to bring limitless inspiration. To the sociology of Herder, whereby the creative life of the individual reproduced an ethnic — and thereby a universally human — life, the philosophy of Schelling added an idealism whereby the creative individual could rise to the Idea itself and become the voice of the "Absolute." By such a process of justification, the socially isolated member of an intelligentsia which scrutinized in critical aloofness the cultural formlessness of Russian life could acquire not merely a sense of direction but an exalted sense of vocation. In the tradition of German cultural philosophy and romantic idealism, the intelligentsia already forming in the twenties and thirties could find a fixed point around which their restless activity, continuously threatened by aimlessness, could rotate. This was not the first or the last time that the Russian "radical" discovered a place outside Russia on which to stand to move the world of Russian reality.

The character and organization of the young radicals who cultivated the study of German philosophy in the twenties and thirties is perhaps as important as the character of the philosophy itself in determining the place of German thought in Russian life. For the position which these young students of philosophy occupied in Russian society and the corresponding eagerness which they brought to their study conspired to create out of an already familiar philosophic teaching a cultural force which was new. At least as early as Karamzin (1766–1826) the Russian intellectual had been aware of the existence of German philosophy. Before the twenties Vassili Zhukovski (1783–1852) had succeeded in introducing a cult of German poetic themes and works in a period of Russian preromanticism. But the drama of German philosophic influence in Russia properly begins rather with the official persecution of German philosophy after 1825. This early reaction in official circles toward the new philosophy gives an initial indication of what was to be the fate of German philosophy in Russia throughout the following decades, during which continuing official persecution was to have two important consequences: a limitation of the freedom and originality of the professional teachers of philosophy, and a consequent movement among the more earnest students in favor of the study of philosophy within secret student societies.

While leaving unanswered the debatable question of how profound was the understanding of Schelling among the Russian professors, it is still possible to credit their services as popularizers of philosophy and as evangelists to zealous students. However incomplete the scholarly analysis of Schelling may have remained at their hands, the Russian professors could still perform a major intellectual function if only by the fact that they stood in the manner of Pavlov "at the doors of the Department of Physics and Mathematics and halted students with the question: 'You want to understand nature? But what is nature? What is understanding?' " [18] The fact that it was a generalized philosophical interest and not only a concern with aesthetic theory that attracted Russian youth to Schelling, is indicated by the nature of the professors' work. For of the major academic teachers of Schelling, only one — Alexander Galich (1783–1848), in St. Petersburg — busied himself primarily with aesthetics.

So diffuse, in fact, became the thought and work of professional Russian students of Schelling, that Schelling himself was more than once denounced by Russian critics as a charlatan. But for all its vagueness, the study of Schelling in the Russia of Nicholas I was officially viewed as a threat to orthodox ways of thought. Philosophy was driven underground — and thereby endowed with a prestige which it could hardly have acquired under a liberal rule of free opinion. For not only did philosophy acquire thereby a more tenacious hold upon the imaginations of young students, but it came to be more closely identified with radical critical attitudes toward the social and cultural *status quo*. Only by realizing this process of identification is it possible to understand how the abstruse theory of a Kant or a Schelling could provide intellectual substance for nonconformist views upon Russian life.

The tradition of the private circle or society had been established in Russian intellectual life well before the twenties and thirties. It goes without saying that the formation of intellectual and literary clubs is not peculiar to Russia; but they were destined to perform a particularly important function within a society in need of intellectual direction and cohesion. The idealization of friendship which marked such societies in Russia is a measure of the need which individual members felt for establishing close personal bonds in refuge from an uncongenial reality. This very process of joining together in small, intimate groups existing apart cultivated an intellectual independence and a moral self-sufficiency in the members of the group, who now saw themselves as a dissident minority.

The private society devoted to the critical scrutiny of Russian life was by no means obliged to attack the political authority and might even be devoid of any political character whatsoever. Thus the student circles of the twenties continued a tradition of philosophical rather than political protest. Indeed, the famous Raich circle, established in Moscow in 1823, was mainly devoted to the study of Greek and Latin classics, and some of its meetings were "worthy of the presence of Prince D. V. Golitsyn, the Governor-General of Moscow, who was loved and esteemed by all" — although even here the less academic and less innocent questions of history and philosophy "dared to raise their voice," if "only furtively and from time to time." [19] Meanwhile these same students attended secretly the meetings of another circle, called "The Philosophical Society." Its secret activity was — the study of German philosophy. So dangerous had the study of Kant and Schelling become, indeed, that with the Decembrist uprising of 1825, the group discreetly disbanded.

Perhaps even more important than the government's official attitude is the attitude of these young men toward their own activities. The debate was apparently general and politically safe; but the debaters were in revolt against their world. The skeleton which Prince Odoevski, the president of the group, kept in the room where the Philosophical Society met bore on its cranium the motto "Dare to Know" (*Sapere Aude*). Knowledge — even the knowledge of abstruse philosophy — promised daring possibilities. Under such circumstances, even the most vaporous metaphysical speculation could become an expression of "radicalism."

The critical rejection of the world around them, transcending the wish for merely political reform, thus became one of the chief marks of the early disciples of German philosophy in Russia. The secret society becomes a symbol of the exclusiveness peculiar to the forming intelligentsia — itself an unformalized secret society, entered into by all who shared a common concern for the radical critique of things as they are; a minority group, a party of the opposition. To this aloof and critical intellectual elite, German idealism, especially during the decade of the thirties, carried an effective appeal. Already in the twenties German thought was being received with something like religious enthusiasm. Such words are not too strong for describing the reception which the young Russian "philosopher" gave to Schelling in particular. And it is not hard to see the attraction for Russian intellectuals in Schelling's systematic effort (however imperfect its success) to elaborate a philosophy which preached creativity and not withdrawal, and which at the same time turned the attention inward to an inner existence which the rootless Russian intellectual was sure to prefer to the empirical world that lay in darkness about him. The systematic philosophic recognition of the self as the vessel of reality provided a respectable justification for personal exclusiveness at the same time that it dispersed the apathy engendered by aristocratic aloofness.

Schelling's dual emphasis upon idealistic dynamism and artistic creativity thus became immediately applicable to the Russian intellectual situation and in particular to current hope for national self-expression in art. The youthful members of the Philosophical Society, who seem at times to have departed from this world toward a world of the ideal, were of the same generation who argued that literature should be the expression of the character and opinions of a people. While seeming to be swept into an otherworldly transcendentalism, the young philosophers of the twenties and thirties thus refused to abandon the cultural problem posed by their realization that artistic expression is national expression.

Instead of healing the painful breach in Russian intellectual life between the ideal and the actual, German romantic thought, especially through its representation in Schelling, worked to justify an egocentric idealism and at the same time to encourage a critical disparagement of Russian actuality. For by its very emphasis upon a creativity which was at the same time personal and national and universal, German cultural philosophy could only serve to impress its disciples in Russia with the sterility of their own native achievement. A philosophy which glorified the creative individual, by relating him to an ethnic and also to a universal life, easily made its home in a country like Germany, where a cultural renaissance with few parallels in modern history had just been taking place. But in a nation like Russia, already desperately aware of its own cultural deficiencies, the glorification of artistic creativity was bound to accentuate all that seemed uncreative in Russian national life. From this it followed, in Russian minds, that the creative artist must somehow be used to lead the way toward national enlightenment. In the working out of that proposition, a whole future drama lies.

T
he gulf between the real and the ideal in Russian
life — between the complaint over Russia's cultural sterility, which
patriotic sentiment made only more poignant; and the quest after
meaning in life and expression in art, which the spirit of German
philosophy helped to guide and encourage — underlies the entire
career of Belinski. He came to maturity precisely at the time when
the problem of Russian nationhood had become a central intellectual issue. Not only did he share a common intellectual interest
in that problem, but the circumstances of his life provided him
with personal reasons both for despising the world of Russian
actuality and for joining ties with the idealism of young Russia.
He was fated, indeed, to bring the abstract problem of Russian
culture into a concrete articulation which no contemporary succeeded in equaling. That destiny was forced upon him by means
of both the opportunities and the hardships of his personal and
intellectual career.

The remarkable degree to which Belinski's private life with its
intellectual and emotional tensions reproduced the life of his
generation has earned him general recognition as a representative
man of the thirties and forties. His title to a place as a central
figure among his contemporaries rests not so much upon particular
characteristics of his thought or achievements of his work as upon
the faithfulness with which the dialectic of his career parallels the
direction of his time. Perhaps his claim to being the true father of
the Russian intelligentsia should be made to depend upon specific

Early Formation

qualities of his thought, such as his social idealism, his passion for reform, his disrespect for tradition, his disinterested zeal.[1] But none of these characterizations, however valid, adds up to Belinski's representativeness, which consists, more than in a mere sharing of dominant radical convictions, in a sensitivity to the prevailing winds of doctrine in his day and a quickness to take up into himself the currents of intellectual and spiritual life that moved through his world. Indeed, Belinski stood, in several dramatic passages of his career, quite apart from the main stream of "radical" thought; but precisely by his independence he succeeded in demonstrating how far he was willing to be carried by the conflicts of his time.

Belinski's career, like the life of his time, is torn by the struggle between pessimism in the face of Russian actuality and a correspondingly lofty idealism in regard to the potentialities of Russian creativity. Belinski's private existence could only corroborate pessimism, but the terms in which he thought about life were always chosen for its justification. Indeed, his personal discomfort only worked to spur him on in his philosophic quest. The intimate knowledge of the brutalities of Russian life which he learned from daily living kept him seriously at work devising a happy solution of the problems of Russian culture. A Chaadaev or a Prince Odoevski could come to a clear intellectual understanding of the ills of Russian cultural formlessness, but it was the unhappy privilege of a commoner like Belinski to have lived in the shadow of that popular darkness which the Russian aristocrat, however sensitive, could behold only at a distance.

Belinski's closeness to the common life, which gave a solid foundation to his critique of Russian national culture, at the same time helped to determine the direction of his idealism. Above all, he was thereby saved from that idealization of the people which continually threatened critical thought in Russia and which made a particularly seductive appeal in days of hunger and thirst after national identity. For all his enthusiasm for "national character" in literature, Belinski nowhere speaks with tenderness of the unenlightened masses. His idealism is drawn instead from intellectual sources, from the world of enlightenment to which Western Europe belonged and to which Russia could hope to belong. In

Belinski's life, reasons for taking a critical view of Russian reality were amply given; the idealism had to be learned.

So much is evident from what we know of Belinski's biography. Although many details are missing, the main features are clear. What is lacking in commentaries and documentation is made up for by Belinski's own prolific output of articles, which often reveal as much about their author as about the subject he is discussing. It is within the pages of his literary criticism, supplemented by his private correspondence, that the main story of his life is told. Outside of this drama of ideas, Belinski's life was uneventful. Externally, his career separates into the period of his provincial upbringing from his birth on May 30, 1811, until his arrival in Moscow as a university student in 1829; then the ten-year period in Moscow, lasting until his move to St. Petersburg in October of 1839; and finally his activity in St. Petersburg, where he died on May 26, 1848. The second half, the active half of his life, from 1829 to 1848, is thus almost exactly divided between Moscow (1829–1839) and St. Petersburg (1839–1848). His intellectual movement is less orderly.

Vissarion Grigorevich Belinski was born in what is now Finnish territory, the first child of a ship's doctor on duty with the Baltic fleet. Five years later, the family returned to the father's native province in Russia, where Belinski's grandfather had spent his days in the undistinguished role of village priest. In this small village of Chembar, where the family settled, in the province of Penza, southeast of Moscow, Belinski's father served as a district physician until his death in 1835. A relative in whose home Belinski spent many hours has testified that the Belinski family, now including three sons and a daughter, lived in moderate circumstances.[2] But before his death in 1835 (by which time Belinski was settled in Moscow) the doctor so aroused the antagonism of his fellow villagers, at first by his professed atheism and reading of Voltaire and finally by his drunkenness, that he finally refused to visit his patients for fear of being attacked.

The violence and fear of violence which poisoned the father's last days had disturbed the home throughout Belinski's childhood. Not only did the child witness fierce quarrels between his parents, but he also received rough treatment at their hands. The father's hostility toward the village joined with the mother's fiery temper to trouble the child's world. Belinski's later laments upon his early home life ("I was a stranger in my family") leave no doubt of his bitterness toward a harsh father and a severe mother. Obviously the early years in Chembar gave Belinski as a boy little delight in the life of the Russian village. After private tutoring, young Vissarion attended school in Chembar until his matriculation in 1825 at the *gymnasium* at Penza, eighty miles away. His material situation at Penza is thought to have been at least comfortable, provided the standard of comfort is not set too high. Somehow he was able to afford at this time to develop a love of the theater which he was later to express in rapturous flights of prose in his critical writings.

A school inspector in his memoirs has recorded his impressions in 1823 of the intelligent pupil, who apparently already showed that owlish seriousness which Belinski later recognized in himself.[3] Seriousness of interest seems to have marked Belinski's career throughout his stay at the Penza *gymnasium*, where through friendship with a professor he gained access to books (for example, Sir Walter Scott) and to current journals, in which he found, among other things, the articles of Nadezhdin, who was one day to be his first editor. The Russian literary traditions he first knew were mainly "classical" (e.g., Derzhavin) and sentimental ("I wept while reading [Karamzin's] *Poor Liza*"), although he was not unacquainted with Pushkin at this time. His own attempts at original verse were in "pure classical and completely sentimental style," as he later said. He adds: "With the romantic style I became acquainted only after the rage to versify had passed in me." [4]

Through Belinski's intellectual comradeship with the professor of the Penza *gymnasium*, and even more notably in the home of relatives, the Ivanovs, in Chembar, where he found books to read, literature began its service of providing release for the young adolescent from the disharmonies of the life around him. A commentary upon his home life, as well as upon his life at school, is provided by the fact that the Ivanov home offered him asylum when he was finally expelled from the Penza *gymnasium* for failure to attend classes. In that friendly refuge he spent much of his time until his enrollment at the University of Moscow, where he succeeded in forcing an entrance despite poor coöperation from home and where he managed somehow to stay, at state expense, despite financial difficulties. The major benefits of university life for Belinski were not those provided by the curriculum. Perhaps the first service which the University performed in his life was to attract him to Moscow, currently the center of Russian intellectual life.

The University itself, to be sure, played a leading role in the life of the thirties and forties, during years when a great number of famous writers and intellectuals attended its classes. After the darkness of suppression that descended upon Russian intellectual life after the troubles of 1825, it was Moscow University which became, as Herzen said, the "first visible object to emerge from the universal fog." [5] In spite of the abolition of the teaching of philosophy in 1826, the thirties were marked by a growing vigor of university teaching. But it was Belinski's misfortune to be required to end his university career before that new life had fully flowered. Nadezhdin, for example, who along with Pavlov was one of the most stimulating professors of the decade, had only begun his university career in Moscow at the time of Belinski's expulsion from the University in 1832. Similarly the influential student circle which formed around the student Stankevich was only beginning its activity when Belinski's university years came to an end.

Among Belinski's noteworthy activities as a student were the "literary evenings" of which he was a cofounder and which were held in his room. According to the reminiscence of a roommate, Belinski engaged in these literary discussions as a zealous defender of romanticism, with heavy attacks against false rhetoric and empty phrasemaking. Evidence of the group's interest in the philosophic aspects of literary study is offered by a translation made by one of its members of a German treatise on aesthetics written by one K. F. Bachmann, a follower of Schelling.[6]

The only literary document which provides insight into Belinski's thought during his student years is his play, *Dmitri Kalinin*, which may have been a primary cause for his early dismissal from the University. As revealing as the play itself is the courage or the foolhardiness with which he offered it, against the advice of wiser friends, to a committee of University censors for their approval, as a preliminary to submitting it for publication. Belinski's hope to make a financial profit from the play ("at least around six thousand," he wrote to his parents in March of 1831) and thereby to earn freedom from his ignominious status as a student on state support, leaves little question of his innocence in making public what he called his "dramatic tale."

The tragedy of *Dmitri Kalinin* is the tragedy of a good man's defeat by the inscrutable injustices of fate. In Belinski's portrayal of this theme, the passionate Dmitri is forced to pass through all the tortures of melodrama. As the illegitimate son of a noble landowner, he must live among his father's family in the position of a menial, frustrated in his love for the daughter Sophia. His final doom is to kill Sophia and then himself, a hopeless victim of circumstance.

The author hoped that the reader would see in his play "only the passion of an ardent soul athirst for all that is exalted and beautiful. . . " But he had written for his hero Dmitri an impassioned attack upon the arbitrary cruelties which result from "the fatal right of certain persons to enslave by force the will of other human beings like themselves" — to which he was prudent enough to add at least a footnote of thanks to a "wise and solicitous government" that such tyrannical excesses as the play portrayed "already are beginning to be completely wiped out." [7] Obviously a play in which a disinherited hero shakes his fist at all pretense of justice, human and divine, was not likely to charm the official censors. But perhaps even the rejection of God's universe would have been more tolerable to them than a direct attack upon the specific injustice of a Russian institution. If we compare Belinski's play with his lively hopes for its success, it is only possible to conclude that the young playwright still had much to learn about the world in which he was to live.

The more obvious heresy of the play's attack upon serfdom may conceal the fact that *Dmitri Kalinin* is primarily a statement not of social protest but rather of philosophical anxiety over the order of the universe. This concern of Belinski's early thought is worthy of note, since in a crude fashion it points the way to the problems about which he was to speculate most earnestly and persistently. But the deficiency of the play as a work of art so reduces its power to illuminate Belinski's mind that out of justice to the author no extreme claims should be made for its significance. Without being required to see in the play "the seed in which is contained *in potentia* the entire later development of Belinski's view of the world," [8] one can nevertheless regard Belinski's first literary work as the spirited beginning of his lifelong struggle for a personal ideology.

Belinski's expulsion from the University may have had a more genuinely academic ground than biographers are willing to believe. Whatever the whole reason, his studies were terminated in September of 1832, more than a year after the incident of the play, on the formal charge of "ill health as well as limited capacities," and specifically for failure to take and pass any examination during his three-year residence (although this was not exceptional). The expulsion was both a shock to his self-esteem and a loss to his intellectual training. Of the two, the moral shock is perhaps the more important. His delay until May of 1833 in breaking the bad news to his parents well shows his refusal to make his terms easily with his misfortune.

It is clear, to be sure, that Belinski's intellectual equipment was imperfect, even by his own admission, as illustrated by a sentence from the "Literary Reveries," written in 1834: " . . . I have a love for truth and a desire for the general good but perhaps no basic knowledge." Although he tutored a student in German on at least one occasion and translated a number of French works, including *Le Père Goriot*, he was reputed to have known no German and to read French with difficulty; and Panaev noted that Belinski was still struggling in 1841 to learn French.[9] In Russia during the thirties and forties, such deficiency in Western languages was a serious handicap.

But more important than gaps of information or knowledge, which at least can be filled, was the conception of himself which an uncompleted education helped to form. Part of this feeling was the sense of broken training and the resulting weakness of system in his work. From such deficiencies grew feelings of inferiority before literary antagonists like Professor Shevyrev, who in an at-

tack upon Belinski in *The Muscovite* (*Moskvitianin*) once spite-
fully referred to him as "a student who failed to complete his
course." [10]

The frustrations of Belinski's university career, and especially
the circumstances of his dismissal, thus added cause for growing
feelings of protest against his world, feelings which were only to
be further offended by the succeeding years of grave insecurity.
Between the fall of 1832, when he left the University, and the
spring of 1833, when he began to translate from the French for
Nadezhdin's journal *The Telescope* (*Teleskop*), he survived pre-
cariously in Moscow upon odd jobs of teaching and translation.
Detailed information about these years before 1834 is spared us.

On the basis of relatively superficial information for the years
of Belinski's boyhood and early youth, it would be rash to adopt
an opinion of his psychological formation. But it is not impossible
to see a relation between Belinski's personal life even of his early
years and the pattern of his intellectual attitudes. During these
formative years, as throughout his life, he displays the figure of an
essentially noble person struck again and again by misfortune in
an uncongenial world. A nobility of character which consists only
in personal chastity and sobriety (with which Turgenev credited
him) may be an overrated virtue; but Belinski is honored with
greater qualities than these, qualities also more relevant to his
intellectual career.

Perhaps chief among his moral virtues is an unflinching devotion
to the truth as he saw it, when none of the circumstances of his
private or public life made purity of conscience profitable. The
readiness to abandon the security of authority in favor of seeking
his intellectual fortune, the insistence that "amicus Plato, sed magis
amica veritas," as he likes to repeat in his articles, reveal the earnestness of the independent mind which marks the best of his generation. With or without the evidence of his contemporaries, Belinski's whole career is hardly even understandable unless recognition
is given to his moral and intellectual probity. In few of his contemporaries could a match be found for the tenacity with which
Belinski clung to his own truth, even when he suspected that it
was leading him into absurdity.

The conviction that truth is dearer than all the authorities, imposed upon Belinski a combination of belligerence and humility which easily left him the prey of rivals or enemies. His good friend Panaev said of him that "with all his inner powers and energy, he was a powerless child in life. . . " [11] Thus the publisher of the *Moscow Observer* (*Moskovski Nabliudatel*) paid Belinski some worthless amount, and then not always on the dot, for the editorship. While he made the literary fortune of the journal *National Notes* (*Otechestvennye Zapiski*) in the forties, the publisher Kraevski exploited him notoriously.

A vulnerability, in childhood and throughout maturity, to being put upon by the world, surely helped to create the emotional extremism and frustration from which Belinski continued to suffer and which early earned him the name of "the violent Vissarion" (*neistovy Vissarion*). He was as quick to admit the vehemence of his temperament as his friends were quick to discover it. His emotional and intellectual progress is a continual dizzy vacillation between extremes of apathy and excitation. This inner movement between extremes of mood parallels an outer movement between a discouraging reality and an intense intellectual stimulation. In a letter written in 1843 Belinski said of himself: "In me there was always a deep thirst, a torturing hunger for intellectual activity and a capacity for it; but it found no nourishment, no basis, no atmosphere. Passionate souls in such a position become the prey of their own fantasy and try to create for themselves a reality outside actuality." [12] By experience and by temperament Belinski was thus naturally brought to a readiness to embrace German romanticism in the form in which it had entered Russian university life. Romanticism of any species was likely to find a devotee in one who could say of himself, as he says in a letter of March 1, 1841, written to his friend Botkin, that "for me thinking and feeling, understanding and suffering are one and the same thing," and in a letter to Bakunin of March 8, 1843, that "fervor constitutes the major element of my noble spirit." Meanwhile, Belinski's life until the beginning of his career as a literary critic had brought him to look with little love upon Russian life as he knew it. His recognition of the formlessness of Russian life could find ample inspiration in a personal animus against the irritations of his own private experience. He could take the problems of Russian cultural existence as his own because the events of his life made them such.

As the early years of the thirties in Moscow brought to Belinski that dramatic clash with his world, his dismissal from the University; so these same years acquainted him with the philosophical activity of the student circle, in which a systematic apology was being sought for the reality against which Belinski had thus far been struggling. The student group to which he came to be more and more closely drawn was the famous Stankevich circle, which faithfully continued the tradition of Prince Odoevski's Philosophical Society of the twenties. With this circle of Stankevich's, all of Belinski's closest Moscow friends — Michael Bakunin, Vassili Botkin, Michael Katkov, Constantine Aksakov — came to be affiliated; and it was consequently to this circle that Belinski's personal life in Moscow was almost exclusively bound.

It goes without saying that the mutual influences exerted within the student circle were predominantly personal in character. Several major consequences flow from that fact. In the first place, the intellectual positions toward which the thought of the circle moved came to be built into a way of life. Far from remaining a mere intellectual or scholastic exercise, the philosophy of the circle tended to exert an influence which covered all of life. Personal friendships were at stake in the fortunes of intellectual allegiances. The very fact that the most active discussion of philosophical questions was removed from the more formal atmosphere of the university classroom and was relegated to the intimate setting of a private club, gave to the pursuit of intellectual problems a pertinence and an immediacy which no academic study could have duplicated.

At the same time, reliance upon the conversation of friends as a major source of the interpretation of philosophical doctrine created the danger of stimulating enthusiasms which might or might not be philosophically valid. The comparatively great freedom allowed to the circulation of foreign works in their original language by a government censorship which disapproved of the same works in translation, helped to separate a student like Belinski from the original sources of the philosophical thought which the student circle taught him to admire. The power of the circle to arouse intense interest in works of philosophical speculation to which it did not always provide an authoritative guide worked to place a member like Belinski in an unfortunate position of intellectual dependence. Such intellectual dependence carried with it a psychological dependence upon more learned friends; and to this dependence Belinski's imperfect education made him particularly susceptible. The fact that such a large measure of Belinski's philosophic knowledge thus came to him at second hand was to constitute one of the principal sources of the extravagance and frequent distortion of his philosophical creed.

The degree to which the student circle cultivated a personal loyalty which at times approached adulation is dramatically illustrated in Belinski's regard for Nicholas Stankevich (1813–1840), the leading spirit of the society. Stankevich was obviously more than the chairman of a club; in the words of Belinski, he was "the life of our circle." Even at the end of the thirties, when Stankevich had been abroad for several years, Belinski, although in the midst of a personal war against all that the circle had meant to him, could still write to Stankevich, "What the devil good would there be in me if I cooled toward you?" [13] Such depth of personal regard is especially impressive in a relationship which apparently never achieved a friendly intimacy, by Belinski's witness: in 1842 he wrote to Botkin, "I could not consider Stankevich my friend, for inequality did not allow the possibility of that either from his side or from mine. . ." [14]

The personality of Stankevich offered many possible appeals to the young Belinski. The embodiment of the youthful idealist, sensitive to the point of fragility, poetic in temperament, "created only for revery," as one Russian literary historian has described him,[15] Stankevich was at the same time one of the first in his generation to undertake a serious program of systematic philosophical study. Inevitably his intellectual search led him to the school of German romanticism. Although his career was to carry him beyond Schelling through Fichte to Hegel, his years at the University of Moscow (1830–1834) correspond to a time when Schelling dominated his thought.

The influence of Schelling found one easy channel into the student life of Stankevich: he lived during his years at the University in the home of Professor Pavlov, who along with Nadezhdin was one of the chief popularizers of Schelling at the University. By 1834 Stankevich had read Schelling's *System des transcendentalen Idealismus*, and already in 1833 his article "My Metaphysic" ("Moia Metafisika") revealed an adaptation of central themes from Schelling's transcendentalism: that every form in creation is the particularization of the universal and eternal life of nature, expressed in man by feeling; that thus the central force of human life is love, by which beauty and truth are joined.

The teachings of Schelling as they were taken up by Stankevich were raised in the enthusiasm of his early youth to a personal cult of the infinite unattainable, which left to its vulgarity the crass reality of the real world: "Imagined happiness is preferable to real happiness. . . How fine it is to renounce the vulgar happiness of the crowd, to create a world of one's own and to aspire to it, even without attaining it!" [16] Longing for union with the infinite and despair at the failure to attain to it could be dissolved only in the fire of "fierce, burning love": "May its destructive fire pass over all my miserable being . . . may it turn to ashes my anguished suffering and disperse the troubled visions which wander through the darkness of my soul!" [17] Such excess of romantic zeal was destined to pass for Stankevich into an ultimate realization that "apparently for the fullness of happiness something of the real world is necessary." [18] That such realization could come to him as a discovery should provide sufficient revelation of the kind of "transcendentalism" which preceded it.

It may be natural to feel a passing regret for the youth and enthusiasm expended upon such impossible heaven-storming. But the flight from reality which inspired philosophical idealism and romantic transcendentalism was in its fashion a pursuit of another reality, one which might be more believable and enduring than an unendurable present. The quest led away from the vulgarities of social and political circumstance, but the withdrawal from life was made precisely in the interest of more and richer life: "life in the Absolute," "the full life of the spirit," in the phraseology of the circle.

The collapse of this "nobility of spirit" which Belinski was to condemn in himself in numerous self-analyses, marks the personal evolution of Stankevich, which in many ways parallels that of Belinski. After continued passionate pursuit of an ineffable ideal, Stankevich came to feel that he had only been hiding his head in the clouds; in 1838 he wrote to Bakunin: "Reality is the arena of the truly strong man. The weak soul lives in the *Jenseits*, in a vague aspiration; . . . as soon as this vague something becomes *etwas* definite, such a soul again throws itself beyond the limits of reality. . . That is my story and the obvious cause of all my unhappiness." [19]

This concept of the "noble spirit" (literally, "beautiful soul"), a figure at first glorified and then condemned by Stankevich and his circle, was originaly drawn from German thought. This was the "schöne Seele" whom Schiller described and portrayed, in whom spontaneous will and feeling are so perfectly in harmony with moral obligation that he is virtuous by instinct, as it were. This ideal of special nobility becomes at length for the philosophers of the Stankevich circle an unreal abstraction inhabiting an impossible dream world. With the rejection of that ideal existence in the "Absolute" which the early Stankevich had striven to attain, the term "noble spirit" is debased to mean the person of lofty aims who is unable to realize them in actual life, who is thereby condemned to inhabit a kind of purgatory between the actuality from which he has divorced himself and the life in the ideal which he has not attained. Living in this shadow world of marginal existence, the "noble spirit" becomes the "superfluous man," separated from actuality by his "noble" protest against its emptiness and vulgarity.

The personal bankruptcy with which a sustained flight from actual life threatened the idealist of the thirties finds comic relief in extreme examples. Even Michael Bakunin, whom Annenkov called "the father of Russian idealism," must have smiled at a young disciple's despair over the fact that he seemed to have no capacity for suffering.[20] In the same vein Panaev describes a glutton who explains his quite temporary loss of appetite by the fact that it is "intolerable to live in this savage, vulgar social order." [21] Even the fair-souled Stankevich can appear ludicrous by finding consolation for an unhappy love affair in the renewed study of Kant.

But such caricatures should not be taken to disparage the very real spiritual and intellectual turmoil through which all the knights of the Stankevich round table were to pass. Belinski, Bakunin, Katkov, Constantine Aksakov, Stankevich — each went his separate way, but the quest of each remained a continuing search for a reality which the circle in its early years hoped it had defined. Whatever its possible exaggerations, the philosophical effort was far from frivolous. Perhaps in none of the members of the circle is the personal rejection of "life in the Absolute" more poignant than in its young chief, whose untimely death abroad at the age of twenty-seven may well have been hastened by failure to come to terms with his world. The tragedy of an entire life of the mind is implied in the constant refrain of his latter-day advice to correspondents: "Do not reflect too much."

Perhaps only in Belinski is it possible to find the equal of Stankevich in the zeal with which he applied an acquaintance with philosophical thought to the construction of a personal creed. That Belinski's first serious introduction to philosophical idealism was made in a student circle which revolved around Stankevich is perhaps the major fact of Belinski's early intellectual life. The personality of the young Stankevich was sure to have a sharper effect than any amount of philosophic study in arousing another young zealot like Belinski, prepared by the dissatisfactions of his personal life to become a willing disciple in the first respectable school of idealism to which the accidents of his life might lead him. The frequency of Belinski's succeeding laments over the hopeless idealism of his years in the student circle, the unhappy realization that "it is sad to recall that narrow exclusiveness with which we looked upon the whole world," [22] bear ample testimony to the influence of the Stankevich circle over his moral and personal as well as intellectual character.

If only by reason of his literary unproductiveness, the influence which Stankevich exercised was primarily that of a friend, working through the medium of conversation; and this evanescent character of the relationship between Stankevich and Belinski leaves in doubt the precise limits of Stankevich's influence. Perhaps Belinski's own declarations of regard for Stankevich have given an exaggerated notion of the latter's influence upon him.

But however persistent may have been Belinski's slowness to adopt the gospel of Schelling according to Stankevich, by the time of the "Literary Reveries" of 1834 the author had clearly become a willing disciple of Schelling. Until the arrival of Bakunin, which occurred after the writing of the "Literary Reveries," Stankevich remained "the life of our circle," as Belinski called him. The appeal for Belinski of this restless spirit and earnest mind must have been given even greater force by the qualities of the colleagues who surrounded him: the "young men distinguished by intelligence, culture, talent, and nobility of feeling," who "force me at times to forget my misfortunes," as Belinski wrote to his brother Constantine in 1833.[23]

If an unhappy personal life supplied Belinski with the ground from which to take a pessimistic view of Russian reality, the idealism of the Stankevich circle helped to inspire a flight toward a spiritual existence in which the disharmonies of actuality could be resolved. By the time of the writing of the "Literary Reveries," the pattern of conflict between an unacceptable reality and an extravagant idealism had become visible.

Belinski's Activity as a Critic

The formative influences of Belinski's early life quickly carried him into the main stream of the intellectual currents of his day. The combination of pessimism and idealism which had provided the substance of critical thought among the Russian intelligentsia, at least since the days of the Philosophical Society, passed into Belinski's thought as a private heritage. But if he joined the generation of his contemporaries in the major directions of his thought, he was required to stand alone in the task of applying a tradition of critical judgment to the exacting job of practical criticism. Necessity required that he become a day laborer while many of his more fortunate colleagues could afford to be unproductive. In this circumstance of Belinski's life resides surely one of the most important consequences of his social status, with its attendant deprivation of financial independence.

This assignment to solitary toil is only the first condition of Belinski's loneliness, which is both personal and intellectual in character. He was not friendless, to be sure. Yet not only did the fortunes of his career and the displacements of his friends cut him off from the opportunity of permanent attachments, but also his intellectual independence cost him the estrangement of friends as dear and close as Michael Bakunin. In St. Petersburg, where he spent approximately half of his mature life, he was forced to forego the consolations of the intimate Moscow circle of his youth and rejoiced at the occasional visits to St. Petersburg of Botkin or Herzen or Ogarev.

Yet more significant than the relative isolation of Belinski's personal life is the loneliness of the post to which he was assigned in a continuing intellectual battle. Above all, he was caught up in a private ideological conflict which all aid from without was ultimately powerless to help him resolve. The fact that literary criticism became the field in which he pursued a private philosophical quest constitutes perhaps the primary feature of his critical activity.

The effort which Plekhanov has made to find at the foundation of Belinski's literary judgments a systematic code of aesthetic principles is necessarily fated to remain sterile or at best superficial.[24] The drama of Belinski's critical career consists precisely in the speed with which he was willing to move from one major position to another. The fact that the principle of change resided more in the critic's private and emotional life than in any purely intellectual or aesthetic doctrine determines the outer disorder of his critical activity and at the same time its semblance of inner coherence.

The changeableness of Belinski's critical philosophy came to be not only recognized by the critic himself but asserted and defended. It was more in a spirit of self-assertion than of self-accusation that he once wrote of himself: "I break with an old idea with difficulty and pain, I reject it to the limit, and pass over into the new with all the fanaticism of a proselyte." [25] His continual emphasis upon the changing character of his ideas, his insistence upon intellectual dialectic, may always be taken partly as an *apologia pro vita sua*. The contention that dynamic conviction necessarily leads to abrupt and radical change brought Belinski to a pronounced contempt for foolish consistency, as reflected in such statements as: "The only person who has never changed his convictions is he who never felt the need and the thirst for conviction." [26] Meanwhile he could only hope that when change occurred it might be change for the better, that he had "changed a kopeck for a ruble." [27] But he knew that the working of the dialectic was not always so profitable.

Belinski's inconsistencies cannot all be justified, of course, as the result of intellectual fervor. The sheer pressure of work on the journals which employed him, and in which all his critical writing appeared, certainly helped to destroy the equilibrium of his literary activity. He habitually wrote his articles hurriedly at the end of the month for an edition due to be published at the beginning of the following month. Little wonder that it seemed to him an "impossibility to write well for a journal." [28] Thus the anxiety of the deadline gave him little rest throughout his prolific writing career. His private letters contain more than one hint of quiet desperation, as when he writes to Botkin of the *National Notes* and his employer–publisher Kraevski: "Kraevski snarls. I haven't even half an idea in my head. I don't know how I'll begin or what I'll say. I take up the pen, and the article will be ready — how, I myself don't know; but it will be ready." [29] Such unleisurely circumstances of authorship help to explain the disproportion, the incompleteness, the lengthy digressions, the repetitiousness which disfigure even the most important articles.

But after considerable allowance has been made for the external pressures under which Belinski was forced to work, the irregularities of his style must also be referred to the irregularity of his thought. However graceless and turgid his writing at its worst becomes, it is always inspired by a fervency of intellectual life which lends an almost lyrical animation even to his heaviest passages. The validity of the argument that he was by nature "not a critic. . . but a tribune," as the novelist Goncharov put it,[30] who asserted his critical convictions in "the style of a manifesto," as Professor Cizevsky has said,[31] is grounded in the almost humorless seriousness with which he attacked the job of criticism. Belinski's frequent condemnation of the literary artist or critic who looks upon his work as a pastime provides an almost tiresome reminder of Belinski's own grimness of purpose, relieved only by the personal affection with which he embraced every artist or thinker who brought his gift of creativity into Russian life: "His [Stanke-vich's] death struck me *personally* and — will you believe it? — *just so* was I struck by the deaths of Pushkin and Lermontov. I consider them *my* losses, and there continues to sound within me the discordant, poignant realization that these are my personal losses, by which my own life has been depleted." [32]

This disinterested passion caused Belinski's personal convictions to press too hard upon his theory to allow him to develop into a great or original philosophical mind. It is hardly fair or exact to characterize Belinski as "a person who never controlled his ideas but was always controlled by them" [33]; yet it is obvious that his enthusiasms were too quickly adopted and too violently exchanged for control over them to have been sure and constant. His thought is too fragmentary and his intellectual positions too easily vulner-able to permit of a systematic elaboration of original ideas.

By this very failure to attain the intellectual self-sufficiency of the disciplined philosopher, Belinski remained close to the urgent intellectual needs of his time. By his very breadth of sympathy, his concern with aesthetic judgments never could remain free from involvement with the larger spiritual and social requirements of his day. Perhaps his misfortune was, in fact, to have been as much of a philosopher as he managed to be. Perhaps a native sense of concrete reality was submerged rather than expressed by the struc-tures of abstract theory which he persisted in building. The or-ganization of his longer critical essays, with their interminable theoretical disquisitions, often only barely relevant to the topic, all too often suggests the presence of a gulf between theory and ap-plication. And the clash between literary preferences and theoreti-cal doctrine continues, throughout his progress as a critic, to throw his "philosophy" into confusion.

Assigned to the heavy task of working out a critical theory which could satisfy the needs of a personal ideology and at the same time account for an unpredictable succession of literary works, Belinski deserved the support and guidance of collaborators wise enough to enlarge his perspective, to clarify his thought, even to share his enthusiasms. But in fact what intellectual aid he did receive was not only insufficient but often of doubtful benefit.

What he got from friends like Stankevich and Bakunin was more an arbitrary creed to which he struggled to make his own thought conform, than assistance in the ordering of his intellectual life. This solitariness of Belinski's position was further sharpened by the fact, already referred to, that no one of his friends was actively engaged at work even similar to his own, partly because they could afford not to be. It was Belinski's privilege to be at some time the chief literary critic of each of the major "progressive" literary organs of his time: *The Telescope, The Moscow Observer, National Notes, The Contemporary*; but the privilege was also an onerous obligation to be discharged with little help from the members of his intellectual camp.

Meanwhile Belinski's lifelong effort to evolve a critical theory whereby the service of Russian literature to Russian society might be defined could draw little support from contemporary currents in Russian journalism. Russian critical thought in his day moved toward two extreme positions: either toward an inadequate conception of the potentialities of Russian literature or toward a narrowly nationalistic conception of Russian life. Even such enlightened critics as Nicholas Polevoi, who preceded Belinski in the serious effort to establish literary criticism on a systematic foundation, inclined to a literary and philosophical eclecticism which reflected an easygoing preference for French romanticism and German philosophical thought (studied through secondary sources) and the absence of any serious concern with the thorny questions of a native cultural life in Russia. Toward another pole moved the tendencies of a narrow nationalism which was given its most extreme and irresponsible expression in the journalistic activities of the St. Petersburg triumvirate composed of Grech, Bulgarin, and Senkovski. To a failure to understand the age and its requirements they added a political and literary opportunism which at least served to bar them from serious influence. A more respectable defense of the nationalistic bias came to be made by Professors Shevyrev and Pogodin in Moscow, where a budding Slavophilism was provided at the beginning of the forties with a literary organ in the journal *The Muscovite*. Between these two extremes of an ineffective and uncreative interest in the literary and philosophic traditions of the West and a jingoistic exaltation of Russia over the "rotten" West, a creative theory of Russian culture was forced to make its way.

Amid the conflict of ideologies which found its expression in journalism, it is perhaps not surprising that the journal of the thirties which contributed least to a serious discussion of current issues achieved the greatest popular success: Senkovski's *Library for Reading* (*Biblioteka dlia Chteniia*). In the number of subscribers, the latter publication far outdistanced important journals like Pushkin's *The Contemporary* (*Sovremennik*) or *National Notes*, in the pages of which many of Belinski's most important articles appeared. Such data may serve as a passing suggestion that among the obstacles to a serious interest in Russian literature must be counted the discouragement of popular indifference.

Among the obstacles, both intellectual and practical, to serious critical thought, an unenlightened censorship must be added. Against the frustrations imposed by a censorship which disqualified all liberal ideas, "for example," as Belinski bitterly explained, "that two plus two equals four, and that winter is cold and summer hot," [34] Belinski's protest is raised throughout his correspondence: "Nature sentenced me to bark like a dog and to howl like a jackal, but circumstances order me to mew like a cat and to swish my tail like a fox." [35]

The effectiveness of the control imposed upon free expression may even seem to leave in doubt the fidelity with which Belinski's published writings reflected his private thought. Even his personal friends could be left to wonder how intimately they knew his mind. Yet in spite of all the qualifications which official authority was liable to impose, the main lines of Belinski's critical theory proceeded through an ideological dialectic which was hardly accessible to censorship. In scrutinizing a changing system of speculative theory frequently awash in abstruse generalities, even the most watchful eye of the most alert censor could hope to discover only random and superficial deviations from orthodoxy. In spite of any external changes which the censor may have imposed, Belinski's articles reflect an inner logic which alone is enough to prove that the main evolution of his ideas has been preserved intact.

CHAPTER FOUR

The Argument of The Telescope
(1834–1836)

B*elinski's* first literary effort, the play of his student years, *Dmitri Kalinin*, was rejected by the censors during the winter of 1831. In September of 1834 he made his professional debut as a literary critic with the first article in a series of "Literary Reveries," signed "on-inski," and published in *The Report (Molva)*, a weekly supplement to Nadezhdin's journal *The Telescope*. Between these two events lay an interlude of minor publications and unimportant translations from the French, largely inspired by financial need.

During his university years only two insignificant works went to the publisher from Belinski's hand: a short poem, called "A True Russian Tale," written in the style of a folk ballad and printed in May, 1831, in the single-sheet publication, *The Leaflet (Listok)*; and, in the following month, a brief article on Pushkin's *Boris Godunov*. After expulsion from the University he turned to the job of maintaining himself by translations. The French works which he translated at this time prove little about him except that he was willing to publish anything which he could sell. During Lent in the year 1833, he met the professor–editor Nicholas Nadezhdin, for whose *Telescope* and *Report* he proceeded to translate French books and journal articles.

Information about Belinski's literary activity and personal life during these years preceding the "Literary Reveries," and even until 1837, is limited. Perhaps informative documents and correspondence were destroyed during the official investigations which followed the suppression of the *Telescope* in 1836. One fact at least seems clear: that between the spring of 1833 and the autumn of 1834, Belinski's fortunes and spirits improved. He must have achieved at least temporary well-being in the city of which he could write: "Moscow is for me a city never to be forgotten, close to my heart; and my favorite dream . . . is to settle in it for good."[1] Letters to his family during the first half of 1834 announce a general improvement in his affairs, state that he was able "to begin to breathe more freely," and even contain a promise of money for his father. By August of that year he wrote to his brother that Nadezhdin had gone off on a trip and left him, Belinski, in charge of both his journal and his house. During the following month Belinski appeared in the pages of *The Report* as literary critic, apparently not against the wishes of his absent employer; and from May to December of 1835, he again served as Nadezhdin's editor.

Belinski's career as a professional literary critic properly begins with the publication of his "Literary Reveries," which appeared in ten numbers of the weekly supplement, *The Report*, between September and December of 1834. This initial period of literary activity was brought to an abrupt and unexpected end in 1836, when *The Telescope* was suppressed because of the publication in it of Chaadaev's famous first "Philosophic Letter." Belinski's critical writing during these two years is notable primarily for two long articles: the "Literary Reveries" ("Literaturnye mechtaniia") of 1834 and the essay "On the Russian Story and the Stories of Gogol" ("O russkoi povesti i povestiakh Gogolia") of 1835.

The task to which Belinski was to devote the major effort of his career as a critic consisted in elaborating a theory by which to define the function of Russian literature in Russian cultural life. For the performance of that task he was equipped, as his first important essays show, with a dual intellectual heritage: a pessimistic judgment upon Russian cultural life, and an idealistic aesthetic. The disparagement of Russian reality and enthusiasm for a romantic idealism drawn largely from German philosophy combined to determine the main direction of thought among the young intelligentsia of Belinski's circle. Such a combination of principles might very adequately fulfill the need of a personal credo for the intellectual willing to remain withdrawn from contemporary actuality. But to the literary critic working with the proposition that literature should become the expression of national life, the theory that the artist rises to the "Absolute" while the national culture remains in formless incoherence could provide little support.

If the "Reveries" demonstrate Belinski's acceptance of both the negativism and the idealism of his generation, the essay on Gogol discloses his capacity to call both those principles into question by his admiration for an artist whose work both glorified Russian life and revealed a new force of literary realism. The two essays considered together supply the first episode in Belinski's continuing struggle to reconcile the tenets of an ideological position with a perceptive recognition of concrete artistic achievement.

As the title suggests, the "Reveries" contain a little of everything. The youthful author wants to tell all he knows. As the first of a long series of frequently chaotic critical expositions, here is perhaps the most chaotic of all. The hints and declarations which constitute the matter of these pages must be marshaled into coherence by the reader himself before their theme, along with its ambiguities, becomes fully clear. By this very character the "Reveries" show what they are: a passing in speculative review of the major critical doctrines and ideological positions which by the time of the writing had come to focus in the mind of Belinski. The rationale for this literary exuberance is provided by the fact that Belinski's problem in these pages is the entire problem of his literary career and of the literary generation to which he belonged: namely, what is and what should be the direction of Russian literature? In sketching a subject of such breadth it was obviously necessary to paint with a large brush. Meanwhile the space allotted for these purposes in weekly editions of *The Report* hardly provided an adequate frame for such a rich portrayal. Perhaps this technical difficulty may at least partly excuse Belinski's dizzying chase across the decades of Russian literary history and in and out through disconnected critical judgments and rhetorical outbursts. The disorganization of these articles must also be ascribed to the inherent disorder of his theme. Into his reveries the young critic had brought elements from a variegated tradition of critical thought. And the author's interest was not so much in bringing order into that tradition (even if he had been able to do so) as in announcing his own enthusiastic acceptance of it.

The "Reveries" present a diffuse panorama of literary history and aesthetic doctrine; the essay on Gogol endeavors to bring into that broad setting a single new literary fact. The limited subject (primarily Gogol's early stories in *Arabesques* and *Mirgorod*) of the second article seems to raise only a minor and incidental literary phenomenon against the wide horizon of the "Reveries." Yet it is the Gogol essay which first shows Belinski's power to recognize new life, to test the discovery against his theory, and to seek to bring literary judgment and ideological doctrine into harmony.

The "Literary Reveries" (*1834*)

To the title "Literary Reveries" Belinski appended a subtitle: "An Elegy in Prose." Apparently the critic was conscious of creating a melancholy counterpart to Pushkin's happier "novel in verse," *Eugene Onegin.* But an elegy, even in prose, remains in spirit a work of poetry, a song. At the outset the suggestion is thus made that if Belinski was to write of Russian literature in a mood of melancholy regret, he was also to express his regret with a lyrical enthusiasm for his subject. This quality of excitement in Belinski's writing is in itself an important character of his criticism. The earnest style demonstrates more effectively than an argument the critic's hope for the national literature even while he expresses his dismay at its contemporary state. The lyrical outburst within the analytical dissection sounds the note of idealism throughout the elegy of negative criticism.

It was, indeed, the impression that a new moral energy had been introduced into the world of criticism, rather than the revelation of any original insight, that aroused readers of the "Reveries" like Panaev, who later wrote of Belinski's article: "Its new, bold, fresh spirit . . . captivated me. 'Is not this,' I thought, 'the new message which I have been longing for? Is not this the very voice of truth which I have wished so long to hear?'"[2] Reacting with similar enthusiasm, the writer Ivan Lazhechnikov (1792–1869) must have given Belinski a welcome titillation of pride by writing him to ask, "Whose are those 'Reveries' of his [Nadezhdin's], so lively and intelligent? . . . Let me know by the first mail who their author is."[3] The new writer had dealt in old themes, familiar to any reader of *The Report*; what impressed his public was the force with which he declared what many knew.

Belinski's opening argument in the first pages of the "Reveries" does not seem to promise much food for exultation. After a brief review of what he takes to be the unhappy state of Russian letters, the young author ends his first article in the series with the apprehensive question: "Is it true that we have no literature?" The following week's installment opens immediately with the answer: "Yes, it is true we have no literature!" Obviously a definition of terms is called for. What is literature? In the answer to that question a major tenet of Belinski's critical position in these pages is announced.

If literature is taken as the sum of all intellectual activity which finds expression in writing, then Russia can lay claim to a considerable literature, exemplified by such works as Karamzin's *History of the Russian State*, the works on natural philosophy of Vellanski and Pavlov, Pushkin's *Boris Godunov*, the odes of Derzhavin. Or if by literature is meant a collection of literary masterpieces, even then Russia is not without honor. But every country, especially one as vast as the Russian Empire, could be expected to have its quota of Lomonosovs and Derzhavins. A third definition of literature is alone acceptable; and judged by its standard, Russian literature does not yet exist. By this definition, literature consists of written works "created as art" which express the spirit of a people and portray their inner life. There are no sudden breaks in the history of a true literature, evolving under the momentum of an inner development of its own which maintains itself against the pressure of external forces. Whereas the history of literary creation in Russia has been, in fact, a long tale of imposed directions and foreign influences, creating a chaos of discordant literary standards.

In an effort to understand what constitutes literature among other peoples, the author notes that the French define literature as the "expression of society." Is such a definition valid? If by society is meant the *beau monde*, then such a definition will hold only for the French. Each people has its own individual character. "Every people expresses in itself some phase of the life of humanity." Thus the Germans are distinguished by a genius for analysis, the

English by activity in the world of affairs, whereas "French life is social life, the life of the salon." And French literature is preeminently the expression of that life. In Germany, on the other hand, "literature is the expression not of society but of the people." Each example seems to illustrate the principle that literature is everywhere "a symbol of the inner life of the nation."

But before Russian literature is discussed in detail, the general nature of art must first be described. Upon this sudden notice, Belinski the analyst of Russian cultural instability is remarkably transformed into the lyric singer of transcendental idealism. He now proceeds to exclaim that all creation is nothing but the breath of the "eternal idea," appearing in manifold form, which restlessly and "continuously creates to destroy and destroys to create." It is this idea which is "incarnated in the brilliant sun, in the magnificent planet, in the wandering comet; it lives and breathes in the stormy ebb and flow of the sea, in the savage hurricane of the desert, in the whisper of leaves, the murmur of the brook, in the growl of the lion and the tear of the child, in the smile of beauty, in the free will of man, in the harmonious creations of genius. . . " The moral activity of the eternal idea appears in the struggle between good and evil, love and egoism, as well as in the physical conflict of expansion and contraction. "Without struggle there is no service, without service no reward, without activity no life." Such is "the movement of the eternal idea, the life of which consists in uninterrupted activity."

Now the aim of art is to express this "idea of the general life of nature." Only the greatest artist is able to depict that life in its entirety. Thus Byron portrays the bitterness of life and Schiller its heroism, but only Shakespeare portrays nature. Ask Shakespeare why he made Lear as he did and he must answer that so it is in the world. The perfect artist shows sympathetic insight into both good and evil.

"When he [the poet] attempts by his works to force you to look upon life from his point of view, then he is no longer a poet but a thinker — and a bad thinker, of dubious intentions, worthy of condemnation; for poetry has no end outside itself. So long as the poet follows spontaneously the momentary illumination of his imagination, just so long does he remain a moral person and a poet. But as soon as he sets himself a purpose and gives himself a thesis, he becomes a philosopher, a thinker, a moralist, and he loses his magic power over me. . . Art is the expression of the great universal idea in its infinitely various manifestations. . . The whole art of the poet should consist in . . . bringing the reader to feel the passing breath of that life which animates the universe.

As the individuality of the artist is defined through his expression of the life of universal nature, so the individuality of every people is defined by its participation in the life of universal humanity. Unless a nation assumes some distinctive role in the realization of the universal design, it does not live but merely vegetates. Just as egoism destroys the artist, so national exclusiveness destroys a people. When Rome came to think of itself as the whole of humanity, it declined morally. For only by moving down the particular roads of particular national cultures does humanity attain its goal. The way which each nation has been assigned to pursue has been established by the cultural heritage of the people. If that heritage is destroyed or impaired, the people is left without a moral identity.

The effects of a division within the Russian national heritage have been observable since the innovations of Peter. Following the imposition of foreign manners and ideas, the people (*narod*) and the society (*obshchestvo*) of Russia formed into separate and opposing camps. Out of this cultural division ultimately resulted the fatal destruction of "national character" in literature — which the great age of Catherine was still able to create, mainly through the dissimilar geniuses of Derzhavin and Fonvizin, successors in the literary tradition which had been fathered by Lomonosov.

Gabriel Derzhavin (1743–1816) and Denis Fonvizin (1745–1792) illustrate a primary distinction between the writer who expresses his age and society by a spontaneous and unconscious sense of the spirit of the people and, on the other hand, the writer who consciously caters to the interests and tastes of a reading public. The validity of the "national character" in Derzhavin's work lies in its "consisting not in a selection of *muzhik* words or forced imitations of the harmonies of folk songs and fairy tales in verse, but in the bent of the Russian mind, in the Russian manner of viewing things. . . He was original and 'national' (*narodny*) without knowing it." Fonvizin's works, on the other hand, "appeared at their time and thus enjoyed remarkable success. They were the expression of the dominant pattern of thought among educated people, and therefore they were enjoyed." By such qualities of timeliness, an author may be recognized as "an intelligent observer and a witty writer, but not as an artist."

The danger to the Russian artist, Belinski continues, in consciously catering to contemporary taste came to be increasingly aggravated by the popularity in Russia of foreign models. By imitation of literary traditions and directions which found no genuine home in Russia, Russian literature failed more and more hopelessly to give voice to the genius of the people. Writers no longer asked how a literary work should best proceed but came to feel secure in the unquestioning adoption of foreign standards and methods. Hence the absence of a genuine Russian literature, despite a proliferation of literary schools growing up like mushrooms and disappearing like soap bubbles. In the absence of a literary tradition of his own, the Russian author was doomed to become a Greek or a Roman, a Frenchman or an Englishman. Even the great Karamzin, the dominant figure of his period in the turn from the eighteenth into the nineteenth century, was the victim of his own imitativeness. His ambitious effort to reconcile the written with the spoken language of his age was jeopardized by his choice of French as a model in preference to the native idioms of Russian. In his crusade to bring to the Russian public a desire for reading, he lowered himself to his public, who grew up to laugh at his sentimentality. By a too-conscious effort to follow the vogue of sentimentalism, which he superficially took to be the spirit of his age, he failed to be true to his own genius and consequently to be honest and natural. By that failure he misused the fine gifts with which he could have performed a substantial service. By this he stands in revealing contrast to Krylov, the writer of fables, which his great talent was able to perfect into enduring works of art because they "originated not accidentally but as an outgrowth of our national spirit."

Yet among all these works of genius scattered through the annals of literary creation in Russia, where is the literature? Where is the coherent literary tradition in the midst of these random literary achievements? "You will search in vain." This discrepancy between the wealth of individual genius and the poverty of native tradition is especially remarkable in the age of Pushkin, whose original achievement stands in bright relief against the pseudo-romanticism of his time. This period shows most clearly the distortions to which Russian literature has been forced by the thoughtless importation of foreign tendencies and controversies. Hence the period of Pushkin was filled with the argument between classic and romantic, although the classicism under discussion was an alien creation and romanticism in Europe implied reaction against the very fault of imitativeness of which the Russian romantics were most guilty. "In Europe classicism was a literary Catholicism," to which the French criticism of Boileau and La Harpe provided an Inquisition and for which the sacred objects were Corneille, Racine, and Voltaire. When the artificial eighteenth century breathed its last, literary taste turned to seek a renewal of life in romanticism. "This romanticism was nothing but a return to naturalness and hence to independence and 'national character' in art. . . " In Russia, on the other hand, just as classicism was "nothing more nor less than a weak aftertone of an echo from Europe," so romanticism remained a fragment of the intellectual life of Europe, "the echo of which came to us across the Baltic Sea."

In such a time of servile imitation Pushkin stood out by virtue of his spontaneity and originality. Precisely by reason of not obeying the superficial demands of a time of pseudoromanticism, Pushkin was saved from Karamzin's error of becoming the victim of his age. For "his work was the unconscious work of the artist. . . " By remaining superior to the passing vogue of a borrowed romanticism he succeeded in dominating the romantic decade of the twenties. "The extreme influence of Pushkin proceeded from the fact that in relation to Russia he was the son of his time in the full sense of the word, that he moved forward in step with his nation and was representative of the development of its intellectual life; hence his authority was legitimate." By virtue of his artistic integrity he himself came to be imitated — by those who mistook a capacity to imitate for the ability to recreate in words "the manifestations of the universal life of nature." Thus Pushkin was imitated in those harmonies which are only his external form

rather than equaled in his deep and passionate feeling, which alone
is the source of artistic creativity. His imitators, on the other hand,
slip over the reality of life and nature without penetrating into its
depth; "they only describe objects or reason about them, as it
were, but do not feel them." Hence the period of Pushkin is
marked by a plethora of poets who for the most part succeed only
in pleasing and seldom in captivating the imagination.

Thus it was the misfortune of the age of Pushkin to produce
works of superficial imitation and to bring forth only rare works
of genuine national expression. So of Kozlov: "What a pity that
he wrote ballads. A ballad which does not express the character
of a people is a false genus and can arouse no feeling. Moreover he
tried to create a kind of Slavic ballad. The Slavs lived long ago
and are little known to us. . . " Whereas the great Griboedov,
"called to be the creator of Russian comedy, the creator of the
Russian theater, . . . carried away too many hopes with him to
the grave." For "the drama is, if not the best, the genre of poetry
closest to us." Among the arts it is the drama which "represents
man in his eternal battle with his own ego and with his vocation,
with his everlasting activity, the source of which is the striving
for some shadowy ideal of happiness which he rarely comprehends
and still more rarely attains."

"What, I ask you, is the theater? . . . Oh, it is the true temple
of art, at whose entrance you for a moment separate yourself from
earth, free yourself from day-to-day relationships. . . Here your
cold ego disappears in the fervent ether of love. If you are tormented by the burdensome thought of your life and the weakness
of your powers, here you forget all that. If your soul at some time
thirsted for love and ecstasy, if in your imagination there ever
flashed, like a bright vision of the night, some captivating form,
long forgotten like an unrecoverable dream, here that thirst will
flare up in you with new, unconquerable power; here that image
will appear to you, and you will see its eyes straining upon you
with love and longing; you will be enraptured by its captivating
breath, you will be startled at the fiery touch of its hands. . . "
But, alas, we have no real Russian theater.

Yet, for all its failures, the age of Pushkin was the age of richest
flower in Russian literature. If Russia did not yet have a true litera-

ture then, at least it had the suggestion of one and was almost willing to believe that it really did possess a literature. But with the year 1830 a new period began. At that time there occurred another of those sudden breaks in Russian literary evolution which most clearly prove the absence in Russia of a genuine literary history. In Russia no literary development becomes the successor of another, no movement takes its impetus from a related movement in the past. "The history of our literature is nothing but the history of unsuccessful attempts to create, by means of blind imitation of foreign literatures, a literature of our own. But such attempts do not create a literature. It is created as a national language and national customs are created: by a people, without their will or forethought."

So the age of Pushkin suddenly died and its numerous literary journals along with it, as if from the cholera epidemic of 1830. The journals succumbed to the common illness which infects the whole of Russian literature: they had been created not out of spontaneous need but to relieve idleness or to make a noise, and so with few exceptions they achieved no independent character and consequently no influence. "Not one of them followed the advance of enlightenment, not one of them brought to its readers the progress of humanity in its career of self-perfection."

With the end of the age of Pushkin, Russian literature entered upon a new epoch. Thus far no major literary figure dominates the present period as Lomonosov, Karamzin, and Pushkin each dominated his period. But one fact is clear: as the age of Pushkin was an age of poetry, Russian literature has now entered upon an age of prose. By itself this fact signifies a decline rather than a step forward. Yet even in this present age of literary interregnum a good work is possible, as good works are always possible. "Every creation, in whatever genre, is good in all ages and at every moment if by its spirit and form it bears upon itself the stamp of its age and satisfies all the demands of that age."

But the present generation in Russian letters, precisely by its "lively sense of the instability of our imitative literature," has been carried to the other extreme of a factitious "national character" in literature. Just as every writer formerly tried to be a romantic, now all set themselves up as "national." But this deliberate cult of the national is a perversion of true nationality in literature. Did Krylov succeed in expressing the Russian national character because he consciously set out to do so? Rather he became the spokesman of the genius of the Russian people because he could not help being so. By his spontaneous participation in the life of his people he was able to give spontaneous literary expression to that life. Meanwhile in their failure to penetrate to the depth of true nationalism, lesser artists turned to themes deliberately drawn from the simple world of the uncultured masses of the people. Such a distortion of true national character in literature, which in its genuine form is the re-creation of a national physiognomy, was doubtlessly inevitable in Russia, where a national physiognomy is hardly observable. Since the area of Russian life which has been least affected by artificial imitation is the world of the uncultivated mass of the people, it was inevitable that the search for national individuality should lead the literary artist to the simple people. But a nation is not composed solely of the popular masses. As the head is the most important part of the body, so the middle and upper classes comprise the most important elements of a nation. And only a literature which reproduces the life of the whole people can claim to be a truly national literature. A disproportionate interest in the lower strata of the national life must necessarily result in narrowness. But until the upper levels of Russian life are freed from sterile foreign influences, the poet who seeks to express the national character will continue to turn to the lower classes and to pre-Petrine Russia, however poor the sustenance which those sources can provide, for a literature which is a genuine expression of the Russian people. This is a result which few writers, until now, have achieved. Among others, Gogol, the author of the well-known *Evenings on a Farm near Dikanka*, "belongs to the number of unusual talents. . . May he fully justify the hopes he has raised."

The present age has emerged as the age of a prose literature dedicated to the depiction of Russian actuality. But this present tendency will constitute merely one more literary fashion in a literary history of many fashions, until there is created in Russia a society which has taken clear shape as an expression of the physiognomy of the Russian people. Such a national identity is sure to be achieved. "We have no literature — I repeat it with enthusiasm, with pleasure, for in that truth I see the guarantee of our future success. . . Noble poverty is better than visionary riches."

Russia needs enlightenment first of all, created by native labors on home ground. In the interests of literature itself, "what we need is not literature, which will come in its time without any effort on our part, but enlightenment. . . What we need at present is study, study, study!"

Externally, the striking feature of the "Reveries," which is noticeable even in the preceding brief reproduction, is their disjointedness. The piecemeal manner of composition and publication could only have aggravated that fault; yet some of the most abrupt movements in the writing appear within a single short installment. Perhaps the most remarkably sudden transition is that made from the introductory definition of literature to the unexpected manner and thought of: "God's whole limitless, beauteous world is nothing but the breath of the one, eternal idea. . . " A similarly sharp turn in the discussion is the movement from the analysis of the drama to a rapturous declamation upon the theater "at whose entrance you for a moment separate yourself from earth," and so on. And each of these shifts occurs within a single article as it was printed in *The Report*. No transition between separate articles is less smooth than these internal changes of thought, manner, and address. This abruptness of movement from analysis to lyricism, from a negative view of Russian literature to an exalted declaration of the significance of art, shows on the very surface of the "Reveries" the conflict they contain: namely, the conflict in mood between a negative critique of Russian cultural life and a positive glorification of art, drawn largely from German sources.

At first sight, indeed, the "Reveries" appear to contain nothing original but to constitute a disorderly passing-in-review of critical propositions widely shared. The influence of Nadezhdin in particular has been suspected in these pages. The title itself suggests perhaps Nadezhdin's article, "Literary Apprehensions," which appeared in 1828 in the *European Messenger* (*Vestnik Evropy*). In the general direction of his thought Nadezhdin had preceded Belinski, first of all in bringing his criticism to transcend a purely

literary interest — a feature of the "Reveries" which has been
advanced as a claim for Belinski's originality in that work.[4] This
tendency in Nadezhdin's critical writing is apparent not only in
the "Literary Apprehensions" but also in his 1830 doctoral dissertation, "On the Present Abuse and Distortion of Romantic
Poetry," as well as in a later article, "Chronicles of the National
Literature; Report for 1831." So apparent, in fact, is the external
resemblance between the two authors that, in the opinion of one
observer, "a visitor to Nadezhdin's lectures would have found it
hard to believe that these 'Reveries' were written by Belinski and
not by Nadezhdin." [5]

The existence of parallel ideas in Nadezhdin and Belinski may
not solve the difficult question of Nadezhdin's influence over
Belinski's thought, if that were necessary. But such parallelisms
at least show in what large measure Belinski filled his "Reveries"
with reflections which were not new to readers of the literary
supplement in which they appeared. Both the pessimistic criticism
of Russian cultural life and the idealistic philosophy of art which
mark the "Reveries" are observable in Nadezhdin's earlier writings.
Even in the detail of his thought Belinski recalls Nadezhdin.

The argument which runs through those writings of Nadezhdin
which have been referred to is that literature should be "the flower
of our national culture"; but that the contemporary state of
Russian letters is lamentable; that individual geniuses in the history
of Russian literature stand in bold relief against a backdrop of
"general emptiness and sterility," which only showed itself more
clearly in Russia's thoughtless imitation of Europe; that the
national literature can be vitalized only by an infusion of the
naturalness of the "national character" appropriate to an age in
which the individual's membership in the national community
"constitutes the essential character of the period in which we are
living"; since the function of poetry is to be "a faithful echo of
reality." In all this, Nadezhdin appears as the obvious predecessor
of Belinski. In at least one place, Belinski with his refrain "study,
study, study," repeats the very phrase used by Nadezhdin in his
dissertation: "to study, to study, by all means to study."

Alongside a negative analysis of Russian literature, Nadezhdin,
as a student of Schelling, had placed an idealistic aesthetic —

which Belinski was also to announce. Having described art as the "echo of reality," Nadezhdin defined reality, in its highest form, as the "divine harmony . . . in all the unnumbered phenomena of the world"; it follows that "the job of art is to harken to the secret echoes of the eternal harmony." For "what is beauty if not the most perfect harmony?" — a harmony served by "poetry, that sacred daughter of heaven and handmaiden of eternal beauty . . . "

Yet despite such occasional references to "divine harmony" and "eternal beauty," Nadezhdin nowhere attempts to relate his professions of idealism to the critique of Russian literature which he is constructing. The only enthusiasm which properly belongs to his critical theory is that which he holds for a future time when a new realism of social consciousness will combine a "classic" moral authority with a romantic individualism. For all his suggestion of a new departure in criticism, Nadezhdin's thought finds its main point of origin in a traditional opposition of classicism and romanticism. His achievement is to have found an equilibrium in "the sanctification of *social* bonds" whereby the literature of the future might avoid both the "academic servility" of classicism and the "insanity" of romanticism.

The young Belinski, of a new generation which had outlived the Russian quarrel of the ancients and the moderns, showed in his first important article an unmistakable disregard for the literary debate which inspired Nadezhdin's criticism. But the emphasis upon citizenship in the national community at which Nadezhdin had arrived in his resolution of an old literary dispute, could be taken by Belinski as a point of departure. By 1834 the doctrine of "national character" in literature was no longer a discovery; at least in Belinski's view, that doctrine had become the literary principle of the thirties. Thus Belinski's problem begins where Nadezhdin's had left off. Nadezhdin had found a synthesis of "classicism" and "romanticism" in his new emphasis upon the social. In moving on from that point, Belinski encountered the problem: once the doctrine of "national character" is recognized as the literary credo of the future, how shall it be interpreted and justified? It is largely to the problems inherent in the literary ideal of "national character" that the "Reveries" are addressed.

The title of the "Reveries" itself suggests their illogical structure and irregular pace; it may also suggest their brokenness of theme. Partly because so many reflections have been brought together, and partly because one thought seems to contradict others, the reader is liable to feel that no critical position whatever has been declared. Yet within this disorderly discussion, rambling over the whole field of modern Russian literature, the outlines of a theory can be discerned. According to the initial stages of the discussion, the subject of the "Reveries" is the nonexistence of Russian literature. Russia cannot claim to have a literature, because literature rightly defined is the expression of the national culture, and Russia is as yet without a coherent national culture.

In this initial and central argument, Belinski shows that he is concerned more with making a dramatic judgment upon Russian literature than with presenting an argument of perfect logic. For if literature properly defined is "an expression of the inner life of the nation," may not the character, however chaotic, of Russian literary tradition in its way constitute a faithful expression of Russian life? Wherein lies the logic of denying a "literature" to Russia simply on the ground that deficiencies appear to mark the cultural life which that literature expresses? Just as French and German literatures differ (according to the argument of the "Reveries") in the nature of what they express, does this difference not imply that Russian literature may in its turn exist to express some third character appropriate to the Russian people?

To meet such an objection Belinski would be required merely to make explicit what he had already begun to imply: that the major fault of Russian literature lies not with the literature but with the national culture which that literature is obliged to portray. A fully consistent pursuit of that argument, however, would have left no place for the dramatic statement that "we have no literature" — which if not perfectly sound literary criticism is probably good journalism.

Yet however phrased, the argument remains that Russian life fails to represent "a symbol of the inner life of the nation." From that major assertion, the critique of Russian cultural life proceeds to an explanation of how "the inner life of the nation" has been disunified by the cleavage between an enlightened minority and the uncultured masses of the people. By this cleavage the enlightened minority, to which group the artist and poet by definition belong, is frustrated in any effort it may make to create a national art. For whether it turns to an imitation of European models or, at the other pole, to a cultivation of themes and styles drawn from the life of the masses, no truly national art is created. For in neither direction lies the whole life of the nation.

This analysis of the predicament of the creative life in a stratified society constitutes one of Belinski's most substantial arguments in the "Reveries." By that analysis he succeeds in lending credibility to a claim which otherwise might have remained empty rhetoric: that "we have no literature." But into the midst, as it were, of this analysis there intrudes the seemingly irrelevant definition of the aim of art as the expression of the "idea of the general life of nature," which is "incarnated in the brilliant sun, . . . in the growl of the lion and the tear of the child. . . " What connection exists between this burst into idealism and the critical account of Russia's cultural incoherence? The remarkable fact is not that the connection between cultural negativism and aesthetic idealism does not exist, but that Belinski failed to make a more explicit assertion of that connection. For it is implied throughout the course of the "Reveries."

The following diagram may clarify what the author of the "Reveries" leaves in scattered formulae:

Poet
|
Nation
|
Humanity
|
"Eternal Idea"

Just as the "eternal idea" finds particular expression in humanity, so humanity in the nation, and so the nation in the true poet. Thus the theorems that art is the expression of the general life of nature and that art is the expression of the inner life of the nation, appear as equally valid statements of the same ideology. The national life is made the vehicle of the "idea in the general life of nature." As

Belinski insists, "every people expresses in itself some phase of the life of humanity."

It is within this schema of the creative life that Belinski arrives at his chief insight here into the relation between literature and nation. His doctrine is that the line in the above diagram between "poet" and "nation" should have the same value as the line between "humanity" and "nation" and that between "eternal idea" and "humanity." In other words, just as humanity is the spontaneous expression of the "eternal idea," and nation a spontaneous expression of humanity, so should the relation between poet and nation remain spontaneous. The farther up the scale we proceed, the less likely it becomes that spontaneity will be preserved. The poet who seeks consciously to give his work a distinctive national character thus finds a parellel in the nation which seeks to demonstrate its special mission among humanity. Just as egoism destroys the artist, so national exclusiveness destroys a people.

Put in its simplest form, Belinski's prescription for the poet is that he "be himself" as the best way of giving expression to the national character in his works. By expressing "the general life of nature" the poet is also on the way to expressing "the inner life of the nation," for the latter is itself a particular manifestation of the life of nature. Just as the national life is defined by its participation in the life of universal humanity, so the poet depends for his life upon the larger life of his nation. It is the national life which creates the national poet, and through him a national literature. Even the greatest poetic genius, even a Pushkin, cannot create a national literature when the national life is divided.

As the above diagram served to illustrate the ideological system of the "Reveries," so the following diagram may serve to indicate the fundamental fault which the critique of the "Reveries" diagnosed in Russian life:

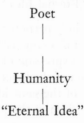

Poet

|

|

Humanity

|

"Eternal Idea"

That is to say, Belinski found that for Russia the weak or absent stage in his ascending order was at the level of the national life. According to his analysis, the function of the nation in the universal hierarchy had been impaired in Russian life by the disastrous cleavage within Russian society. The Russian poet's natural function as the poet of the whole Russian people was thus in its turn impaired. As a consequence, every effort by the poet to express the national character was bound to become a too-deliberate effort and thus to be threatened by falsification. Whereas the only true national poet is a poet like Krylov, who became the spokesman of the genius of the Russian people because he could not help being such.

By their failure of spontaneous participation in the life of the whole people, lesser literary artists turn to sources which are inevitably uncreative, Belinski argued. Thus a Fonvizin, or even a Karamzin, by catering to the arbitrary fashion of his time and milieu, seems to represent his age but in truth has lost touch with the common human life of the nation. On the other hand, a deliberate turning to the life of the unenlightened masses as a source of inspiration is equally ineffective. For the nation which the truly national poet knows and portrays is the whole people, not the common people without its leaders, not the national body without its head.

By such a diagnosis of the dangers of a false "national character" in literature, Belinski argued that the nation is properly not so much an object of the artist's portrayal but rather the particular medium through which "the eternal life of nature" and humanity is transmitted to him. In this interpretation of the national life as a particular mode of the development of mankind Belinski repeats the gospel of humanity which had found its most eminent apologist in Herder.[6] And precisely by means of such a philosophy of national life he is enabled to subordinate the demands which a narrow nationalism would make upon the artist to an idealism which transcends the very national life in which that idealism finds its expression. So long as Russian national life stood in urgent need of enlightenment, so long as it failed to achieve an organic unity, the literature which belonged to that life would remain subject to those sudden breaks and arbitrary influences which left Russia without an autonomous literary history. But since the ultimate end of art is to depict "the manifestations of the universal life of nature," to which the national life is only an avenue, even in Russia there can exist, despite the absence of a national literature, great artists like Pushkin and Krylov, whose genius for expressing the Russian national character remains the by-product of a human truth which transcends any national particularity.

For all their disorder, the "Reveries" may thus be taken to contain a theory which brought into approximate reconciliation the negative criticism of Russian cultural life and the idealism which had filtered to Belinski from German sources. But the conflict between that negativism and that idealism was not to disappear in Belinski's thought. Rather it was fated to undergo new provocation in the years just ahead, and first of all by the necessity of accounting for a new event in the world of Russian letters: the first major work of the young writer Gogol.

"On the Russian Story and the Stories of Gogol" (*1835*)

The article "On the Russian Story and the Stories of Gogol" appeared in *The Telescope* in the autumn of 1835, just a year after the "Reveries." If only by the familiar adjacency of the themes of realism and idealism, the Gogol essay clearly belongs to the period of the "Reveries." But the work of Gogol presents a troublesome test for the theory of the "Reveries." The subordination of the national reality to an "eternal idea" as the ultimate end of art finds little apparent corroboration in the work of an artist whose genius seems to lie in his portrayal of unadorned Russian actuality.

The essay on Gogol begins by joining the skepticism of the "Reveries" to a promise of new life in a literature to which the "Reveries" had barely allowed legitimate existence. In spite of its insignificance and even of doubts concerning its very existence, Belinski proceeds to argue, Russian literature has undergone a great variety of literary influences and has followed many literary directions. The literature of modern Russia began in an age of pedantic scholasticism, which in the time of Karamzin gave place to sentimentalism. To the latter importation from eighteenth-century Europe, Zhukovski added a mystical and fantastic element, which, although a valid contribution, provided only another variant of sentimentalism. By the age of Pushkin the romantic poem had come to be the preferred literary form. At the present time this is no longer true. "Now all our literature has turned into novels and stories," and the romantic poem is a thing of the past. Novels and stories alone are profitable on the contemporary market. Only in these forms is human life portrayed, along with "the principles of morality, the systems of philosophy, and, in a word, all the sciences."

What has caused this change? No individual, but "the spirit of the times," partly determined, of course, by external influences. So dominant have the novel and the story become that they have surpassed even the drama in popularity. In what lies the cause of this "dominant spirit of the times"?

Poetry embraces and reproduces by two methods, as it were, the phenomena of life. These methods are opposed to each other, although they lead to a single goal. The poet either re-creates life according to his own ideal, which depends upon his way of looking at things and his relation to the world, to his age, and the people among whom he lives; or he reproduces existence in all its naked truth, in fidelity to all the details, colors, and shadings of actuality. Poetry may thus be separated into two divisions, as it were: *idealistic* and *realistic*.

The poetry of every early people is hostile to reality, which is thought to be insipid. Only the mature individual or the mature people admires reality. For the sun to become an object of interest to a simple people, it must be made into a chariot of Phoebus. Thus the early Greek preferred the hymn and the ode to the depiction of actual life and would have considered the novel vulgar. Likewise his drama was not concerned with the human realism of a Shakespeare but constituted a form of religious ritual. Drama and poetry both selected from the reality of life only its noble and exalted moments.

But "poetry also has its ages, which are always parallel to the ages of a people." If it fails to develop it dies. Thus a false poetic coloring came to be applied in Alexandrian times to a Greek poetry which had lost its magic. Such artificiality is dominant in both Latin and French classical literature. The nobility and exaltation of French classical drama is a servant decked out in his lord's dress coat. With Christianity there developed the idea of the individual as separate from a people. With this sense of the individual as interesting in his own right, there developed the novel in its original form of the romance. It was the achievement of Cervantes to kill the false idealism of the outmoded romance, and of Shakespeare to create a poetry of real human emotions by depicting real persons in their human truth. In the eighteenth century, Goethe and Schiller followed Shakespeare in this creation of a poetry true to human life. In the nineteenth century the chief successor in this tradition of realism was Sir Walter Scott. Perhaps history itself will one day replace the novel, as the novel replaced poetry.

The present day, Belinski continues, is witness to the efflorescence of "realistic" poetry, "the poetry of life, the poetry of actuality, the true and actual poetry of our time. Its distinctive character is its faithfulness to reality. It does not transform life but reproduces, re-creates it, and . . . reflects its varied manifestations, selecting out of them whatever is needed for the creation of a complete, living, and unified picture." The hero of this poetry is the free individual working out his understanding of himself. The poetry which is closest to us portrays life "in all its nudity, in all its frightening formlessness. . . We demand not an ideal of life, but life itself, as it is. It may be good or bad, but we do not want to beautify it. . . Where there is truth, there is poetry."

As for "idealistic" poetry, it also exists with us in the contemporary lyric. But our lyricism is more plaintive than victorious. We see life more as a problem than as a gift. If the modern poet turns to nature he does so not to praise it but to find his own mystery in it. "Reflection — that is the subject of his inspiration."

It is not easy to see why our age is poor in the drama form. Perhaps the novel is better fitted to depict reality by reason of being freer and more formless. The popularity of the story is not hard to understand: it is short and quick and at the same time light and deep. So prolific have been our writers in this form that all our stories taken together would constitute another *Thousand and One Nights*, which if collected could all appear under the title: *Man and Life*. Above all, the novel and the story are the only two forms which appeared in our literature more from inner necessity than from imitation.

The story in its contemporary form began in Russia only in the twenties. Marlinski, its real founder, was soon joined by many rivals, including Odoevski, Pogodin, Polevoi, Pavlov, Gogol. But of them all, only Gogol is the genuine poet, "the poet of real life." He alone fulfills the demand of the chief question in all critical judgment: "Is this work really artistic? Is this author really a poet?"

"The capacity for creation is a great gift of nature. The act of creation in the creative soul is a great mystery. The moment of creation is a moment of great solemnity. Creation is purposeless in its purpose, unconscious in its consciousness, free in its dependence — such are its basic laws."

The artist feels a need to create which is independent of his will. "He can name neither the day nor the hour nor the minute of his creative activity." The need to create brings its artistic conception with it. Such a conception — for example, the idea of jealousy — is borne by the artist as a mother bears a child, while he hopes to present his idea in concrete form to others. The figure of the African Othello appears as in a vision in which increasing clarity brings out more and more detail. The final act of the artist, and the least important, is to give to his creation a visible, communicable form. For the creative moment in the artist's activity is the moment of secret vision, seen in "poetic somnambulism." "While the artist's creation is still a secret from the world, before he has yet taken pen in hand, he already sees his creatures clearly, he can already count the folds of their clothing, the wrinkles on their forehead, lined by passion and misfortune; he already knows them better than one knows his own father, brother, friend, mother, sweetheart; he knows even what they will say and do; he sees the whole thread of events which will entangle them and bind them to each other. But where has he seen these figures, where has he heard of these happenings? What is this creation of his? The consequence of a long and various experience? Of precise observation, of a profound ability to note similarities and to delineate them in sharp outlines? . . . Oh, certainly not, not in the least. . . Nowhere has he seen the figures which he has created; he has not made a copy of actuality. He has beheld it all in a prophetic vision; in the brilliant moments of poetic inspiration, in those moments known only to talent, he has seen with the all-seeing eyes of feeling. And such is the reason why the characters he has created are so true, so exact, and so well formed; that is why the plot, the dénouement, the transitions and the course of his novel or drama are so natural, so true to life, and so free. . . " Where conscious effort replaces the vision of the creative moment, creation suffers. "Inadequacies always appear where creation leaves off and work begins." It is in this sense that the artist is purposeless in his purpose and unconscious in his conscious effort; thus the creative act is accomplished independently of the artist while being at the same time dependent upon him. "To all this it is not at all difficult to relate the works of Gogol, as facts to theory."

The chief impression left by Gogol's work is: how simple, natural, and true; and yet how novel and original! The reader feels that he has long been familiar with these characters which the artist has created, that he has himself lived with them, that he could almost remind the author of certain of their features which have not yet been mentioned, so true to life are the personages which he has created. And in this very ordinariness of subject, this matter-of-fact, everyday quality of the events which he describes, resides the true mark of the artist. Indeed, "the more commonplace, the more squalid, so to speak, the content of a story is, . . . the greater is the talent which it reveals in its author." Thus an author shows his marvelous power when he can "force us to take a lively interest in the quarrel between Ivan Ivanovich and Ivan Nikiforovich and can make us laugh until the tears come to our eyes at the stupidity, meaninglessness, and utter foolishness of these living caricatures of humanity. . . But to require us then to take pity on both these idiots, pity from the bottom of our heart; to require us to take leave of them with a certain feeling of deep sadness, to force us to exclaim along with the author himself, 'This is a sad world, gentlemen!' — that is art which is truly divine, that is creativity; there is the artist who finds poetry wherever there is life."

The job of "realistic" poetry is "to abstract the poetry of life from the prose of life and to move our spirits by a true depiction of that life. But how powerful and profound is the poetry of Mr. Gogol within its external appearance of plainness and pettiness! Take his 'Old-World Landowners.' What do you find there? Two parodies of humanity, who in the course of several decades drink and eat, eat and drink, and who then, as has always happened, die. Where is the fascination in that? You see all the banality, all the ugliness, of this bestial, misshapen, ridiculous existence; but at the same time you take a real interest in the characters of the story, you laugh at them, although without spite, and then you sob with Philemon over his Baucis, you share his profound, unearthly grief and you are enraged at the worthless heir who squanders the property of those two simpletons! And then you have such a realistic conception of the actors in this stupid comedy, you see their whole life so clearly — you who perhaps have never been in the Ukraine and have never seen such scenes or heard of such people! Why is this? . . . Because the author has found poetry even in this vulgar and stupid existence. . . You weep for people who only ate and drank and then died! Oh, Mr. Gogol is a true wizard, and you cannot imagine how angry I am at him for almost having forced me to weep for people who only ate and drank and then died!"

Or "take 'The Diary of a Madman,' that disfigured grotesque, that strange, capricious fantasy of the artist, that good-natured smile at life and at man — at the pitiable condition of both life and man — that caricature, in which there is such depth of poetry. . .

"Yet none of this is manufactured, it is copied neither from tales nor from real life, but guessed at by feeling, in a moment of poetic inspiration."

While the stories of Gogol are to the highest degree genuine portrayals of Russian reality, their national character is not a special quality consciously imposed but a necessary condition of the true work of art, which by definition reflects the manners of a people. True national character is to Gogol as his shadow:

without his thinking about it at all it attaches itself to him. In this, it is like originality. For while Gogol's originality lies in his individual humor, his humor consists in his fidelity to life and not in the caricature of reality.

The humorous or the comic in Mr. Gogol has a special character of its own; it is a purely Russian humor, a quiet, good-natured humor, in which the author assumes the air of a simpleton. . . But this is only his manner; the real humor in Mr. Gogol consists in a true vision of life and . . . in no wise depends upon caricature. . . Objectivity is his idol. Evidence of this can be found in *Taras Bulba*, that marvelous epic, painted with a wide and bold brush, that penetrating sketch of the heroic life of a nation just coming into maturity, that broad picture in a narrow frame, worthy of Homer. Bulba is a hero, Bulba is a man with an iron character and an iron will; in describing the triumphs of his bloody vengeance, the author rises to a lyric tone and at the same time becomes a dramatist in the highest degree; but all this does not prevent him from showing you his hero from time to time in an amusing light. You shudder at Bulba coldbloodedly separating the mother from her children, killing his own son by his own hand . . . but you also laugh at him taking his son on in a fist-fight, drinking with his sons and rejoicing that they can keep up with the old man, and expressing his satisfaction that the teachers at the seminary thrashed them soundly. The basis of this humor . . . consists not in the author's ability or tendency to see the funny side of everything, but in his remaining true to life. If frequently Mr. Gogol does deliberately make fun of his protagonists, he does so without malice or hatred; he understands their foolishness but is not incensed at it; he even shows, as it were, his affection for it. . .

In this refusal to distort reality resides Gogol's morality. He "allows himself no sententious judgments, no moralizing; he merely depicts things as they are, without being concerned with their state, and he portrays them without any purpose but solely for the pleasure of portraying them. After [Griboedov's] *Woe from Wit* [*Gore ot uma*] I know nothing in the Russian language so distinguished by its purest morality and having so powerful and so beneficial an influence upon morals, as Gogol's stories. . . Morality in a work should consist in the complete absence of any claim by the author to a moral or immoral purpose." The work of art is moral by being true, and only a genuine talent is capable of truth; hence only genuine talent is moral.

Gogol's power to seize and to portray the whole of life is

clearly demonstrated in his story "The Nevsky Prospect." This is a creation which is both "profound" and "fascinating." For it moves between "the two opposite poles of life" and places "the sublime and the ridiculous side by side": the poor artist Piskarev and the gay lieutenant Pirogov. "Oh, what meaning is hidden in this contrast . . . Piskarev and Pirogov — the one in his grave, the other satisfied and happy. . . "

Although Belinski does not expound the "hidden meaning" which he finds here, it is clear from his excitement that the story has touched an inner chord: for surely the story of "The Nevsky Prospect" constituted for him, among other things, an image of the familiar conflict between the "real" and the "ideal" with which he was even now grappling — a conflict which all of Gogol's stories helped to sharpen in his mind.

What, Belinski now asks, is Gogol's place in Russian literature? Perhaps it is enough to say that he is a poet — a word which has lost its noble meaning in an age of many writers and no poets. To be sure, Gogol's career is only beginning and permits a judgment mainly of his hopes for the future. But it is clear that his possibilities are great. "At least at the present time he appears as the chief of our literature, the chief among our poets; he stands in the place left by Pushkin."

In a certain journal (Shevyrev's review of *Mirgorod* in *The Moscow Observer*) a strange request was addressed to Gogol: that he try his powers on a depiction of life among the upper classes — as if a poet can say to himself, I shall compose a work of such and such a kind, or in such and such a form. Or as if the subject which he treats makes any difference in the value of his work. As if it were not axiomatic that "wherever there is life there is poetry." Gogol can write only what his inspiration tells him to write. "The freedom of the artist consists in the harmony of his own will with some higher will not dependent upon him."

Perhaps no aspect of this discussion of the artistry of Gogol is more remarkable than the abrupt movement between "realism" and "idealism" which continues the vacillation of the "Reveries." Thus the discussion of Gogol's simplicity, nationalism, and perfect fidelity to life is broken into by a theory of the creative act according to which the poet receives his inspiration "in the prophetic dream" of "poetic somnambulism." Having outlined a theory of art whereby the artist is removed as far as possible from the concrete fact of empirical reality, the author proceeds by means of that theory to try to account for the stories of Gogol, which impress him most by their closeness to commonplace, even vulgar, actuality. Thus it seems clear that the realism of Gogol, far from being perfectly at one with Belinski's present ideology, asserted itself against the idealism of the theory which the "Reveries" first announced. The assertion that "to all this [i.e., this theory of art] it is not at all difficult to relate the works of Gogol" serves mainly to call attention to the effort which Belinski is compelled to make: namely, the effort to reconcile an aesthetic idealism with an artistic realism. But instead of a reconciliation, a new break is announced: poetry comes to be divided into "realistic" and "idealistic." And not only is the ideal separated from the real, but the move is clearly made to discount the ideal in favor of the real. "Idealistic" poetry finds its purest expression among simpler peoples, among whom it remains "in harmony with life but in discord with reality"; whereas the "realistic" poetry of mature peoples depicts a life which by being "divested and denuded of its false colors" would seem to the primitive idealist "desiccated, tiresome, insipid, and impoverished prose." How close to earth Belinski stands here (at least for the moment) after his flight into the empyrean of Schelling's *Welt- seele* on which the "Reveries" had recently carried him!

The crucial discovery which Belinski made about the early tales of Gogol was that their author, by the power of his artistry, had glorified Russian reality — the unbearable reality against which German romantic philosophy had been invoked in psycho- logical and intellectual defense by a whole generation of the in- telligentsia; the sordid reality which by reason of its sterility could not nourish a continuous national literature but only the random works of occasional genius. And it was to just such a random masterpiece, created by the individual genius of Gogol, that Belinski, the theorist of literature as national expression, turned as to a momentous revelation. Clearly the "physiognomy" of Russian national life had not become perceptibly clearer or more coherent when Gogol's artistry declared itself. The need for an enlightenment which was to precede the establishment of literature in Russia had obviously not been met. Gogol's artistic achievement apparently derived from another source.

The disparagement of Russia's national formlessness which the "Reveries" had asserted and the consequent readiness to allow for an art which in the absence of a coherent national physiognomy drew its inspiration directly from "the general life of nature" thus comes into collision with Gogol's achievement in creating art out of the commonest materials of Russian life as it existed, "in all its nudity, in all its frightening formlessness." Confronted with the work of Gogol, Belinski was reduced to insisting that his theory could account for the discovery, but the claim serves only to call attention to Belinski's own recognition of his difficulty. All his effort had been expended on transcending the fact of Russian reality as it then existed, of explaining art in terms of that transcendence. Gogol appeared with an art which found its basis precisely within that reality which all of Belinski's theoretical effort had striven to transcend. Clearly the artist had surprised his critic by the potentiality for art which he had found in the materials whose rejection Belinski, the eager disciple of the Russian cult of Schelling, had been struggling to justify. Met with Gogol's power to evoke the humanity of such people as the "old-world landowners," "who only ate and drank and then died," Belinski has good reason to exclaim, "You cannot imagine how angry I am at him for almost having forced me to weep for [them]. . . "

What is impressive in Belinski's critical recognition of Gogol is, first of all, that he accomplished it. But it is equally noteworthy that he proceeded to account for his literary judgment in terms of his idealist theory. Notwithstanding the abrupt introduction of the conception of art as a depiction of life "in all its nudity, in all its frightening formlessness," Belinski is unprepared to accept such a conception, which goes undeveloped at his hands. He insists upon introducing the "eternal idea" which his theory had declared essential to artistic creation. He therefore proceeds to find in the art of Gogol a penetration of the commonplace by the ideal, through which alone the vulgar reality of the contemporary scene can become an object of artistic inspiration. He thus insists formally that the stories of Gogol illustrate the theory of the genesis of artistic creation out of a "poetic somnambulism." But the hypothesis remains hypothetical, and immediately following its formulation the critic goes on quickly to dwell upon the simplicity and naturalness of Gogol's work.

Thus Belinski did not reject the often vulgar realism of Gogol but turned instead to the job of reconciling it with his own theoretical position, established upon an idealistic rejection of the very reality which Gogol's genius had transformed into art. The high post to which Belinski assigned Gogol as "the chief of our literature, the chief among our poets," who "stands in the place left by Pushkin," is proof of the impact which Gogol had made upon Belinski's thought. But all of Belinski's aesthetic formulations up to this time scarcely prepare us for his recognition of Gogol. Having accepted Gogol's realism, Belinski was left with the task of accounting for that acceptance in theoretical terms.

It is this enthusiastic search for the terms by which he could harmonize the ideal with the actual, that embarked Belinski upon the critical passage of his life and thought which lay just ahead. That the reconciliation of Gogol's realism with the idealism of his own theory remained in his thought unsatisfactory and incomplete, notwithstanding the preliminary effort of the 1835 essay on Gogol's stories, is proved by the necessity of his further search, which led him inexorably into succeeding crises. Before he could fully grasp the impossible remoteness of the transcendental idealism toward which his thought had been oriented by his intellectual heritage, he was required to play out, in the years immediately following his affiliation with *The Telescope*, a metaphysical drama which involved his entire personal and intellectual life. Into the development of that drama intruded new influences which met him at crucial turns. But notwithstanding an appearance of unstable sensitivity to the pressure of arbitrary influences, the evolution through which he was to pass has a human logic of its own which alone makes the extremism of the succeeding years comprehensible.

CHAPTER FIVE

The Rationalization of Reality
(1836–1841)

The Locked Paradise

In the fifteenth number of the journal *The Telescope* for the year 1836, Professor Nadezhdin, the editor, decided to publish Chaadaev's famous first "Philosophic Letter" — evidently not a work to delight the censors. Nadezhdin had preceded his decision with the announcement that he would "revive his drowsy journal or bury it with honor." The upshot, as the word "bury" seems to anticipate, was the suppression of *The Telescope*. Whatever honor the journal could claim at the time of its burial was largely the work of its twenty-five-year-old critic, Vissarion Belinski. For it was he who, mainly by his "Literary Reveries" and long article on Gogol, had transformed *The Telescope* into a journal of serious criticism. Even Russia's first poet, Alexander Pushkin, had been impressed by this young critic who had promoted Gogol to "the place left by Pushkin" and who dared to pass judgment on Pushkin's own journal, *The Contemporary* (predicting — accurately — that it would not sell). Pushkin at one time considered employing him.

Between the closing of *The Telescope* in the autumn of 1836 and the publication of *The Moscow Observer* (*Moskovski Nabliudatel*) in the spring of 1838, Belinski was left professionally, although not intellectually, unemployed. This interlude of literary inactivity is marked by a personal drama of such significance that upon its dénouement Belinski emerged in the pages of *The Moscow Observer* in 1838 with a critical position which had obviously undergone a major alteration since his last public ap-

pearance; indeed, he appeared to have effected something like a
complete about-face.

The struggle of the years which closed with *The Telescope*
had been engaged between an idealism which transcended actuality and a criticism which subjected actuality to a negative
judgment. By neither term of that argument was reality justified
or accepted. With the first articles printed in *The Moscow Observer*, on the other hand, a major emphasis appears to be placed
upon a systematic acceptance of things as they are. The "national"
poet as presented by Belinski in the pages of *The Telescope* had
been the poet who expresses "the inner life of the nation" by
seizing "the idea in the general life of nature" and in "the life of
humanity." The argument of *The Telescope* had thus sought to
sustain, in the interpretation of "national character" in literature,
an idealism which allowed no place for narrow nationalism. But
in Belinski's articles of 1839 on Zhukovski's poem, "The Anniversary of Borodino," and Glinka's *Sketches of the Battle of Borodino*, the critic seems to be announcing an unqualified patriotism,
a *mystique* of Russian life in which national faults become almost
national virtues.

How can such a reversal of position be explained? How, indeed, can a critic apparently so mercurial be absolved from the
charge of arbitrary judgment? Or have accidental influences from
without inflicted upon Belinski's own thought that same fragmentary quality which he was so quick to diagnose in the Russian
literature of his day?

There is, of course, no doubt of the power with which influential minds (in the years just ahead, chiefly Fichte and Hegel)
were to appeal to Belinski, through the mediation of influential
friends (now chiefly Michael Bakunin). But if influences from
without now seemed to dominate Belinski's intellectual and emotional life, it was because they answered to a spontaneous and
self-conscious personal experience.

Although the main direction of Belinski's evolution at this
time seems clear enough in its psychology, precise chronology is
not easy to establish. This fact is partly due to the difficulty of
setting time limits to the life of the mind; but it is also partly due
to the scarcity of documents. There are no critical essays for this

period, lasting roughly a year and a half; and especially for the first half of the year 1837, private correspondence is almost nil. The best first-hand source of information is Belinski's later correspondence, especially the letters of late 1837 and of 1838 addressed to Michael Bakunin, with whom Belinski engaged in lengthy recapitulations of his own spiritual progress. Until the early forties, in fact, Belinski continued to provide voluminous demonstration of an assertion made to Bakunin, in a letter of April 6, 1841, that "all my life is in my letters."

The fate of *The Telescope* was settled in the fall of 1836. The news reached Belinski upon his return from the Bakunin estate, "Priamukhino," situated near the city of Tver, to the northwest of Moscow. The coincidence of these two events may be taken to forecast the immediate future in Belinski's life. Materially reduced to indigence by the loss of his only source of income, intellectually he was being raised, by the help of Bakunin, to new heights of personal idealism. The gap was thus widening perilously between his material condition and his metaphysical effort.

In these years of the mid-thirties, Belinski seems, on the evidence of his subsequent confessions, close to being intellectually hypnotized by the spell of his new friend, the young Michael Bakunin (the famous anarchist of later years), to whom he once confided, in a letter of June 20, 1838, "After Stankevich, you are the one to whom I owe more than to all the others." By his own admission, the chief attraction which he found in Bakunin must have been approximately the same as that which he had found in Stankevich: the appeal of a vigorous personality embarked on the same philosophic quest which Belinski himself knew. In his own words (from a letter of October 12, 1838, written to Bakunin) what Belinski found impressive in Bakunin was "the savage power; the restless, uneasy, and profound movement of spirit; the ceaseless striving forward, without satisfaction in the present moment — even hatred for the present moment and for himself in the present; the breaking through to the general from particularities."

It was apparently this common eagerness for philosophic solutions which had earlier attracted Stankevich to Bakunin in 1835 and had inspired the two young metaphysicians to study

Kant together during the winter of 1835–36 — a decision which brought Bakunin to Moscow, where he was subsequently to occupy an increasingly important place in the Stankevich circle. Upon Stankevich's departure abroad in August of 1837, Bakunin succeeded him as the leader of the circle.

These years are the time of Bakunin's hold upon Belinski, who soon, in a letter of June, 1838, was to cry, "Michel, I stood, I groaned under your authority." What seems to have impressed Belinski most and to have influenced his thought most decisively was the compelling, the almost bewitching capacity for generalization at which he marveled in Bakunin. Another contemporary, Paul Annenkov, said of Bakunin, "All life appeared to him through the prism of abstraction, and he spoke of it with striking enthusiasm only when it was translated into idea." [1] This was the power by which Bakunin was to charm Belinski, in a spell which Belinski was to throw off only by the most painful exertions. Bakunin was to become for Belinski the wielder of a fatal influence, the one who (as Belinski complained in a letter written to Bakunin on August 17, 1837) "introduced into my life the idea — which I do not like. . . " By "the idea" Belinski meant not some particular conception, but the whole life of abstraction which Bakunin seemed to incarnate and against which Belinski's sense of concrete reality was compelled to assert its claims.

Perhaps even more decisive for Belinski than the character of Bakunin was the character of Bakunin's current philosophic enthusiasm: the philosophy of Johann Gottlieb Fichte. In 1836 *The Telescope* ran a translation by Bakunin from Fichte's *Several Lectures on the Vocation of the Scholar* (*Einige Vorlesungen über die Bestimmung des Gelehrten*). In these lectures, originally five in number, delivered at Jena in 1794, Fichte declared in popular form the philosophical doctrine which was to determine his appeal for his young Russian disciples: namely, an egocentric idealism. As the vocation of the individual as such is "a perfect harmony with himself" — an infinite goal to which it is man's vocation to continue to aspire — so the vocation of the individual in society is to assist all other individuals toward that goal; and of the scholar to preserve the ideal of the "moral nobility of the whole person." [2]

This exhortation to the moral perfection of the individual through a "perfect harmony with himself" was provided by Fichte with a doctrinal basis in his conception of the ego as the central reality. By this emphasis the external world, the "non-ego" (*Nicht-Ich*), becomes essentially a set of materials for the working-out of the ego (*Ich*). As Bakunin reproduced Fichte: "The soul must be its own object; it must not have any other object." By the interpretation of Bakunin, the external world of the non-ego became artificial, of no real substance in itself but merely the creation of the inner life of the ego, which alone could claim autonomy.

The significance of Fichte for Bakunin at this time lies in the fact that, far from suggesting a departure from the subjective idealism which Russian students had found in Schelling, Fichte placed his emphasis upon a still greater assertion of the ego. However unsuccessful, Schelling's effort had continued to be a reconciliation of the subjective and the objective within some kind of philosophic identity. Fichte represented a step backward, so to speak, from that effort of reconciliation, by his deliberate assertion of the subjective self.

This doctrine of the autonomy of the self and the validity of subjective intuition was provided with something like a material setting on the Bakunin estate at Priamukhino. Here Bakunin had set himself up as a sort of spiritual guide to his adoring sisters. Here Stankevich had visited in the autumn of 1835 as the suitor of Liubov Bakunin, whom he charmed less than he did her brother Michael, eager to hear of Stankevich's sallies into German metaphysics.

From August until mid-November of 1836, Belinski remained at Priamukhino, under the attentive patronage of his new instructor in German idealism and surrounded by the unfamiliar consolations of feminine solicitude. In the years ahead Belinski was never shy about describing the impact made upon him by the little universe of Priamukhino. "By inviting me to Priamukhino," he wrote Bakunin in August of 1837, "you resurrected me. My spirit softened, its bitterness passed away, and it became amenable to happy impressions, happy ideas. The harmony of Priamukhino was not merely of assistance to you in my awakening; it was the chief cause. I felt that I was living in a new sphere; I beheld myself in a new world. Everything around me breathed of a harmony and a beatitude which penetrated partially even into my own soul. . . "

It is not hard to imagine the allure held out to a young literary day laborer by a nobleman's country estate where he could find the stimulation both of a congenial philosophical mind and of young women whom he found attractive. Without much doubt this was Belinski's first intimate glimpse of a happy home life graced by all the embellishments of easy material circumstances. He stood as a restless intellectual, condemned to a bleak and precarious existence "in Moscow . . . where my only anchor of salvation is *The Telescope* — and that an unstable one," [3] before the warm hearth of what looked to him like a serenely happy family. This family circle, with its "half-philosophic, half-mystical German tone," as Panaev described it, in which "one of Bakunin's sisters, under the influence of mystical ecstasy, sometimes, it was said, even saw visions," was sure to impress young Belinski with its "mystical mood, which he took for poetry." [4] Perhaps overawed at the outset by his abrupt introduction into the private life of the nobility, the needy young author, laboring through a time of graceless hardship and unrelieved struggle, was easily brought to look upon Priamukhino as a moral enclosure in which the Bakunin family was living out an idyllic existence of harmonious self-sufficiency.

But the significance of Priamukhino in Belinski's life is that it became much more than the scene of a pleasant interlude. For in this harmony of Priamukhino Belinski saw the materialization of the "free life of the spirit" toward which the zealots of the Stankevich circle were forever reaching — almost the visible form of that "harmony of a rational creature with itself" which Fichte had set up as the ideal of man. Until now the harmonious life had remained for Belinski a subject of disembodied speculation; here for the first time such life appeared incarnated in the visible world of concrete existence.

It was during this momentous summer of 1836 on the Bakunin estate that Belinski finished writing his last important article to be published in *The Telescope*. This was the review of an 1835 work by a certain A. Drozdov entitled *An Essay upon a System of Moral Philosophy*. Upon completing his review in mid-September of 1836, Belinski read it to the Bakunin sisters, whose lively approval of it helps further to make it a document from the little world of Priamukhino.

Belinski used the Drozdov essay as a springboard from which to attack the notion of a pragmatic moral philosophy. "The idea must explain the facts," Belinski declared in the course of his review, "and not be deduced from the facts. Otherwise matter could determine spirit and spirit would become the slave of matter," whereas "external objects only serve to give impulses to our ego and to inspire in it the conceptions with which those objects are then endowed."

The servitude of spirit to matter, Belinski continues, marked the eighteenth century, "the century of experiment and empiricism," which led to "skepticism, materialism, disbelief. . . " But the theories of the Encyclopedists have vanished like soap bubbles. Where did the aesthetics of the eighteenth century lead? "To the utter destruction and disparagement of art. . . " And this because of a desire "to create an ideal for art from external models inherited from antiquity rather than to deduce one from the spirit of art itself.

"It is said that they [the Encyclopedists] knew only Greek and Latin literature and hence they judged only by the creation of those literatures; that they were ignorant of Shakespeare, unfamiliar with the literature of the Middle Ages, with the literatures of Eastern peoples, that they lived before Schiller, Goethe, Byron. Well, what of that? They had no need to know all that, because they possessed something more stable than the works of Schiller, Goethe, and Byron: they possessed reason, the self-conscious human spirit; and in that reason, in that spirit, there was contained the ideal of art, an obscure, uneasy intuition of genuine creative works. . . Poetry is the unconscious expression of the creative spirit, and . . . hence the poet at the moment of creation is a being more passive than active, and his creation is a captured vision shown to him at a bright moment of inspiration from above; hence it cannot be the invention of his brain or the conscious creation of his will." Works not so created are false. When inspired by mere imitativeness, poetry becomes an ornament, a pastime, like cards or dancing.

Only from the Germans did humanity learn what art is and what philosophy is; whereas the French showed us, instead of art, something in the style of the shoemaker's trade; and in the place of philosophy, something like a game of jacks. Speculation is always based upon laws of necessity, whereas empiricism is based upon the conditional appearances of a lifeless actuality. Hence the former is a house built on rock and the latter a house built on sand. . .

The Drozdov review was thus devoted to a forthright assertion of idealism. Belinski's own idealism, become somewhat uncertain, had found in the world of Priamukhino and of Fichte a new strength, of which he "took hold," as he later said, "with energy, with enthusiasm." [5]

Yet the ultimate result of his summer and fall sojourn at Priamukhino was to be not an elevation of spirit but, on the contrary, a moral and psychic despair. What began as an "awakening," a "resurrection," soon became such a disillusionment that he could later write, in a letter of October 12–24, 1838, addressed to Bakunin, that "my major period of disintegration and abstractness was the time of my stay at Priamukhino in 1836."

Now met face to face, as it were, at Priamukhino, by the world of the ideal toward which he had been straining and which he had come to recognize as the only reality, Belinski was suddenly overwhelmed by a momentous realization: he saw that this ideal existence was beyond his grasp. The world of the "idea," to which he had been willing to ascribe a fuller reality than to actuality itself, had now come into concrete realization before his eyes; and he saw to his dismay that he was obliged to stand outside its gates, that "divine grace had merely become available to me; it had not yet come into my full possession. . . " He was suddenly forced to the bitter realization that his own life was still so lost in the "external" life of the non-ego, that clearly for him the ego was far from reaching "perfect harmony with itself." The experience of Priamukhino, as interpreted by the philosophy of Fichte, thus ended in showing him that his own existence was haunted by "the fearful phantom of external life," of which he lamented that it "poisoned my best moments." His

introduction into what seemed to him the paradise of Priamukhino, far from rescuing him, only served to highlight his "moral
deficiencies." His fitful success in rising to "life in the Absolute"
only sharpened the contrast between his own spiritual imperfec-
tion and what he took to be genuine beatitude: "When I compared my momentary fits of exaltation with that even, harmonious
life [of Priamukhino], proceeding without breaks, without gaps,
without ups and downs; with that progressive movement forward
to infinite perfection — I was terrified at my own nothingness."
However ardent had been his pursuit of the ideal in life, he had
never achieved more than spasmodic lunges into the state of
moral harmony: "At times I found a true balm for my sick spirit
in the self-respect which I achieved through momentary energetic impulses of love for the truth — those rare and brilliant
flashes of emotion which would flame up in me. But sometimes
I saw in all that . . . a certain appearance of brilliance without
substance, a magnificent building without a foundation, a tree of
luxuriant foliage without roots; and I became repugnant to myself."

To one under such a curse of self-condemnation, the very sight
of the fortunate was liable to suggest a reproach. The long confession to Bakunin continues: "In the absence of your sisters . . .
I imagined that their presence would calm my spirit. But when I
saw them again, again I was convinced that the sight of angels
inspires in devils only the realization of their own fallen state." [6]
The "awakening," the "resurrection," had turned into a "disintegration." The momentous meeting with life-in-the-ideal brought
into actuality had finally served only to show Belinski the un-
availability of that life for him. He "had attained thereby not
complete felicity of life but only the objective consciousness of
it." [7] "I learned of paradise only to convince myself that merely
an approach to its gates — not the enjoyment but only the foretaste of its harmony and its aromas — is my only possible life."
He had met moral despair at the end of an experience which had
begun in renewed devotion to the ideal: "Ideal life and real life
had always been separated in my conceptions. The harmony of
Priamukhino and my acquaintance with the ideas of Fichte,
thanks to you, for the first time convinced me that ideal life alone

is real, positive, concrete; and that so-called real life is negation, an illusion, nothingness, emptiness." [8] Here in "the harmony of Priamukhino" there was immediately observable that ideal life which alone could claim to be real — and the unhappy Belinski was driven to realize that he stood far from full participation in that life: "There [at Priamukhino] I collided for the first time face to face with the idea — and I was terrified at my own emptiness. This was a fearful period in my life." [9] This is the time which Belinski later called the "Catholic period" in his life, the time of his conviction of gracelessness, "when I was convinced with all my soul that I was without feeling, without intelligence, without talent, without ability of any sort, without life, without fire, without warm blood, without nobility or honor; that I was the worst of God's creatures; that I was the most despicable and worthless thing alive." [10]

Such a profound sense of estrangement from the "life in the ideal" toward which all his previous aspiration had been directed could not endure for long. He could not continue to operate under a sentence of complete moral "nothingness." His rejection from paradise could have only one desperate remedy: the rejection of such a paradise. Within the context of Belinski's ideology this meant a rejection of the abstract ideal which had won his former adoration; a search for a means of bringing the "idea" down into actuality. The concrete world of real existence must be saved from "illusoriness" and "nothingness." The ideal must be brought to penetrate life, not allowed to glimmer afar in some inaccessible Eden. If the ideal alone is real, then it must be brought into the concrete world where one's life is lived. One obviously cannot continue forever as a phantom cut off from reality.

Such is the ideological setting for the subsequent move toward that "reconciliation with reality" which came to seem such an extravagant absurdity to Belinski's friends, and ultimately to Belinski himself. But for all its extravagance, the reconciliation which Belinski tried to force was an effort toward a new realism. In protest against an inaccessible ideal, he idealized the actual. In this ambitious metaphysical enterprise he was assisted by an able guide: Georg Wilhelm Friedrich Hegel.

In the subsequent period of "reconciliation," Belinski found consolation in looking back upon the "Catholic period" to which his "Fichteanism" had brought him, and in recognizing in the moral despair of that time the motivation toward his new reconciliation: "This disintegration and this abstractness were a terrible evil and a frightful torture for me only at the time; but for the future they brought forth blessed fruit by forcing me into a thorough reconsideration of all that I had been quick to accept in the past. . . Yes, I have recognized and admitted the necessity and the great value of this period for me. My present belief in myself and all that is now good in me — for all this I am indebted to this period, and without it there would be nothing good in me." [11]

It may be asked whether Belinski in the years just ahead merely traded one set of abstractions for another. But in any event the earlier idealism, cut off from the real world of concrete life, had received a mortal blow: "Now . . . I must break with my beautiful dream, although this is painful to my 'nobility of spirit' . . . [But] I shall never forget that this event opened my eyes to the view of a truth to which I had been blind; and if I now see notable progress in myself from time to time, I owe it to this occurrence in my life." [12]

Reconciliation with Reality

The struggle which the Priamukhino episode of 1836 symbolized in the life of Belinski found no conclusive resolution in the following months and years. Rejection and acceptance of the old ideal of "life in the Absolute" continued to contradict each other throughout a long and weary private argument, to which almost every energy seems to have been devoted during the last months of 1836 and throughout 1837.

In literary production, 1837 turned out to be the least creative year of Belinski's career. His main literary prospects lay with a Russian grammar, the first part of which appeared in the spring of 1837 under the title: *Fundamentals of Russian Grammar for Elementary Instruction*. But Belinski's mind was hardly fitted for the writing of textbooks. The critic–friend on whom he called to sponsor his work had so many doubts of its selling that he refused even to discuss it with a publisher, since, he argued, "it is not at all for children, being more a philosophical grammar." [13]

Meanwhile Belinski's brother and nephew were obliged to depend upon him for their support. Even under these increasing responsibilities and diminishing financial prospects, it is noteworthy that an invitation which he received in January, 1837, to work for a literary publication, was answered by his insisting on complete freedom of expression for himself as an essential condition of employment. He did not get the job.

Throughout all the years ahead, Belinski barely managed to pay his own way. Sometimes it was Vassili Botkin, the son of a rich Moscow merchant, who advanced or donated money; sometimes it was Alexander Herzen; sometimes a number of friends together. In the last year of his life, when he had accumulated many painful experiences of financial dependence, it is no surprise that he should write to Botkin, in a letter of January 29, 1847, "I tell you frankly, this living on charity is becoming unbearable to me."

Financial insolvency was only one of the shadows that lay over Belinski's career: his failing health, undermined by the tuberculosis which killed him, made increasing demands upon both the invalid and his friends. He lived through all the years of his active career the victim of a mortal illness. The serious, sometimes grimly serious, mien of the gaunt face which portraits of him show betrays the victim of a struggle which was not only intellectual and moral but also practical and physical. It becomes easier to appreciate the dead-seriousness of Belinski if one keeps in mind the image which more than one of his contemporaries create of him: pacing the room in the fever of an argument, coughing blood into his handkerchief.

After the closing of *The Telescope* and the spiritual "disintegration," as he later called it, brought about by his experience at Priamukhino, the winter of 1836–37 was presumably one of the darkest periods in Belinski's life. The following spring, his friends took up a subscription of money to send him away for his health to take the waters at Piatigorsk. From June to September he lived in the Caucasus, existing on gifts and loans.

Belinski found in the Caucasus that charm which constitutes a familiar theme in Russian literature. In a letter of June 21 to his young friend and protégé, Dmitri Ivanov, he writes that "it is rather gay in Piatigorsk. The countryside is beautiful; the sight of the mountains is bewitching, especially on a clear day." In these agreeable surroundings, health and spirits improved: "I feel better by reason of the journey, the change of scene, the mountain air, the exercise, the early rising (between 4 and 5 o'clock), and the diet. I hope to return to you healthy."

But the old ideological battle continued to rage within. In a letter to Michael Bakunin written in August he admitted: "Never have I reflected so much upon myself in relation to my ultimate purpose as here in the Caucasus."

Upon his return from the Caucasus in September, 1837, Belinski is still to be found standing like an outcast looking across into the paradise of "life in the Absolute." In a letter of that month he confessed to Bakunin: "Better and more clearly I contemplate the mystery of life in the Absolute. I see myself far from it, but I do not despair of approaching it." Yet this life in the ideal is recognized at the same time as "fantasy," "illusion," as he admits to Bakunin in a November letter: "I hide in fantasy from actual life, and my return from the realm of fantasy is a bitter awakening. In that life there is beauty, but I realize that such life is an illusion, because true life is concrete with reality." In the throes of spiritual struggle, he desperately looks for consolation to the notion that suffering is itself the sign of a noble spirit: "Suffering is . . . a mark of the presence of a higher life . . . an earnest of the possibility . . . of passage into the full life of the spirit." [14] But the futility of the struggle, the recognition of hopeless odds, leads to a desperate moral weariness, a will to give up the pursuit of an illusion: "Tortured every moment by the thought of debts, of poverty, of beggary, of my years . . . of my lost youth . . . can I forget myself in pure idea? Welded by iron chains to external life, how can I rise to the Absolute?" Throwing idealism aside, he begins to reflect that perhaps his condition would be helped if he paid more attention to bringing his "external affairs" into order: "I saw myself disgraced, despicable, lazy, good for nothing . . . and I saw the cause of it all precisely in my external life. This thought gladdened me: I had found the cause of the disease — medicine would not be hard to find." [15] Certainly Belinski's was a pitifully poor external life to find much consolation in. But in this unlikely direction he had found the clue to his release into the empirical world of actuality. "Weary of abstraction," as he told Bakunin, he "longed for an approach to reality."[16] Weary of abstraction, Belinski was to find refreshment in Hegel.

The dramatic significance for Belinski, at this juncture, of the philosophy of Hegel is that it provided exactly what he most required: namely, a prepared theoretical position into which to move, whereby the real world from which he could no longer escape might be philosophically vindicated. As it turned out, this reconciliation with the world of things as they are held dangers of its own. The Hegelian rationalization (as he understood it) met such a desperate personal need for Belinski that he quickly drove it to death. Thus the extremism of Belinski's Hegelian phase shows how urgent was the demand which Hegel seemed to answer.

It happened that Belinski's personal search coincided with the intensive study of Hegel in the Stankevich circle, in which the intellectual leadership had passed to Michael Bakunin upon Stankevich's departure abroad in August of 1837. Presumably the autumn of 1837, when he returned from the Caucasus, was not the first time that Belinski had heard of Hegel. His acquaintance with Hegelianism began in all probability gradually, even while he was still close to Stankevich. It can surely be assumed, for example, that Belinski read Stankevich's translation, published in an 1835 issue of *The Telescope*, of a French "Essay on the Philosophy of Hegel."

Meanwhile Belinski's own thought was moving independently toward some kind of reconciliation with reality. The fullest evidence of this is a long letter of August 7, 1837, written from the Caucasus to his young friend Ivanov. But while this letter develops the theme of acquiescence to the "external" world (especially the world of politics), such acquiescence is justified not by any moral justification of the external world but on the contrary by a doctrine of withdrawal into the self, in safe seclusion from vulgar actuality. It is true that throughout this revealing letter overtones of Hegel as well as of Fichte and Schelling can be heard, and the letter mentions the names of all three. But the mixture

remains an original concoction served by the hand of Belinski.
The Fichtean "ego" appears, but not the Fichtean moral assertion;
the reality of "pure idea" is announced, but the "idea" remains
within the close confines of the subjective:

Throw out your political economy and statistics; all partial knowledge lowers, vulgarizes a person. Thought, or the idea, in its disinterested, universal meaning — that is what should be the object of a
man's study. Outside of the idea all is illusion, a dream; the idea alone
is substantial and real. What are you yourself? An idea, clothed in a
body. Your body will rot, but your ego will remain. . . Philosophy —
that is what should be the object of your activity. Philosophy is the
science of pure idea. . . But it will be impossible for you to begin
directly with philosophy. For this you must prepare yourself by means
of art. . . By art you must cleanse your soul of the leprosy of earthly
vanity, of cold self-love, of the lures of external life, and prepare it
for the acceptance of pure truth.

. . . Only in [philosophy] will you find answers to the questions
of your spirit; only it will give peace and harmony to your soul and
supply you with that happiness which the crowd does not even suspect and which external life can neither give nor take away. You will
not be in the world, but the whole world will be in you. In yourself,
in the secret sanctuary of your spirit you will find your highest
happiness. Then your little apartment, your miserable, narrow room
will be a true temple of happiness. You will be free because you will
be asking nothing of the world; and the world will leave you in peace,
seeing that you ask nothing of it. Most of all, leave politics alone and
oppose every political influence upon your manner of thinking. Politics with us in Russia has no sense. . . Love the good and then you
will necessarily be useful to your fatherland without thinking how
you can be or without trying to be useful to it. If each one of the individuals who constitute the Russian people came to perfection by
the way of love, then without any politics Russia would become the
happiest country in the world. Enlightenment — that is the way to
happiness.

. . . All the hope for Russia lies in enlightenment and not in revolt,
not in a revolution and not in a constitution. In France there were
two revolutions and as a result of them, a constitution. What then?
In France with its constitution there is much less freedom of thought
than in autocratic Prussia. Because constitutional freedom is a conditional freedom, whereas true, unconditional freedom advances in
states along with the progress of an enlightenment based on philosophy, on speculative and not empirical philosophy; on the rule of pure
reason and not of vulgar common sense. Civic freedom should be the
fruit of the inner freedom of each individual. . . And by this same

splendid road our Russia will achieve freedom. . . Our government forbids writing against serfdom, but meanwhile it is gradually freeing the serfs.

Into this interesting intellectual amalgam Belinski had mixed a philosophical subjectivism which looked back to Fichtean doctrine, along with a political conservatism which looked forward, as Belinski's thought was to move, to a rationalization of reality inspired by Hegel. Partly by the aid of a subjective idealism which he had been struggling to reject, the stage was set for Belinski's reception of Hegel.

According to Belinski's account, the dramatic meeting with Hegel, as introduced by Bakunin, occurred immediately upon his arrival from the Caucasus, in September of 1837.

I arrive in Moscow from the Caucasus; Bakunin arrives; we live together. That summer he had been looking over Hegel's philosophy of religion and law. A new world opened up before us. "Might is right and right is might." No, I cannot describe to you with what emotion I heard those words; it was a liberation. I understood the meaning of the downfall of empires, the legitimacy of conquerors; I understood that there is no crude material force nor conquest by sword and bayonet, nothing arbitrary, nothing accidental. . .

Before this, Katkov had conveyed to me as well as he was able, and I had received as well as I could, certain conclusions from the *Aesthetics*. Good heavens, what a new, bright, infinite world!

. . . The word Reality became for me the equivalent of the word God. In vain you advise me to look more often at the blue sky, the image of the eternal, so as not to fall into a cookhouse reality. My friend, blessed is he who can see in the image of the heavens a symbol of the eternal; [but] more blessed is he who can illumine the cookhouse by the idea of the eternal.

If one can trust this account, written in a letter of October 2, 1839, to Stankevich, and thus two years after the fact, it is clear to what degree Belinski's original knowledge of Hegel was gotten at second hand, from teachers possibly more enthusiastic than exact. According to the statement above, his heart seems to have been won first by a slogan: that "might is right and right is might" — a slogan which hardly does justice to the Hegelian conception of "right." But this was a slogan which had resounding overtones of personal meaning for him. For out of it rang the good news that the eminent German philosopher had elaborated the very conception which Belinski most earnestly sought to discover: namely, that the existence of things as they are can be morally and philosophically justified.

The impact of the doctrine of Hegelian realism, as he understood it, was perhaps exaggerated in retrospect by Belinski, whose personal correspondence during this time and after shows a continuing struggle with a lofty idealism. Within the month, for example, he was to write, as already quoted, "I hide in fantasy from actual life, and my return from the realm of fantasy is a bitter awakening. . ." There had to be a gradual transition in the move toward the new gospel of reality. For all the suddenness of his liberation, his break with the past was in no sense abrupt and complete.

It is not until the fall of the following year, 1838, that Belinski finally declares his newly-adopted doctrine of reality. Already in this first declaration, the ambiguous character of the concept "reality" is clearly hinted. The manifesto of reconciliation contained in the letter of September 10, 1838, written to Michael Bakunin, is dedicated with almost religious fervor to "the great word 'reality.'" "Reality" is thus introduced at the outset as almost an ideal, rather than as a conception of empirical fact and circumstance. In this initial phrase is given the first clue to the discovery that Belinski had been won over not to the state of things as they are but to a new way of thinking about them.

At first sight, Belinski's evolution in this passage seems clear: "I look upon reality, which formerly I had so despised, and tremble with secret elation when I recognize its rationality, when I see that it is impossible to subtract anything from it. . . Reality! I repeat it getting up and lying down, day and night. Reality surrounds me; I feel it everywhere and in everything." But a strange ambiguity shades this apparent clarity of mood: "It would be a stupid lie if I said that I am real and have attained reality. But I say the truth in stating that I have made a great new step toward it." Obviously Belinski is far from having accepted "reality" as a frustrated idealist might, in a spirit of cynical disillusionment. He is careful to distinguish himself from "the idealistic man [who], meeting his ideal woman nowhere, because she nowhere exists, falls into despair and is convinced that low and vulgar reality is the true reality."

For the "reality" which now fires his thought is still a goal to attain — almost a special state of being, as appears in the revealing phrase: "more full of love and hence more real." Yet at the same time the notion of reality includes the inexorability of the actual: "Reality is a monster equipped with iron claws and iron jaws. If one does not give himself over to it willingly, it seizes him forcibly and devours him."

The exclusive attitude of the Stankevich circle, which saw humanity divided between those capable and those incapable of pursuing "life in the Absolute," now makes way in Belinski's life for a closer jostling with the world of men into which he hopes to sink his old transcendentalism: "I begin to find in conversation mutual interests with people with whom I should never have thought I had anything in common. . . Now my one effort is that everyone knowing me in the literary world and seeing me for the first or for the hundred-and-first time shall say, 'There's Belinski — he's like everyone else!'"

Out of the medley of declarations by which the author of this crucial letter of 1838 reveals himself, there emerges a clear indication that Hegelianism not only had provided him with philosophical reasons for repudiating his bankrupt idealizations, but had done so by means of an analysis which remained within the tradition of philosophical idealism.

The ego-centered systems of both Fichte and Schelling left unfinished an account of the bond between the ego and the environing reality (in Fichte, the non-ego; in Schelling, nature). Fichte had recognized the self as the effective moral reality, working its will upon the plastic materials of the external world. Schelling extended the definition of the ego to create out of the self the culmination of Nature. But even for Schelling the ego still remained counterpoised against the material universe. Schelling's glorification of the creative ego as the focus of universal life had the effect of leaving the external world, which lay outside and beyond the self, out of focus and nebulous.

Hegel arrived at his distinctive achievement by working within the tradition of philosophical idealism at a correction of its ego-centrism. His theoretical discovery was that all existence depends upon relationship; that the ego exists only in a relationship with a universe within which it grows in self-consciousness until "spirit" recognizes that "nature" is only itself objectified. Under Hegel's illumination, the ego crossed the artificial boundary of selfhood; the self and its outer environment were seen as two aspects, the subjective and the objective, of the same reality. External reality lay not outside the self but implicit in the self.

Putting his emphasis upon the idea of relationship, Hegel showed that the qualities of the external world could be understood as objective images of the categories of subjective consciousness. This systematic philosophical statement of a relationship between the world and the self is the major contribution which Hegelianism made to Belinski's intellectual progress. Whatever faults may have marred Belinski's understanding of Hegel's message for a generation of romantic idealists, he grasped its main emphasis, by the very witness of the release which he found in it. The primary contribution which Hegel had to make to philosophical idealism was, in fact, the one which Belinski was best prepared to assimilate, at least in spirit if not in full technical understanding. The Hegelian destruction of egocentrism met Belinski's current need by permitting him to return to concrete reality without sacrificing the moral sustenance of philosophic idealism. Just at the time when his image of the ideal had moved off into an inaccessible remoteness, leaving him with an increasing disgust at the utter emptiness of his concrete existence, he was able to find in Hegelianism a rejuvenated sense of a reality which was both concrete and spiritualized: a recognition of the world of external fact and historical event as the material through which the "idea" worked. For Schelling's transcendental idealism, Hegel had substituted a dialectical idealism. To the focus upon the creative and purposive ego in the systems of Fichte and Schelling, Hegel applied the centrifugal force of an emphasis upon relationship. But it is important that Hegel saw in the form of relationship the same basic reality which Fichte and Schelling tended to see focused in the self: namely, "idea." Thus Hegelianism could return Belinski to the world of external actuality fortified by a new dispensation of philosophic idealism.

After his dramatic encounter with Hegel in the fall of 1837, Belinski continued until the end of 1839 to record, mainly in his correspondence, an experience which is nothing short of spiritual liberation: liberation from empty abstraction, a sense of redis- covery of himself and the world about him. During these years this sense of a new-found freedom is frequently renewed. Thus in November of 1838 he writes to Stankevich: "Since spring I have awakened to a new life. I have decided that whatever I may have been, I *am myself.* . . Now I am not under law but under grace." By the following spring of 1839 he is still rejoicing at his fresh discovery of the world of concrete reality: "I am appalled at my past life, so well known to you, when I compare it with my present life. Happiness and inner life come to me most of all from the widening of my receptivity to beauty. . . A good plaster cast of the Venus de' Medici is worth in my eyes more than the stupid happiness which I used to seek in the solution of moral questions. Good heavens, what a fearful life that was! The moral point of view almost destroyed for me all the color of life, all its poetry and charm." [17]

Meanwhile the paradoxical result of Belinski's rediscovery of the real world was already in the making. Having been brought, after futile soaring, back to the real world, he set about fanatically to justify all that he found there. With something like the religious fervor of the recent convert, he drew from his new realism an inspiration to prove that whatever is should be. Such an effort required the suppression of any individual moral protest against the march of unalterable law. And for this, also, Belinski was prepared, by having passed through a poignant experience of recognizing his own "nothingness," of looking upon his individ- ual will as an "illusion."

This energetic disavowal of all individualism and personal self- assertion is given its most specific expression in his change of heart toward his former idol, Schiller, whom he now denounces for "his subjective–moral point of view, his fearful notion of duty, his abstract heroism, his fair-souled war with reality, for all that for which I suffered in his name." In the poetry of Schiller he now detects "an abstract ideal of society, isolated from geograph-ical and historical conditions . . . built on air." [18]

Rejection of Schilleresque "abstract heroism" constituted merely one episode, however, in a sweeping disparagement of the old abstraction. In the midst of such a violent repudiation of abstract idealism, even a secondhand acquaintance with Hegel-ianism was enough to provide a satisfactory philosophic refuge. In this eagerness to find release from an old bondage lies the reason why "Belinski acts toward the philosophy of Hegel like a young man in love," invoking the philosopher's name and repeating his ideas even when they are irrelevant to his purpose, in the spirit of a kind of "verbal fetishism." [19]

Simply upon the evidence of Belinski's reliance on secondhand sources for his knowledge of Hegel, it is unlikely that his under-standing of Hegelian philosophy could have been full and precise. Indeed, there is no reason to think that he was interested in be-coming an expert on Hegel. He sought in Hegel a philosophically adequate solution of his own ideological problem, the fulfillment of an intimately personal intellectual and spiritual need. If he can be considered a faithful follower of Hegel it is because, in spite of useless repetition of Hegelian terms and Hegelian formulas, he continued to work toward a conviction that reality is justified and that art is justified only by its fidelity to reality.

A systematic exposition of what Hegel meant by "reality" is out of place here. A systematic exposition of what Belinski meant by "reality" is out of the question. Yet in Belinski's defense it can be said that he grasped the meaning of the principle that noth-ing is real except idea, and that his vacillation between a reality of idea and a reality of appearance is inherent in Hegel's original doctrine. To say that nothing is real except idea does not limit the area of idea, which in the Hegelian system tends to be all-embracing. If Belinski in his excesses of political conservatism seems to have misinterpreted the Hegelian formula, "What is ra-tional is real and what is real is rational," perhaps the original formula can be accused of containing the seeds of its own misin-terpretation.

In the spring of 1838, Belinski became editor of the new *Moscow Observer*. The journal had already been appearing, but with little success; Belinski and his friends (including "foreign correspondents" Granovski and Stankevich in Germany) gave it a new start in a new direction.

The first announcement of direction was made in the first numbers of the *Moscow Observer* by Bakunin's translation of Hegel's "Gymnasium Speeches." It was in his introduction to this translation that Bakunin reproduced the Hegelian formula, "What is rational is real and what is real is rational." This aphorism Bakunin presented to the readers of the *Moscow Observer* as "the basis of the philosophy of Hegel."

The second indication of the direction of the *Moscow Observer* was a second translation from the German, made by another member of the Stankevich circle, Michael Katkov. This was an essay by the German Hegelian, H. T. Roetscher, entitled *The Relation of the Philosophy of Art and Criticism to the Individual Work of Art (Das Verhältniss der Philosophie der Kunst und der Kritik zum einzelnen Kunstwerk)*. Bakunin had introduced Hegel as the theorist of rational reality; Roetscher, via Katkov, introduced the "philosophic criticism" of the work of art, according to which the "idea" of every work of art becomes the principal subject of critical concern. Both these emphases belong to Belinski's so-called "Hegelian period," and the theme of each article may be considered a starting point of Belinski's development in the immediate future. From the slogan that "everything real is rational" Belinski proceeded toward a rationalization of reality which ended in a remarkable excess of political conservatism. In the field of criticism, Belinski undertook to apply Roetscher's doctrine of "philosophical criticism" and so moved toward a new emphasis upon the integrity of the work of art as a self-contained creation. The instability of this period lies not in his conception of art but in the separation he made between art and life. The breach kept widening as his political conservatism became more and more extreme. It was this reactionary philosophy of Russian life which was ultimately to make his "Hegelian" position untenable.

At the same time, Belinski's philosophy of art was also unstable. And for Belinski its instability lay precisely in the doctrine of the self-sufficiency of art. To another critic at another time, that emphasis is likely to seem the beginning of all critical wisdom.

A later Russian critic has argued that even Belinski was at his best as a critic while he held this position.[20] But the whole weight of cultural circumstance and the whole significance of Belinski's critical activity worked against his championing the independence of art.

By 1840, in an article on the German critic Menzel, Belinski came to declare, "Art must not serve society except by serving itself. Let each go its own way, without hindering the other." For all its wisdom, the statement is clearly extreme. The phrase "without hindering the other" is obviously destructive of the tension between life and art which vitalizes both. And no critic was quicker than Belinski — no age was quicker than his — to emphasize the relationship between art and life. It is inevitable that neither Belinski nor the cultural milieu from which he emerged could long support a notion of art and society which would require each to go "its own way, without hindering the other" (whatever that could mean).

Meanwhile the increasing extremism of Belinski's political and social views had the effect of forcing the artist into a more and more false position. During the *Telescope* period, Belinski had found what justification he could for Russian national life in seeing the nation as an expression of a life of humanity and of a universal nature which transcends the national particularity. Raising his eyes to this transcendent life, he could look beyond the formless and unenlightened culture of Russia. He could preach a doctrine of national character in art while at the same time repudiating Russian reality.

The "reconciliation with reality" which his understanding of Hegel brought him was a new resolution of this old conflict between a transcendental idealism and the disparagement of Russian national life. He now saw the life of the nation, with all its apparent contradictions, as the very manifestation of Reason, of a rational reality which moved behind the façade of "appearance." If the social and political progress of the national life was thus carried forward by an inexorable dialectic, then the artist was allowed to relax, so to speak, in his function of national enlightenment. National life no longer required the justification of art. And art, as an expression of the universal dialectic, had received a higher mission than the glorification of the national life. "Let each go its own way, without hindering the other." This reconciliation with reality toward which Belinski proceeded to draw both politics and art, involved him in a campaign which cost heavy casualties: first the career of the *Moscow Observer*, then the respect of friends and followers, and finally his own equilibrium.

As for the *Moscow Observer*, it flourished hardly a year under the new management. Belinski's argument, set forth in a letter to Stankevich, that it was Bakunin's introductory article on Hegel which ruined the journal, may seem a crude effort to deflect the blame from himself. Or perhaps Belinski also meant that it was the doctrine which Bakunin offered in that article which had begun, in himself, the work of destruction. A simpler explanation is that the *Moscow Observer*, like any other literary journal, could not afford to cater to the philosophical interests of the staff while it neglected the interests of its subscribers, as it inclined to do. Belinski even publicly chided his readers for wanting to be entertained rather than enlightened; in an article which he published in the journal he remarked: "Many readers complained about our publishing Roetscher's article, 'On the Philosophic Criticism of the Work of Art,' finding it unclear and hard to understand. . . [But] not all articles are placed in a journal *only* for the satisfaction of the readers. Sometimes learned articles are necessary, and such articles require work and thought." [21] Such an amazing statement helps to prove Annenkov's criticism that the *Observer*, reflecting Belinski's grim determination to master Hegel, wore out both Belinski and his collaborators.[22] Panaev adds that the "conciliatory direction" of the *Observer* had become "a direction with which the public could in no wise sympathize." [23] Belinski's own patience and self-assurance weakened visibly, until the year 1839 found him desperately eager to get away from himself by going to St. Petersburg.

As early as November of 1837 Belinski had written to Bakunin that he seriously considered moving to St. Petersburg, "which will divide my life into two halves." He had good reason to hesitate. More than all else, St. Petersburg meant exile from the family of his Moscow circle. Yet this very consideration seems to have attracted him with the possibility of liberation from a past against which he had turned, and especially from its outworn idealism. Belinski had thus been preparing himself for a move long before the occasion appeared. By 1839 the *Moscow Observer* had failed and he was out of a job. Through the good offices of Belinski's friend Ivan Panaev, the publisher Alexander Kraevski offered a place on his *National Notes* (*Otechestvennye Zapiski*), published in St. Petersburg. Belinski accepted the offer and moved to St. Petersburg in the fall of 1839.

In St. Petersburg, Belinski was destined at first to find little sympathy or support. The literary circles of the capital had little reason to welcome him. The reigning triumvirate — Grech, Bulgarin, and Senkovski — in the world of St. Petersburg journalism were an incarnation, especially in their narrow nationalism, of all that Belinski despised. They had been the favorite enemies of *The Telescope* and the *Moscow Observer*, and Kraevski's revival of *National Notes* in 1839 was mainly inspired by a wish to do battle with them. Just as Belinski had assumed leadership on *The Telescope* and the *Moscow Observer* in matters of critical doctrine, so he was destined to provide Kraevski's journal with its doctrinal basis. His arrival in St. Petersburg was thus at the outset a move into enemy territory.

Belinski's intellectual loneliness in St. Petersburg was reflected in his style of life during the first years after his arrival. For a while he lived with Panaev, but by the winter of 1840 he rented two rooms off one of the main thoroughfares: one big cold room and one small overheated one, as Annenkov reported.[24] Here he lived an ascetic existence filled with hard work and cut off for weeks at a time from all social contacts.

In this alien world, Belinski was left to play out the often melancholy drama of his personal philosophy. He is the first to contend that it was his life in St. Petersburg that worked the radical change in his thought which distinguishes these years. In coming from Moscow to St. Petersburg, he felt he had come into a new intellectual climate; in 1844 he devoted an essay, "St. Petersburg and Moscow," to describing the difference in "spirit" between these two cities. At least there is little doubt that his break with old Moscow ties helped him to break with old ways of thought. But there is also good reason for seeing in the radical

intellectual changes of these years the evolution of a pattern of
thought which has little connection with geographical place. The
rationalization of reality which he was working through at this
time was in any case bound soon to reach its limit, whether in
Moscow or in St. Petersburg.

If the main writings of Belinski's "Hegelian" period are examined consecutively, it becomes clear that the period is marked
by an inner development which finally works out into a crisis of
thought. The crisis is arrived at gradually, in an inevitable movement that would have pleased Hegel; Belinski's effort at reconciliation with reality appears already at the outset to contain the
seeds of its own destruction.

Articles of Reconciliation

Belinski's first critical article of his "Hegelian" period, written
in Moscow in the spring of 1838, was a review of Shakespeare's
Hamlet, currently being played by the celebrated Russian actor,
Mochalov. Belinski develops the thesis that Hamlet's career is in
effect a struggle with "reality," toward which he is at first reconciled in an unstable idealism; against which he struggles upon the
knowledge of his uncle's crime; and which he is finally obliged to
accept. In Belinski's analysis, Hamlet begins as an idealist who is
content with his life because reality has not yet invaded his innocent dreams. Hamlet admires the nobility of his own subjective
will but not yet the beauty of an objective reality from which he
is isolated. His moral immaturity is inevitably followed by breakdown. But as a model of the best among men, Hamlet is able, by
dint of inner struggle, to move from the breakdown of an old,
factitious harmony into a new realism. By the tragedy of his
father's death Hamlet is brought to learn that life and dreams
are not identical. Having once protested that life, and not his
dreams of life, was false, he is forced to recognize the reality of
an objective world often hostile to his dreams. Hamlet's drama
is the drama of his own weakness. And "what is the nature of
that weakness? It is disintegration, the passage from an immature,
unconscious *harmony* and *self-satisfaction* of spirit into disharmony and struggle, which constitute the necessary condition for

a passage into *mature* and *conscious* harmony and self-satisfaction of spirit. . . What brought [Hamlet] into such fearful disharmony, what threw him into such a tormented struggle with himself? *The discrepancy between reality and his ideal of life. . .*" *

Thus begins Belinski's "Hegelian" period. It is possible to detect here in his review of *Hamlet* the Hegelian framework of thesis, antithesis, and synthesis. But for one thought of Hegel it is obvious that the author had two thoughts of himself. Hamlet had become not so much the vehicle of the Hegelian triad as the image of Belinski's own self-identification. Hamlet's passage from idealism to its disintegration and from thence to "reality" is precisely the movement of Belinski's own career to the date of his writing.

If in its central thesis the first article of this period is more a work of self-recognition than of Hegelian analysis or Shakespearean criticism, nevertheless it is clear that Hegel is being introduced. Already suggested is one mark of Belinski's Hegelianism: the search for one main idea which the form of the work of art shall express — found in *Hamlet* in the idea of "weakness." The Hegelian disparagement of abstraction likewise finds conscious expression here, in Belinski's praise of Shakespeare's power to create a "living character with nothing abstract about him, taken as it were whole and without alterations or corrections, from everyday reality." Indeed, Belinski here gives Hegelianism a formal introduction, albeit not by name, as "that world-embracing, final philosophy of our age, which has developed like a magnificent tree from a single seed and which held concealed in itself, according to a free necessity, all the stages of the evolution of spirit." But the introduction is quietly made within a context of the old Schellingesque idealism which had animated the "Literary Reveries": "Behold the wide world in all its marvel; everything

---

* Professor Harry Levin has pointed out a similarity between Belinski's interpretation of Hamlet and that of Wilhelm Meister. Goethe's hero likewise found his key to *Hamlet* in the theme of the Prince's disintegration before an overwhelming reality. Wilhelm as a critic sounds very much like the critic Belinski when he argues that in Hamlet "a beautiful, pure, noble, highly moral nature, lacking the strength of feeling of which heroes are made, sinks beneath a burden which he can neither carry nor throw off; every duty is holy to him, but this one is too heavy." (*Wilhelm Meisters Lehrjahre*, bk. IV, chap. 13.)

in it shows beauty and wisdom: both the worm crawling through
the grass and the lion roaring in the African grassland, terrifying
everything that lives and breathes; the wafting of the breeze on
a calm May evening and the hurricane whirling up the sands of
the Arabian desert. . ." This spirit of the universe, whose every
manifestation is beautiful and sublime, ultimately reaches its highest development in humanity, after having proceeded through the
whole series of organic particularizations; every stage of history
is a phase of the evolution of spirit, and each stage has its chief
exponent. Shakespeare was one of these.

In this essay, with its thumbnail sketches of its author's conver-
sion from the old Adam to the new, the poet remains what he
had always been for Belinski: the singer of a universal reality.
But that reality has begun to change character: if page one of
the essay is painted with pictures of lions and hurricanes, its theme
is Hamlet's struggle with a reality "armed with iron claws and
iron jaws" — a reality which forces the transcendental idealist to
pass through moral disintegration into the achievement of a new
reconciliation.

But reality is still not the reality of accidental appearance:
reality consists only in "idea." And the artist's portrayal of reality
is a portrayal of an idea. Hence the substance of every work of art
is an idea. It is for this reason that the criticism of art must be
primarily the criticism of the idea which the work incorporates.
"The idea is the content of the work of art and is general. Form
is the particular manifestation of the idea. Without having grasped
the idea one can neither understand nor appreciate the form. But
it is possible to get at the idea only by abstracting the idea from
the form. . . The first problem is: Is the idea concrete which
has been taken as the basis of the work of art? . . . For only a
concrete idea can be incorporated into a concrete poetic form.
Poetry is thought expressed in images, and hence when the idea
which the form expresses lacks concreteness, or is false and hollow,
then the form necessarily fails to be artistic." [25]

Roetscher's essay on the relation of the philosophy of art to
art criticism had supplied Belinski with the support he may have
needed — and he expressed his gratitude openly in a denunciation
of the "French principle" in criticism, whereby the work of the

artist is taken to be "the work of the *external* circumstances of his life," in favor of the principle of German criticism: "even while being empirical it displays an effort to explain the appearance of spirit by the laws of spirit." [26]

Yet however obvious may be the influence here of the Hegelian criticism of art and the Hegelian apology for reality, Belinski is clearly still his own master, in full control of certain basic principles which hardly needed an abstruse philosophic argument for their justification. The conception of art as the portrayal of reality in the form of concrete image seems reliable enough. The conception of reality as being often at odds with subjective fancies and ideals seems wholesome enough. What could overthrow such an apparently solid foundation?

Belinski's next important articles, published in 1839 and 1840 in the *National Notes* of St. Petersburg, were among his most extreme expressions of political conservatism. They make clear the danger of his position. Whereas the essay on Menzel brought his view of the autonomy of art to its fullest expression, his notorious articles on Zhukovski's patriotic poem, "The Anniversary of Borodino" (1839), and Glinka's *Sketches of the Battle of Borodino* (1839) showed him moving farther and farther toward an impossible vindication of Russian national life. Such a cleavage between art and society might appear at first to offer benefits. The glorification of the national life by its very excess might preserve the function of art from servitude to ulterior purposes. So it happened in Belinski's own theory. But it soon appeared what was to be the paradoxical outcome of such a preservation of art: art lost touch with the tangible world. By his increasingly desperate effort to glorify the *status quo*, Belinski was more and more unwillingly forced to push the artist into a refuge, as Panaev noted, in "some supreme, separate world, self-contained, concerned only with eternal truths and having no connection with the annoying trivia of everyday life, with that world in which we move." [27] By dint of keeping art "pure," Belinski succeeded ultimately only in making it remote. Meanwhile the rationalization of the world of everyday life was becoming more and more extreme and less and less tenable.

Nowhere does Belinski set forth an argument for art-for-art's-

sake with more effect than in the essay on Menzel, published
in the beginning of 1840, at the climax of his period of Hegelian
"realism." Belinski had recently made acquaintance with the literary opinions of the German critic Wolfgang Menzel (1798–1873)
through a Russian translation of his work *Die deutsche Literatur.*
Menzel's book had first appeared in Germany in 1828; a second
German edition was published in 1836. By the time Belinski came
to the book in its Russian version, Menzel had radically altered
his position. But such considerations, even if they occurred to
him, deterred Belinski very little, since it was apparent that he
was only using Menzel as a convenient example. Indeed, so close
do the ideas of Menzel's *German Literature* stand to opinions just
lately held by Belinski himself — particularly Menzel's emphasis
on literature as a national expression — that one might well take
Belinski's attack as an attack upon a disavowed remnant of himself. "In any case," Belinski admits at the beginning of his article,
"the following article is not at all an analysis of Menzel's book,"
and "in speaking of Menzel we mean to speak of criticism in general, having particularly in view a Russian public. . ."

The literary judgment which made Menzel especially useful to
Belinski for his present purpose was an attack on Goethe. Menzel
had criticized Goethe for his failure to assist German literature
to become an expression of German national life; Goethe was
guilty of standing aloof from the world of his time, preferring
even researches in natural science to the performance of his
proper duties toward the German fatherland. Belinski took Menzel's strictures on Goethe as the occasion for a grand-scale defense
of the freedom of art. Not only must the poet, in Belinski's argument, be kept secure from the private opinions of his critics, but
he must also be kept free from the demands of his society; his
freedom from all the interferences of his contemporary world
is, indeed, sacrosanct.

An idea expressed by a poet in his work may conflict with the
private conviction of a critic without ceasing to be true and universal,
provided the work is truly artistic. For a person, being a limited
individual, may be in error and may entertain false convictions. But
the poet, being an organ of the general and universal, an immediate
manifestation of spirit, cannot err or speak a falsehood. Of course
. . . he may fall into error, but only when . . . he ceases to be a poet

and allows his individuality to intrude upon the free process of creation. . .

Whereas "the fundamental idea of Menzel's criticism is that art should serve society. If you wish, it does serve society by giving expression to its own creations and by nourishing the spirits of those who make up society, by sublime impressions and noble conceptions of the good and the true. But it does not serve society by existing for the benefit of society, but by existing in and for itself, by containing within itself its end and its cause. Whenever we demand from art a contribution toward social purposes and regard the poet as a hireling whom we can order at one time to sing the holiness of marriage, at another the joy of sacrificing one's life for one's fatherland, or on a third occasion the duty of being honest in the payment of debts — then instead of works of art we inundate literature with rhymed dissertations on abstract and polemical subjects; with dry allegories, in which is concealed not living truth but dead rationalization; or, finally, with a poisonous progeny of sordid passions and partisan zeal." Such have been many outstanding works of French literature, from the "trite, sententious statements" of the classical dramatists to Voltaire's "bold heresy against everything sacred," to "the stormy frenzy which by glorifying the fury of animal passions brings forth, in the manner of Hugo, Dumas, and Eugène Sue, butchery in the place of tragedy and romance, and libels against human nature in place of the portrayal of the present age and contemporary society."

The freedom of the true artist is so complete that he could not become the hireling of his society even if he so wished. "The inspiration of the artist is so free that he cannot control it but can only obey it. For it has its existence in him but not from him. He cannot choose the themes of his works, for involuntarily there arise in his soul mysterious visions, which he then shows forth, to the wonder of the world. He creates not when he will but when he may. He awaits the moment of inspiration; he does not bring it to pass according to his will. . ."

Menzel accuses Goethe, Belinski continues, of having kept silent during the French Revolution and of failing to express by a single line his opinion of that great event. But this is like blaming

Pushkin for having brought out of the Caucasus Book VII of
Eugene Onegin instead of triumphal odes to the achievements of
Russian arms.

By this we do not at all mean to say that the poet may never respond
with his poetry to contemporary events. No, to say that would be to
fall to the opposite extreme. . . But . . . the poet is least of all capable
of responding to contemporary affairs, which remain for him a
beginning without a middle or an end, an appearance without substance and wholeness, observed through the smoke of passion, bias, and
partisan preference. Hence his inspiration prefers to live in past ages
and to awaken the giant shades of Achilles and Hector, Richard and
Henry. . .

Menzel is angry at Goethe because he refused to be a mouthpiece
or a guide for any political party, because he did not demand an
impossible coalition of dismembered Germany into a single political
body. In every genius there is an instinct for truth, for reality. What
is, is for him rational, necessary, and real; and what is rational, necessary, and real — that alone is. Hence Goethe did not demand and did
not desire the impossible but preferred to find his satisfaction in what
necessarily is.

The business of the Pitts . . . the Talleyrands . . . and the Metter-
nichs is to participate in the destiny of nations and to exert their influence within the political sphere of humanity. The business of artists
is to contemplate "the creation full of praise" and to be its organs, not
to intrude into the affairs of politics and government. . . "Alas if the
shoemaker began to bake pies and the baker to turn out shoes."

As the sphere of art and the sphere of society are separate, so
each has its separate justification in a larger Reason which both
express. "One shouts, 'Society! Let everything perish that does
not serve society!' And another screams, 'Art! Let everything
perish which does not exist in art!' But the truly wise meekly and
without screaming say, 'Let society live and art prosper. Each is
the appearance of one and the same Reason, unique and eternal.
Each contains in itself its necessity for being, its cause and its
purpose.'

"Yes, society must not sacrifice its essential interests to art or
deviate for the sake of the latter from its own goal. Art must not
serve society except by serving itself. Let each go its own way,
without hindering the other."

Although Belinski had undertaken his critique of Menzel with the aim of justifying the freedom of art, it becomes clear in the course of his argument that his effort at justification has taken on the life of society as well as the life of art. His assertion of the autonomy of the artist was accompanied by a rationalization of political life in Russia. These two principles belonged, in his mind, together. Just as in the national life "everything that is, is necessary, rational, and real," so the artist's "instinct for truth and reality" tells him that "what is, is for him rational, necessary, and real; and what is rational, necessary, and real, that alone is." At the end of 1839 Belinski had already shown to what extremes that dubious formula could lead him.

The lengths to which Belinski was now ready to go in glorifying the Russian autocracy in particular and the power of the state in general, can be seen in two remarkable articles. In 1839, two works appeared in commemoration of the famous 1812 battle of Borodino, at which Napoleon's invasion forces were decimated by Russian arms. A poem by Zhukovski, "The Anniversary of Borodino," mixed a nostalgic reminiscence of Russian heroes fallen on the field of Borodino, with a celebration of the Tsar and the Russian people. The second work published in this year which Belinski used for his purpose was Glinka's *Sketches of the Battle of Borodino; Reminiscences of the Year 1812*. Belinski's essay on Zhukovski's poem appeared in the *National Notes* in the fall of 1839, just after his arrival from Moscow. It was followed in December by an article on Glinka's work. In the former, Belinski presented his own celebration of Russian autocracy; in the second, he supported that outburst of partiotic fervor by a discussion of the general relationship between the individual and society.

In the article on Zhukovski's piece, Belinski announced that "for us Russians there are no national events which have not come from the living source of the supreme authority. . . Yes, in the word 'tsar' there is a marvelous fusion of the consciousness of the Russian people, for whom that word is full of poetry and mysterious meaning. And this is no accident, but the strictest, most rational necessity, revealed in the history of the Russian people. . . In the tsar is our *freedom*, because from him will emerge our new civilization, our enlightenment, just as it is from him that we draw our life. . . Unconditional submission to tsarist authority is not only useful and necessary for us, but it is the highest poetry of our lives — our nationality, if by the word nationality is to be understood the act of fusing particular individualities into a general consciousness of the personality and selfhood of the State."

To show that this glorification of the Russian State had a philosophical foundation was the major purpose of the subsequent essay on Glinka. The idea, familiar from "Literary Reveries," that the individual is to the national as the national is to the universal, here is repeated — with an opposite emphasis. Whereas in the "Reveries" the individual had been conceived as the apogee of the structure of national and universal life, now it is stressed that the individual is dependent upon that structure, that the individual is subservient to the greater reality of the nation. The individual "must renounce his subjective individuality, recognize that it is false and illusory, and put himself in harmony with what is universal and general, recognizing that in the latter alone is truth and reality." The fault of "the subjective person" is that he "is in eternal struggle with the objective world, and hence with society. . ." Whereas in comparison to the life of the individual, the life of his society is "much more coherent, much richer, much more rational and comprehensible." The "poetry" of Glinka's book on Borodino consists in its revelation of "the deep, sublime thought of humanity, of emperors and nations, epochs and events. It will raise you to that lofty sphere where your head is cleared of the poisonous and fetid vapors of petty egoism, of sordid cares about your person and the baser requirements of your life. It will raise you to that high hill from which disappears everything petty and trivial, everything particular and accidental, and there become visible only nations and empires, emperors and heroes. . ."

The enthusiasm with which Belinski hailed these patriotic works of Zhukovski and Glinka did not carry him away, however, from one central conviction: namely, that these were not works of art; that the true work of art could never be forced to swear political allegiance. Thus immediately after elaborating the *mystique* of national life which Zhukovski's poem had called up in him, Belinski concludes: "Of course, as a poem, which did not appear out of the freely ranging impulse of fantasy but was brought to us by a contemporary event . . . it should not be subjected to an entirely strict criticism." Similarly Glinka's book, for all its "poetry," lacks "any complete picture, artistically realized and self-contained. . ." Belinski refused to allow his political philosophy, however passionately held, to infringe upon the autonomous function of the artist.

In fact, the direction in Belinski's present thought which was to lead him to dramatic consequences was neither his extreme patriotism as such nor any false or indefensible conception of art as such. The radical consequences which followed this transitory stage of his thought flowed mainly from one source: namely, the fatal separation he had made between the sphere of art and the sphere of social and political actuality — the insistence that "each go its own way, without hindering the other."

It is also true, of course, that the extremism of Belinski's present political philosophy rendered its existence precarious. Everything in Belinski's life and temperament made it impossible for him to go on singing praises to Russian autocracy.

Gogol's The Inspector *versus* Griboedov's Woe from Wit

The January, 1840, issue of *National Notes*, which carried Belinski's essay on Menzel, included also a long article ostensibly devoted to *Woe from Wit* (*Gore ot uma*), the play by Alexander Griboedov. The occasion for Belinski's review was a second edition in 1839 of this work which had been known in Russian literary circles since 1824. Belinski used the occasion to illustrate the doctrine of art and society which is characteristic of his Hegelian phase. To that end, he introduced, for purposes of comparison, the discussion of a second famous contemporary play: Gogol's *The Inspector* (*Revizor*), which had first appeared in 1836.

It would hardly be disputed that this article on Gogol and Griboedov is the outstanding critical essay of Belinski's "Hegelian" period. In it Belinski not only succeeds in revealing the major elements of his present doctrine, and in illustrating his argument by two major works of contemporary Russian literature; but he also succeeds in demonstrating how his doctrine could be made compatible with concrete literary judgments.

That the two plays are to serve as examples for a general theory

is clear from the structure of Belinski's article, which opens with
a long theoretical statement, constituting nearly half the essay.
Midway through this long disquisition, the author introduces his
now favorite concept:

Reality — there is the password and the motto of our age; reality
in everything: in beliefs, in science, in art, and in life. Our strong and
forceful age tolerates nothing false, counterfeit, weak, diffuse, but
loves what is powerful, solid, real. It boldly listened without trembling
to the inconsolable songs of Byron and along with the mournful singer
deemed it better to forego all joy and all hope than to take satisfaction in the beggarly joys and hopes of the past century. It endured the
critical realism of Kant, the rational position of Fichte; it suffered with
Schiller through all the ailments of the inner, subjective spirit, striving
toward reality by way of negation. And then in Schelling it beheld a
dawn of infinite reality, which in the teaching of Hegel shone over
the world in a luxuriant and splendid light of day. . . Only in our age
has art been accorded its full significance as the reconciliation of a
Christian content with the plasticity of classical form, as a new phase
in the harmony of idea and form. Our age is an age of reconciliation
and is as alien to romantic art as it is to classical art.

By the word "reality" is meant all that is: the visible world and the
spiritual world, the world of facts and the world of ideas. Reason in
consciousness and Reason in external appearance — in a word, spirit
revealing itself to itself — is *reality*; whereas everything that is particular, accidental, and unreasonable is *illusion*, the opposite and the
negation of reality, appearance and not real being. Man drinks, eats,
dresses: that is the world of *illusions* because his spirit has no part in
it. Man feels, thinks, knows himself to be an organ and a vessel of
spirit, a finite particularization of the general and the infinite: that is
the world of *reality*.

Reality is the affirmation of life, illusion is its negation.

This distinction between reality and illusion furnishes the basis
for a distinction between tragedy and comedy. Just as tragedy
is conflict within the sphere of reality, so comedy is conflict
within the sphere of illusion. "The humor of comedy proceeds
from the continual conflict of the world of appearance with the
laws of rational reality. . . The contradiction between actuality
and the laws of rational reality is revealed in illusoriness, finite-
ness, and limitation — as in Ivan Ivanovich and Ivan Nikiforovich. . . ." The two Ivans are comic just because the quarrel between them is based on nothing more substantial than the word
"goose"; "if the author had made the cause of the quarrel some

really insulting oath or a slap in the face or a fist-fight, he would have spoiled everything. No, the author understood that in the world of illusions to which he was giving objective reality, every-thing — amusements, occupations, pleasures, sorrows, suffering, and even offenses — in that world everything is illusory, senseless, empty, and sordid.

At the basis of *The Inspector* lies the same idea which appears in "The Quarrel of Ivan Ivanovich with Ivan Nikiforovich": in both works the poet has expressed the idea of the negation of life, the idea of illusoriness. . . In the latter work we see an emptiness void of all activity; in *The Inspector* an emptiness filled with the activity of petty passions and petty egoism.

Thus the Mayor lives and moves in a world of illusions. He is the very creature of superstitious fears and desperate remorse of conscience. His fears frighten his conscience, and his con-science increases his fears. Thus when he hears that the Inspector from St. Petersburg is traveling incognito and "under secret or-ders," his anxiety immediately prepares him to accept the first stranger as the dreaded Inspector. The fact that the official visitor will come from St. Petersburg increases his awe: "St. Petersburg is a secret country for our Mayor, a fantastic world, the form of which he may not and cannot imagine." The inner logic of his world of fearful illusion makes it quite understandable and even inevitable that he should mistake the idle Khlestakov for the Inspector, that "not harsh reality but an illusion, a phantom, or, better yet, a shadow cast by the fear of a guilty conscience, should be the punishment of this *man of illusions*."

The inevitable logic of this world of unreality is well expressed, for instance, in the interchange between the Mayor and Bobchin-ski, when the latter announces that he has seen the Inspector. Just as the Mayor's anxiety drives him to wish desperately to discount the report, so Bobchinski's pride over his "discovery" drives him to insist that his discovery is genuine.

Finally, "the arrival of the policeman with the news that the real inspector has come ends the play beautifully and gives it the fullness and wholeness of a self-contained world of its own."

The Inspector thus fulfills the chief requirement of the work of art: that everything in it show an inevitable development out of a basic idea, so that nothing remains arbitrary or accidental. Thus "every actor expresses himself by his every word, yet not at all for the sheer purpose of expressing himself, but rather by reason of his inevitable participation in the progress of the play. Every word spoken by every person is related either to the fact that the Inspector is being awaited or else to the fact of his presence in the town. The person of the Inspector is the source from which everything flows and to which everything returns."

The comic absurdity of the play, Belinski continues, is essentially the absurdity of an unreal world of fear and false pride, a world of empty appearance. The "Inspector" of the play is himself the creation of the deluded townspeople. Indeed, Khlestakov is not the protagonist of the play: he arrives in the second act and leaves before the end; meanwhile "the spectator's interest is still concentrated on the people whose fear created this phantom; and the comedy would not have been completed if it had ended with [Khlestakov's departure]. The hero of the comedy is the Mayor, as representative of this world of illusions."

Griboedov's play, *Woe from Wit*, in contrast, lacks any central and unifying "idea" to which all the elements of the play serve as elaboration.

They tell us . . . that there is an idea here, and that it is the conflict between an intelligent and profound person and the society in which he lives. . . But are the representatives of Russian society all Famusovs, Molchalins, Sophias . . . and their like? If so, they do right to banish from their midst a Chatski with whom they have nothing in common, nor he with them. Society is always superior to the individual person and has superior rights over him. Private individuality is a reality and not an illusion only to the degree that it expresses society within itself.

Furthermore, "these people were not representatives of Russian society but only representatives of one part of it; so there were other circles within the society which were closer and more akin to Chatski. Such being the case, why did he . . . not seek a circle more to his liking? Hence Chatski's conflict is accidental and not real. It is not a conflict with society but a conflict with a particular circle within society.

"*Woe from Wit* is not a comedy, by the absence — or, better yet, by the falseness — of its basic idea. . . . *Woe from Wit* is a satire and not a comedy. And a satire cannot be an *artistic* creation. It is in this respect that *Woe from Wit* stands at an immeasurable, infinite distance beneath *The Inspector* as a perfectly artistic creation."

The weakness in Griboedov's central idea is observable in many related weaknesses. Chatski, for example, who is ostensibly the hero of the play, is inexcusably impolite and intrusive, especially with Sophia, on whom he imposes himself from the beginning to the end of the play. Sophia, meanwhile, makes a confused impression upon us by her persistent regard for the despicable Molchalin. Individual parts of the play, far from all conducing to a single development, are sometimes best appreciated when looked at separately. Thus the scene of the ball in Act III, excellent in itself, would be better if Chatski were omitted from it.

Although an imperfect "artistic" creation, Griboedov's play is a "poetic" work with many fine features; and Griboedov is clearly a great writer. But this work shows that he had not yet matured to that "harmonious and objective contemplation of life in which everything is inevitable and rational" — whereby the "poet" of "lyrical outbursts of his own subjectivity" becomes a true "artist," creating "objective reproductions of the phenomena of life."

This comparison between Gogol and Griboedov provides a clear demonstration of the balance which Belinski now had struck between social conservatism and a new insistence upon the integrity of the work of art. Only that work is "artistic" which presents a self-contained "idea" in the form of a perfectly appropriate imagery. The true "artist," as distinct from the "poet," works with an objective world: a world of reality, as in tragedy; or of nonreality, as in comedy. He does not express merely subjective judgments upon his world; to do so is to reduce the "artist" in himself to the "poet," to reduce true comedy, as in Gogol, to satire, as in Griboedov. It thus becomes the work of the true artist to build a miniature world-in-itself, an imaginative duplication of the self-contained world of actuality, in which everything that exists is the unfolding of an inner rationale.

Belinski's respect for the integrity of the work of art was probably never greater than at this time. That he was a good critic during this phase of his thought is perhaps best seen in his article on these two plays. For once, even Gogol, as Belinski reports in a letter of March 14, 1840, was satisfied with Belinski's criticism of his work. But respect for the freedom of art was now joined in Belinski's thought with an impossible social conservatism. The consequence was that he required art and life to exist apart — both threatened, through such a divorce, with the loss of their common humanity. The effort to preserve the purity of art was bound to be made foolish by the first genuine artist who might come along — especially when he was destined, as it turned out, to be Michael Lermontov.

Unreconciled: The Discovery of Lermontov

Belinski's article on Menzel and his article on Griboedov were printed in the same issue (January, 1840) of the *National Notes*; in the sixth issue for that year, published in the summer of 1840, Belinski's next important article appeared — on the subject of Lermontov's novel, *A Hero of Our Time*. Here was an unusual subject for a critic who had just been busy announcing the rationalization of Russian life and the Olympian objectivity of the true artist. What makes Belinski's commentary dramatic is the acclaim which he was ready to accord Lermontov, while at the same time persisting in a critical doctrine by which Lermontov's genius could hardly be grasped. The artist and the doctrinaire in Belinski had quarreled before (and would again); now the quarrel was aggravated by the progressive deterioration of his doctrine.

Theoretical difficulties notwithstanding, Belinski was quick to see that "suddenly on the horizon of our poetry there has arisen a new bright light," which "immediately showed itself to be a star of the first magnitude. We speak of Lermontov. . . ." Although his "Song of Kalashnikov" was slighted when it appeared in 1838, "each of his minor works has generally called forth strong enthusiasm. Everyone saw in them something completely new and original; all were struck by the power of his inspiration, the depth and force of his feeling, the richness of his fancy, the fullness of life and the vividly felt presence of thought in artistic form. . .

"The 'Song of Kalashnikov' shows that Lermontov is able to reproduce the immediate detail of Russian life in the form of a national poetry which alone is appropriate to it; while his other works, animated by a Russian spirit, appear in that universal form which is appropriate to poetry which is no longer merely natural but has become artistic, and which while not ceasing to be national has been made available to every age and nation." Thus Lermontov's art fulfills the requirement that every particular work be "a particularization of a general and universal idea in a particular form. . ."

But the work of art created upon a particularization of a general and universal idea must fulfill a second requirement: it must be "self-contained," having within itself a "wholeness" in which nothing is lacking and nothing is superfluous, where all elements are joined into a single unity as the separate organs are joined to form a total organism.

"All that has been said is quite easy to apply to Mr. Lermontov's novel." *

Lermontov's power to create a work which is self-contained, the movement of which is inherent and not imposed by the author, is demonstrated at the very beginning of *A Hero of Our Time*. The story is brought into being by a succession of necessary developments: the meeting with Maxim Maximych on the road from Tiflis, the offer of rum for his tea, his refusal of the rum, his recollection of the experience which led him to give up drinking, the movement to other experiences among the Cherkess. . . This impression of inevitable development comes home to the reader even more convincingly at the end of the episode concerning Bela. Bela's death, although sad, "does not trouble you with an unrelieved and heavy feeling, for it entered the story not like some frightening skeleton arbitrarily called forth by the author, but in consequence of a rational necessity of which one had already had a premonition; it appeared in the story like a bright

---

* Belinski's protesting claim here recalls a similar phrasing in his 1835 article on Gogol, discussed above, in which he was likewise laboring to relate an artistic work to a theory of dubious applicability.

angel of reconciliation. Dissonance has been resolved in a harmonious accord. With tenderness one repeats the simple and
touching words of the good Maxim Maximych: 'No, she did well
to die! What would have become of her if Gregory Alexandro-
vich [Pechorin] had abandoned her? And that would have happened sooner or later. . .' "

Like the story "Bela," so also the character sketch "Maxim
Maximych" "is an individual and self-sufficient whole" and "leaves
in the mind of the reader a complete, integrated, and profound
impression." In this part "the poet wanted to portray a character,
and he made an excellent success of it: his Maxim Maximych can
be used not only as a proper name but also as a common noun,
along with Onegin, Lenski . . . Ivan Ivanovich, Ivan Nikiforovich . . . Chatski, Famusov, and the like."

In the story "Taman," although we are given "an episode from
the life of the hero of the novel, the hero remains for us as before,
a mysterious person." It can be said of the whole story, in fact,
that for all the "prosaic actuality of its content, everything in it
is mysterious; the people are all some kind of fantastic shadows
fleeting through the evening twilight, in the light of the moon
or of the dawn." The unity of the story is the unity of a lyric
poem; "if one were to quote from it, it would be necessary to
quote the whole thing word for word."

"As for the hero of the novel, he appears here the same mysterious person as in the first stories. You see a man of powerful will,
courageous, unflinching before any danger, thrusting himself into
storms and alarms, in order to be busy with something and to fill
the bottomless void of his spirit, even though with aimless
activity."

Finally, in the story "Princess Mary," there begins the novel to
which all the preceding has been a long foreword. Princess Mary
reveals the character of Pechorin through being made his victim.
"What a fearful person is this Pechorin! Because his restless spirit
demands movement, and activity demands food, and his heart
longs for some absorption in life, the poor girl is obliged to suffer!" The strict moralist may cry out against such a monster of
egotism. But the individual on his way to self-knowledge must
take this road. "The kingdom of truth is the promised land, and

the way to it is an Arabian desert. . . Without storms there is no fertility, and nature languishes; without passions and contradictions there is no life, no poetry. . . We must demand of art that it reveal to us reality for what it is, since, whatever it is, reality will tell us, will teach us more than all the conceptions and doctrines of the moralists. . ." It is with this realization that the present age has turned from the moralizing of the eighteenth century to the truth of what is. "Hence also the art of our age is a reproduction of rational reality . . . according to *the laws of rational necessity*. This being the case, no matter what is the content of a poetic work, it will have a beneficial effect upon the soul of the reader, and thus a moral aim is achieved by itself." Thus modern art "allows in itself dissonances created within the harmony of the moral spirit, but with the object of showing how out of dissonance harmony again rises. . . This is the universal law of life and consequently also of art."

Pechorin is a man who has not yet succeeded in making his terms with reality. Not having attained reality, he is compelled to live in a present condition of illusory appearance. He is a man of "reflection" — divided into two men, one of whom lives while the other coldly observes and coldly analyzes into nothingness every spontaneous movement of his heart and mind. However terrible this state of "reflection," it is a necessary stage between "spontaneity" and "rational consciousness." Our time is *par excellence* an age of "reflection." It is in this respect that Pechorin is the hero of our time.

"A great many readers will surely cry, 'A fine hero!' . . . You say that he is an egotist? But does he not despise and hate himself for this? . . . No . . . egotism does not suffer, does not accuse itself, but is satisfied, self-contented." Granted that Pechorin is no model for all the virtues — but such is to be found "only in classical tragedies and in the sentimental novels of the last century. . . But this is one of those novels

> *In which an era can be scanned,*
> *In which contemporary man*
> *Is realistically portrayed*
> *In all his immorality,*
> *His self-love and sterility. . .**

* From Pushkin's *Eugene Onegin*, chap. VII, stanza XXII.

" 'A fine person, this contemporary man!' . . . But no contemporary man, as the representative of his age, however bad it may be, can be bad, because there are no bad ages, and no one age is worse or better than another, because it is a necessary stage in the development of humanity or society."

Just as Pushkin's Onegin was the representative of an age which is now past, so Pechorin is "the Onegin of our time, *the hero of our time*. The difference between them is much less than the distance between the Onega and the Pechora. . . † As Onegin is artistically superior to Pechorin, so Pechorin is superior to Onegin in respect to idea. But this superiority belongs to our time and not to Lermontov. Who is Onegin? . . . The novel presents him as a man weighed down by culture and high society, who has experienced everything, has grown tired of everything, and whose whole life showed that

> He found the world an equal bore
> In modern or antique décor.

Not so Pechorin. Here is a man who bears his suffering with neither indifference nor apathy. He is on a mad search for life, seeking it everywhere; and he bitterly accuses himself when he loses his way. Questions arise within him incessantly, trouble him, torment him; and he seeks their solution in self-scrutiny. He observes every movement of his heart, examines each of his thoughts. He has made out of himself the most fascinating object of his observations, and in trying to remain as frank as possible in his confession, not only does he openly admit his true faults but even fabricates others which do not exist, or else makes a false interpretation of his most natural reactions."

Having recognized in Pechorin the true "hero of our time," Belinski must somehow reconcile such an unharmonious, unpredictable, unstable image with the principle of rationality which he continues to posit in reality and with the principle of organic self-containment which he continues to require in the work of art. And for all his own lively recognition of the human truth

---

† The names of two rivers in northern Russia from which Pushkin and Lermontov presumably drew the names for their heroes Onegin and Pechorin.

of Pechorin — a truth which Belinski was well equipped to grasp — he proceeds to apply to Lermontov's work his inappropriate critical demands.

Pechorin, in the first place, is vague, contradictory, lacks unity, remains too close to his author, who fails to maintain a proper objectivity. "In the matter of form the portrayal of Pechorin is not completely artistic. The cause of this, however, is not in a lack of talent in the author but in the fact that the character whom he has depicted . . . is so close to himself that he was unable to separate himself from it and objectify it. . . In order to make a true portrayal of any given character it is necessary to be completely separated from it, to look on it as on something finished. But this, to repeat, is not observed in the creation of Pechorin. He is the same incomplete and enigmatic creature when he slips from us as when he first appears before us at the beginning of the novel."

Hence, Belinski argues, Pechorin suffers in contrast to Onegin, whose story and personality are more integrated. "In the *Onegin* all the parts are organically fused; for within the chosen framework of his novel Pushkin exhausted the whole of his idea, and hence not a single one of its parts would it be possible to change or replace. *A Hero of Our Time* represents several frameworks superimposed within one larger frame provided by the title of the novel and the unity of its hero. The parts of the novel are deployed in conformity with an internal necessity; but since they are only discrete occurrences out of a life — although it be the life of one and the same man — they could be interchanged with others. . . There could be similar adventures in other settings and with other characters, although happening to one and the same hero." Lermontov's work is held together "by a marvelous unity of *feeling*" but lacks "unity of *idea*."

Finally, if Lermontov lives up to what he promises in *A Hero of Our Time*, he should subsequently show us a new Pechorin — perhaps after the latter has come to clear recognition of the laws of morality. Perhaps Lermontov "will require him to recognize the rationality and beatitude of life but only to be convinced that this is not for him, that he has spent much of his force in his fearful struggle, has become hardened thereby, and is unable to

make that rationality and beatitude his own possession. . . Or
perhaps he will permit him to partake of the joys of living by
triumphing over the evil genius of his life. . . "

Here at the close of Belinski's analysis of Pechorin, the dogma
of "reconciliation," which he had been careful to insinuate
throughout the essay, stands forth as a kind of concluding moral.
Perhaps one might mark here the first eminent example of that
critical method which was later to be called "utilitarian": the
method whereby a work of art is used as "a set of materials for
making judgments about actuality." [28] Faithful to his philosophical creed of rational reality, for which Pechorin would seem to
provide so poor an illustration, Belinski is obliged to leave a final
word of advice and hope about what Pechorin may, or ought to,
become.

The striking feature of this final tendentiousness in Belinski is
that it closes an essay in which the critic had shown such a penetrating understanding of Lermontov's work. Indeed, Belinski's
whole essay adroitly joins a keen awareness of Pechorin and a
subtle "rationalization" of what Pechorin represents. If Pechorin
had seemed to frustrate any effort to make reality "rational,"
Belinski insists that Pechorin is the dissonance which proves the
universal harmony. If Lermontov's work had seemed to present
a bitter reality and an unreconciled hero, Belinski insists that "we
must demand of art that it reveal to us reality for what it is, since,
whatever it is, reality will . . . teach us more than all the . . .
doctrines of the moralists."

The psychological fact is that Belinski understood Pechorin so
well because he saw himself in Lermontov's hero. The philosophical superstructure which he raises over Pechorin is at the same
time being raised over his own head. But what we know, mainly
through his private correspondence, of Belinski's mind and heart
at this time confirms the impression which we get from his critical review of Lermontov's novel: that the superstructure is already tottering.

Meanwhile one cannot fail to be impressed by Belinski's success
in skewing the structure of his theory in critical recognition of
the one contemporary author whose life and work would seem to

do the greatest possible violence to every major tenet in his present critical doctrine. As he had allowed Gogol to attack his transcendentalism, he now hears in compassion the "wail of pain" raised by Lermontov against the rational reality which he had just been announcing. He is even ready to admit that Lermontov's failure to achieve in *A Hero of Our Time* "that higher artistic self-containment" is "at the same time a virtue of Mr. Lermontov's novel: such is the nature of all contemporary social questions which find expression in poetic works. Here is a wail of pain, but a wail by which the pain is assuaged. . . "

Having emerged from the analysis of Lermontov's novel with his critical sensitivity still vigorous and with an undefeated will to defend his theoretical positions, Belinski might have turned to consider less troublesome subjects. But the following winter of 1841 finds him again involved, now in a review of Lermontov's poetry, published in the January issue of the *National Notes*. Here the lyric cry of Lermontov is clearly heard in protest against the claims of a rational reality and a harmonious, self-contained, objective art.

The dramatic emergence of a new emphasis in Belinski's thought becomes gradually apparent in these pages. Before the close of the article, it is clear toward what position he has moved; innuendo finally gives place to outright declaration. But even as we begin in the first pages to read what seem at first to be stale recapitulations, a crucial shift becomes discernible. Here if in any one place is the point of Belinski's mid-passage from a tentative to a final position.

In the review of Lermontov's poetry Belinski has not proceeded very far before he begins to repeat the familiar notion that "the objects in the world are numberless and various, but in them there is a unity: they are all particular manifestations of the universal. That is why philosophy holds that only the universal exists. . . Particular phenomena are born and die, appear and pass away; just as waves are born in the ocean . . . and wave replaces wave, but the ocean remains grand and deep and life and movement continue over its bottomless, limitless bed; while from one of its crystals there is shed a brilliant reflection of the radiant sun. . .

Each person is a separate and particular universe of passions, feelings, desires, sensations; but these passions, feelings, desires, sensations belong not to some one person but are the possession of human nature, common to all men. Thus he lives most who possesses most that is common; he in whom there is nothing common is a living corpse. By what is a person's participation in the common expressed? By the accessibility to him of all that is proper to human nature. . . in his right to say of himself, 'I am a man and nothing human is alien to me.' "

Within the space of several sentences, what had started out as a celebration of the general, common, universal, has thus been turned into an elevation of the individual: the crystal in which "the radiant sun" is contained, the separate person in whom the universal finds its only concrete life. Belinski's movement of protest against Hegel's lesson of universality had, in fact, only brought him closer to the Hegelian conception of concreteness; but in Belinski's own mind there was being prepared here not a further reconciliation with Hegel but a revolt.

But the revolt was not a sudden *coup d'état*. Almost on the following page of Belinski's article the old formula is repeated: "What is real is rational, and what is rational is real — that is a great truth. But not all is real which exists in reality; while for the artist there should exist only a rational reality." Yet in the very next sentence a crucial qualification is added: "But in relation to it [i.e., to the rational reality of the artist] he is not its slave but its creator; it does not lead him by the hand, but he introduces into it his own ideals, and in accordance with them he transforms it. Thus poetry is life *par excellence*, the essence, so to speak, the rarefied ether, the triple-extract, the quintessence of life. . . Poetry is the pulse-beat of universal life, its blood, fire, light, and sun.

The poet is the noblest vessel of the spirit, the preferred darling of heaven. He is a *man*, but a man who can be worthless without ever being low, who can fall more often than others, but who rises just as quickly as he falls. . .

What is the aim of poetry? . . . Poetry has no aim outside itself, but is an end in itself, just as is truth in knowledge and goodness in action. . . The poet is a painter and not a philosopher. The constant subject of his pictures and portrayals is "the creation full of praise" . . .

For the poet all the phenomena of earth exist for themselves; he puts himself into them, lives their life, and cherishes them in his heart just as they are, without altering their nature according to some caprice of his own. This does not mean that the poet cannot . . . introduce . . . his own ideal, that he cannot exchange the lyre of song, the dagger of tragedy, or the trumpet of the epic for the thunder of noble indignation or even the hoot of satire; or that he cannot leave off prayer for preaching, forgetting for the moment the past, the universe, and the eternal, to turn to the contemporary world and present society. But it is ridiculous to demand that he see the goal of his life in this and that he be obliged to subordinate his free inspiration to various "current requirements."

Whereas the poet had been the passive organ of a rational reality which devours the individual who foolishly refuses to accept it, he now becomes himself its creator, and only by the expression of his own "passions, feelings, desires, sensations" is he ever an effective spokesman of universal reality. Far from being a passive receptacle into which the universal life is poured, the poet is the creative builder of a rational reality which he causes to exist within the context of actuality. He is even superior to nature, because his work is conscious. "The poet does not imitate life but competes with it; and his creations arise out of the same source and by the same process as all phenomena of nature, with the one difference that in the process of his creation there is consciousness, which is absent in the activity of nature. . . Art is superior to nature in so far as every conscious and free activity is superior to one that is unconscious and involuntary."

By the same reasoning, Belinski's recent justification and even exaltation of national life in Russia quietly makes way for a philosophy of critical evaluation of the *status quo*. The creative function of the individual cannot be confined to his own private world, for "there is also society and humanity. However rich and sumptuous may be a man's inner life . . . it is incomplete if it does not take upon itself the interests of the world external to itself, of society and humanity. . . A *living* person bears in his spirit, in his heart, in his blood, the life of society. He is hurt by its misfortunes, tormented by its sufferings, flourishes in its health. . . Of course, in this connection, society takes only its portion from him . . . without subordinating him to itself completely and exclusively. The citizen should not destroy the person, nor the person the citizen. . . Love for fatherland should come out of love for humanity, as the particular from the general. To love one's native land means to have an ardent desire to see realized in it the ideal of humanity and to contribute to that, within the measure of one's powers."

Just as the particular has asserted its claims against the general, so the function of the individual has been identified with the creation of conscious order in a world of unconscious variety, and with the maintenance of a critical concern for the general life of society and humanity. That creative and critical function is, of course, performed *par excellence* by the artist. But the artist does not perform that function so long as art and society "each goes its own way, without hindering the other," as Belinski had recently said they should, in his 1840 essay on Menzel. Nor will independent criticism be encouraged as long as it is held that "society is always higher than the individual person and has superior rights over him," as he had argued in his 1840 article on Griboedov. The bridge between the artist and society is now boldly thrown: "The greater the poet and the more he belongs to the society into which he was born, the more closely is the development, the direction, and even the character of his talent bound to the historical development of his society."

Thus "Pushkin began his poetic career with *Ruslan and Liudmila* — a work which is irrepressibly joyful and playful. . . Lermontov began with a historical poem, somber in content, grim and weighty in form. . . [The first lyrical works of Pushkin were] full of bright hopes, a foretaste of triumph. . . In the first lyrical works of Lermontov . . . there is nowhere any hope, they strike the soul of the reader with their desolate lack of faith in life and in human feeling, along with a thirst for life and an overflow of feeling. . . Nowhere is there Pushkin's revelry at the banquet of life, but everywhere questions which darken the soul and freeze the heart. . . Yes, it is clear that Lermontov is a poet of a completely different age, and that his poetry is a completely new link in the chain of the historical development of our society. *

* Belinski's footnote: "Let us note, for greater clarity and 'accuracy,' that

Lermontov's first piece was printed in *The Contemporary* for 1837.
. . . It is called "Borodino" . . . The whole main idea of the poem is
expressed in the second stanza. . . This idea is a complaint against the
present generation, drowsy in inactivity; a sighing for the greatness of
the past, so full of glory and great deeds. Further on we shall see that
this *longing for life* inspired in our poet more than one poem full of
energy and noble indignation.

In 1838 . . . there was printed his poem "Song of Tsar Ivan Vasilevich, of the Young Oprichnik, and of the Courageous Merchant
Kalashnikov". . . Here the poet transported himself from the present
world of Russian life, which dissatisfied him, into the world of the
Russian past; he listened to the beat of its pulse . . . and extracted
from that life a fictitious tale more credible than reality, more believable than any history. . . This "Song" [shows] the blood-relation-
ship between the spirit of the poet and the spirit of the nation. . . The
very choice of this subject witnesses to the state of mind of the poet,
dissatisfied with contemporary reality and so having moved out of it
into the distant past, in order to seek there life which he cannot find
in the present. But the past could not occupy such a poet for long. He
was bound to feel soon all its poverty and monotony and to return
to the present, [which] awaits its illumination from him, the healing
of its plagues and diseases. He and he alone can accomplish that. . .
In poetic works which express the ills and afflictions of society, society
finds the alleviation of its ills and afflictions . . . a knowledge of the
cause of the illness through a representation of the illness. . .

"Our age is an age of consciousness, of the philosophic spirit,
meditation, 'reflection.' *The question* — that is the alpha and
omega of our time. . . " In an age of self-conscious individualism,
the poet is necessarily a self-conscious individualist. "Hence reflection (meditation) is the proper material for the poetry of our
time, and almost all the great poets of our time have paid it their
full tribute. . . In our age the absence in a poet of the element of
inwardness (subjectivity) is a fault. Even Goethe is blamed, and
not without cause, for the absence of historic and social elements,
for his tranquil satisfaction with reality as it is. This was the
reason why the human poetry of Schiller, although less *artistic*
but more *human* than Goethe's, found among humanity a greater
response than did the poetry of Goethe."

The attack here upon Goethe's "tranquil satisfaction with

in speaking of society we mean only the sensitive and thoughtful members
of the new generation."

reality is it is" — as well as the comparison with Schiller — contains too pointed a reference for Belinski not to have intended thereby a public announcement of his own transformation. Goethe's tranquillity had been precisely the subject of Belinski's defense of Goethe against Menzel, and the phrase "reality as it is" certainly carried resounding overtones of meaning for Belinski. Clearly he is not shy about recanting openly.

In so declaring, under the banner of "the subjective poetry of Lermontov," the rights of the individual in society, the validity of subjectivity in art, and the function of the artist to celebrate those rights by subjective portrayal, Belinski has obviously come a long way from a "Hegelian" exaltation of the universal. Yet at the same time it is apparent from the beginning here that the dignity of the individual for Belinski rests precisely upon the individual's participation in the universal.

In a great talent, a profusion of inwardness, of subjectivity, is a mark of humanity. Do not fear this direction. It will not deceive you, it will not lead you astray. A great poet, in speaking of himself, of his ego, speaks of the universal — of humanity, for in his nature there resides all that by which humanity lives. And so in his melancholy mood everyone recognizes his own; in his spirit everyone recognizes his own spirit and sees in him not only a *poet* but a *man*, his own brother in humanity. While realizing that he is a being incomparably superior to one's self, everyone at the same time recognizes his own kinship with him.

This is what impelled us to pay particular attention to the subjective poetry of Lermontov and even to rejoice that it was more than a work of pure art. By this sign we recognize in him a Russian poet, *national* in the highest and noblest sense of that word: a poet in whom there has found expression a historical stage of Russian society. And all his poetry of this sort is profound and significant. In it there is expressed a nature rich in the gifts of the spirit, a noble human personality.

A year after the publication of the "Song of Tsar Ivan Vasilevich, of the Young Oprichnik and of the Courageous Merchant Kalashnikov," Lermontov again came forth into the literary arena with a poem called "Meditation" ["Duma"]. . . . The poet speaks of the new generation, of how he looks upon it with sadness, saying that its future is "either empty or dark". . . . These verses are written in blood. They come from the depths of an outraged spirit. This is the wail, the groan of a man for whom the absence of inner life is an evil a thousand times more fearful than physical death! . . . And who among the men of the new generation will not find in it the clue to his own despair and spiritual apathy and inner emptiness, and will not answer back with his own wail and groan? . . . If by "satire" we are to mean not the innocuous grin of some gay wit, but the thunder of indignation, the storm of a spirit outraged at the shame of his society, then Lermontov's "Meditation" is a satire, and satire is a legitimate form of poetry.

Since the time of Pushkin's appearance in our literature . . . there has come into use the new word "disillusionment". . . This was the age of the awakening of our society to life; literature for the first time began to be an expression of society. This new direction of literature was fully expressed in that marvelous work of Pushkin, "The Demon". . . This was the demon of doubt, the spirit of meditation, of reflection, destroying all the fullness of life, poisoning every joy. The strange thing is that just when life was awakening, there should appear right along with it the spirit of doubt — the enemy of life. . . Moreover, [Pushkin's "Demon"] brought forth another demon even more fearful and more puzzling. . .

> How weary! how mournful! and no one to grasp by the hand
>   When the heart is dissolving in tears. . .
> Desire! . . . but how useless to follow desire without end
>   As the years hurry on, all the glorious years!
> And love! . . . but who is there to love? . . . and why love for
>   a time?
>   Yet all love is for only a day.
> Look inward: within, of all trace from the past not a line:
>   Every joy, every sorrow has vanished away.
> And passions? But sooner or later their sweet discontent,
>   At the first word of reason, must go;
> And the mind, when on life all its cold concentration is bent,
>   Discovers how empty and stupid a show. . .

. . . This is not a mere moment of special disharmony, of the heart's despair; this is a funeral dirge sung over all life! . . . He who has heard more than once within himself this burial chant, and has seen in this poem only an artistic expression of a terrifying sense long familiar to him, — he will ascribe a very deep significance to it . . . he will give it a place of honor among the greatest creations of poetry. . . . And what simplicity of expression, how natural and free the verse! so that you feel as if the whole piece had suddenly poured out onto the paper by itself, like flowing tears long welling up, like a stream of hot blood from a wound from which the bandage has suddenly been ripped. . .

Recall *A Hero of Our Time*, recall Pechorin — that strange person who, on the one hand, is tired of life, despises it and himself, believes neither in it nor in himself . . . and who, on the other hand, is in pursuit of life, who greedily seeks its sensations . . . recall his love for Bela, for Vera, for Princess Mary — and then you will understand those lines:

And love! . . . but who is there to love? . . . and why love for a time?
Yet all love is for only a day.

. . . "How weary! how mournful!" ["I skuchno! i grustno! . . ."], out of all the pieces written by Lermontov, attracted the special hostility of the older generation. Strange people! They still think that poetry should invent instead of being the priestess of truth, that it should console with a baby's rattle instead of thundering forth the truth!

[Yet] from the spirit of that same poet who sang songs of affliction, freezing the human heart, from that same spirit there could come forth also — [a] prayerful, soothing melody of hope, of reconciliation, and of the benediction of life in the midst of life. . .

" . . . From what rich elements were compounded the poetry of this man, in what varied themes and expressions do its harmonies and melodies roll out and pour forth!" — as in "To the Memory of A.I.O." ["Pamiati A.I. O-go"], "A Prayer" ["Molitva"], "January First" ["1-e Ianvaria"], "The Journalist, the Reader, and the Writer" ["Zhurnalist, Chitatel i Pisatel"], "To a Child" ["Rebenku"], and others.

We shall not call Lermontov a Byron or a Goethe or a Pushkin; but we do not consider it excessive praise to say that *such* poems as "The Water Nymph" ["Rusalka"], "Three Palm-trees" ["Tri Palmy"], and "The Gifts of the Terek" ["Dary Tereka"] could be found only in such poets as Byron, Goethe, and Pushkin. . .

Not long ago someone, holding forth in a newspaper article on the poetry of Lermontov, called his "Song of Tsar Ivan Vasilevich, of the Young Oprichnik, and of the Courageous Merchant Kalashnikov" a childish work and "Mtsyri" a mature work. This profound critic, counting on his fingers the time when each work appeared, very cleverly figured that the author was three years older when he wrote "Mtsyri," and from this circumstance he very soundly concluded: *ergo* "Mtsyri" is the more mature. . . But regardless of the immaturity of the idea and a certain forced quality in the content of "Mtsyri," the details and the execution of this poem are amazingly well realized. . . The pictures of nature reveal the hand of a great master: they are alive with the grandeur and the magnificent brilliance of the fantastic Caucasus. . . Strangely, the Caucasus has somehow been destined to be the cradle of our poetic talents. . . Griboedov created his *Woe from Wit* in the Caucasus: the wild and grandiose nature of that

country, the turbulent life and dour poetry of its sons inspired his
outraged humanity to portray the apathetic, useless crowd of Famusovs, Skalozubs, Zagoretskis, [etc.] — those caricatures of human nature. . . And now a great new talent appears, and the Caucasus becomes his poetic homeland, ardently loved by him. Upon the inaccessible heights of the Caucasus, crowned with eternal snow, he finds
his Parnassus. . . What a pity that that other poem of Lermontov's in
which the action also takes place in the Caucasus, was not printed . . . :
we speak of "The Demon" ["Demon"]. The idea of that poem is
deeper and incomparably more mature than the idea of "Mtsyri". . .
   Casting a general glance over the poetry of Lermontov, we see in
it all the forces, all the elements of which life and poetry are composed. In this deep nature, in this powerful spirit, everything seems to
live, everything is accessible and understandable, everything finds a
response. He is the omnipotent master of the kingdom of life; he
reproduces it in the manner of the true artist. He has the soul of a
Russian poet: in him are alive both the past and the present of Russian
life; and he has a profound knowledge of the world of the spirit. . .
There is everything, everything in the poetry of Lermontov: both
heaven and earth, both paradise and hell. . . For the present we shall
call him neither a Byron nor a Goethe nor a Pushkin, for we are convinced that he will become neither the first nor the second nor the
third, but — Lermontov. . . Already the time is not far off when his
name in literature will become a famous Russian name. . .

In this concluding declaration of esteem for Lermontov, it is
possible to see the climax of a personal drama in Belinski. In singing the praises of Lermontov, Belinski is looking toward his own
triumph over a discredited reconciliation with the world of
things as they are. No longer, as in the essay on Pechorin, is Lermontov asked to show the resolution of dissonance within a larger
harmony. Lermontov as he stands revealed in his poetry, not the
Lermontov who might some day achieve a reconciliation of his
quarrel with life, has become Belinski's hero. Literally within the
space of his essay on Lermontov's poetry, Belinski has moved
from an insistence that reality is rational to a glorification of the
very poet of spiritual discord.

New Resolution

By the beginning of 1841 Belinski had come a long way from
the reconciliation with reality which had allowed art and society

each to go its separate road without hindering one another, as set forth in the article on Menzel, published just a year before, in January of 1840. But the two major articles on Lermontov had made only a public statement of a change which had already been developing in Belinski's thought even while the famous "conciliatory" articles were being written, during the winter of 1839–40. Throughout that winter and the next, the evolution away from the doctrine of a rational reality continued to engage the critic's private thought, as mirrored in his private correspondence.

The rediscovery of reality, the power to reject the old "fair-souled" idealism, had been Hegel's original gift to Belinski. But his interpretation of Hegel had carried him to an extreme of tranquil satisfaction with reality as it is. In that ideological tranquillity he was ultimately forced to recognize a reëmergence of a false idealism seven times worse than the old idealism he had been struggling to exorcise. Formerly he had been in quest of a transcendental "life in the Absolute" — a vain pursuit which was, however, dignified at least by moral struggle; whereas now, by his attempt at a kind of philosophic quietism, he stood in peril, as he thought, of losing his own moral meaning. The creative, critical individual was in danger of being crushed by "that Moloch which philosophy has called the universal." [29]

By the strength of his own moral vitality, Belinski was thus brought to a new desperate realization: having removed the spectacles of a Hegelianism which had once seemed to justify the world of things as they are, he could see only disorder around him. The theories which had rationalized this disorder now seemed vaporous and poisonous. Those like himself and Botkin, who in his "Quixotic fervor" was deluded enough to "cry out about the rationality of life," [30] came to appear ineffectual idealists whose temporary refuge had been "on the desert island which was our circle," while the real business of life went on in "a society in which rascals and mediocrities play dominant roles while the noble and gifted lie in shameful idleness on a desert island." [31]

The refusal to continue justifying a "fearful and disgusting reality" by theories which vanish into "the smoke of fantasy and dreams" was for Belinski far from easy to make, for it cut him loose from more of his past than he could abandon without pain.

Cries of despair fill his private correspondence throughout 1840, as in a February letter: "I see my destruction. . . External conditions are fearful, and the thought of them stings the soul; but there is no possibility of rectifying them. . . What for the future? Only tears and sorrow for a lost paradise . . . and an abiding realization of decline to death forever." [32] Several months later he was still busy elaborating the same doleful theme: "In my soul there is coldness, apathy, unconquerable inertia. . . But the worse I see myself the better I understand reality. I see things more simply and hence more truly. . . I see myself . . . commonplace, such as I really am but as I had never represented myself. The best which is in me is a heart by nature inclined toward good. . . I have made [literature] the chief interest of my life; I torment myself, suffer, deprive myself for it. . . But to make of myself a real and powerful weapon for its service. . . I have already ceased even to think of that." [33]

As a sense of the sordid mediocrity of himself and of his world turned to ashes the grand structure of a rationalized reality, Belinski looked again to a renewal of concrete life, such as he had once discovered not long ago in Hegel and which he now sought through liberation from the Hegelian universal: "Oh, away with that hateful universal, that Moloch, devouring life. . . Better the most vulgar existence than such a universal. . . Let my consciousness be given a small corner of living reality rather than that empty, dry, and egotistical universal devoid of any content, of any reality. . . It is true that I am a rationalizer and a speculator, yet as soon as the marvelous facts of reality are presented to me, in art and in life, I consign my speculation to the devil." [34] From pursuit of the examined life, the search now turned toward the pursuit of life fully lived, for its own sake: "Fullness, fullness! Great, wonderful word! Blessedness is not in the Absolute, but in fullness. . . As for the Absolute, I would give it up, along with my last coat thrown into the bargain, in exchange for the fullness with which some officer hurries to a ball." [35] The separation between art and life, the insistence that each go its way without hindering the other, had made even of art a form of speculation, while the actual life of individual experience was repudiated as accidental and illusory: "The love of Romeo and Juliet is a universal, but the reader's love or need for love is particular and illusory. Life is in books, but in life — nothing." [36]

The rejection of an abstract universality in favor of a fullness of concrete life, even commonplace, joined in Belinski's thought with an ethical sense that only the concrete and particular individual has moral meaning and moral worth. If the rationalization of reality was a fantasy; if in truth reality lay about the individual in disorder; then only in the individual himself did there exist any ethical design or moral purpose. To smother the individual in the universal was not only a false, but indeed an immoral procedure. By such an illumination, it was "time for the human personality to be freed from the base fetters of irrational reality": "I curse my odious effort of reconciliation with an odious reality! Long live great Schiller, noble advocate of humanity, bright star of salvation, emancipator of society from the bloody prejudices of tradition! . . . For me now the *human personality* is above history, above society, above humanity. . . I have become completely absorbed in the idea of the worth of the human individual and his bitter lot — a frightful contradiction!" [37] There can be no rights, no matter how exalted a name they may be given, which can transcend the rights of the particular human person: "For me human nature is the justification of everything. The event is foolishness, to the devil with it, I spit on it. The important thing is the human personality, which must be valued as superior to all else." [38] For it remained to the human individual alone to bring moral order into a disordered world, to wage a moral battle with actuality.

Since it was under the banner of Hegel that he had defended all reality as rational, it was in Hegel that Belinski was bound to see the symbol of all that he now repudiated. By the spring of 1841 his two long winters of private war with his own Hegelianism ended in a personal triumph which he announced to Botkin in lines that carry an unmistakable portent of Ivan Karamazov:

I have long suspected that the philosophy of Hegel is only a phase, although a great one, but that the absolutism of its conclusions is not good, that it is better to die than to be reconciled to them. . . The individual with him is not an end in itself but a means for the momentary expression of the universal, and with him the universal is a

Moloch in regard to the individual. . . . I have particularly weighty reasons for raging against Hegel, for I feel that I was faithful to him (in sense) in reconciling myself with Russian reality. . . . All of Hegel's views on morality are downright nonsense, for in the realm of objective thought there is no morality. . . . The destiny of the subject, of the individual, of the person, is more important than the destinies of the whole world and the health of the Chinese emperor (i.e., the Hegelian *Allgemeinheit*). . . . I thank you humbly, George Frederick Hegel; I bow to your philosopher's gown. But with all due respect for your philosophic philistinism, I have the honor to inform you that if it were granted to me to climb to the highest rung of the ladder of development, at that very point I would ask you to account to me for all the sacrifices to the conditions of life and history, all the victims of hazard, of superstition, of the Inquisition, of Philip II, etc., etc. Otherwise I would throw myself down head foremost from the highest rung. . . . It is said that discord is the condition of harmony. No doubt that is quite profitable and enjoyable for lovers of music, but certainly not for those whose fate it is to express the idea of discord by their participation in it. . . . What is it to me that all will be well with my children or yours, if it is ill with me now, and if it is no fault of mine that it is ill? [39]

The writer of these lines had traveled a long distance in a short time from the justification of things as they are. From being a garment in which the universal "flaunts itself for a while" and which it then "discards like a pair of old pants," the individual has become for him the one effective moral agent in an irrational universe. And the artist, far from remaining the passive "organ of the general and universal," the creature of an inspiration which "prefers to live in past ages and to awaken the giant shades of Achilles and Hector, of Richard and Henry," as he had asserted in 1840 in the article on Menzel, has become, in the 1841 article on the poetry of Lermontov, the conscience of his time and of his society, who "does not imitate life but competes with it."

The spring of 1840 was marked in Belinski's life by two memorable meetings: a visit with Lermontov and a reconciliation with Herzen. Both these eminent figures, appearing thus briefly upon the horizon of Belinski's life at the beginning of the forties, foreshadow the direction his thought was to take throughout the decade. For if Lermontov was now coming to be for Belinski the very voice of human protest against an unenlightened world, Herzen had represented, since university days in the thirties, a tradition of social criticism, as distinct from the philosophic speculation of the rival Stankevich faction.

Belinski's meeting with Lermontov inspired an interesting report, sent off to Botkin in a letter of April 16, 1840:

Profound and powerful spirit! How true is his understanding of art, what a profound and perfectly spontaneous aesthetic sense. . . A marvelous person! I was absolutely delighted to hear him say that Cooper is superior to Walter Scott, that his novels have more depth and more artistic unity. I had long thought so and had yet to meet the first person who thought the same. He shows deference to Pushkin and most of all admires *Onegin*. He rails against women. . . Of men he is likewise contemptuous. But he loves several women and usually sees only them. His outlook is exactly that of Onegin. Pechorin is himself, just as he is. I argued with him that I was glad to detect in his rationalistic, cold, and outraged view of life and of people the seeds of a deep faith in the value of both. When I told him so, he smiled and said, "God grant that it may be so!" Good heavens, how inferior he is to me in his ideas, and how infinitely inferior I am to him in my superiority. His every word is himself, his whole being, in all its depth and wholeness. I am shy in his company: such whole, full individuals exert a restraining influence upon me; I defer to them and humble myself in the consciousness of my unworthiness.

Similarly impressive to Belinski, although for other reasons, was his subsequent meeting with Herzen. To Belinski, Herzen still recalled the Moscow University circle of the mid-thirties which rotated around Herzen and his friend Ogarev, forming the so-called "French" camp, whose interests were primarily in social questions and natural science, in opposition to the "Germans" of the Stankevich group, whose interests were predominantly philo-sophical and aesthetic. The meeting of these two currents of the thirties led into the formation of the "Men of the Forties," with intellectual interests now broad enough to include both political theory and speculative philosophy. In this historic confluence within the intelligentsia of the forties, combining the two main tendencies of the preceding decade, both Herzen and Belinski were representative figures: whereas Belinski was turning toward an interest in questions of society and politics, Herzen was be-coming interested in the philosophy of Hegel.

Belinski's reconciliation with Herzen at this time had another more specific significance. Herzen had cooled perceptibly toward his former fellow-Muscovite following the appearance of Belin-ski's reactionary articles on Zhukovski and Glinka. To make friends again with Herzen meant to celebrate the close of a period which Belinski was now happy to repudiate. Herzen even seemed the more honorable a friend because of his former hostility; on December 11, 1840, Belinski wrote to Botkin in praise of Herzen: "I like that man more and more. In fact, he is better than all the rest. . . That he upbraided me in Moscow for my *absolutist* articles is an additional reason for me to respect him."

The meeting between the two men had taken place in the pre-ceding May or June. Herzen, on a visit to St. Petersburg, came to call on Belinski. Panaev, who recounts the episode, tells how, after a half-hour's conversation between the two, he went into the room to find that the conversation was still somewhat strained. "At the end of an hour," Panaev goes on, "Belinski came upstairs to me.

" 'Well, we've explained ourselves to each other and we seem to have reached an understanding again,' Belinski said to me, taking a deep breath and dropping onto the divan (this meeting seemed to have affected him greatly)." [1]

Belinski as a man of the forties worked at one main task: to clarify in his own thought and to express in his critical writings a philosophy of protest — the protest of the creative individual, of the artist *par excellence*, against the universe of things as they are. That struggle was to animate not only his critical theory but also his personal existence throughout the decade until his death in 1848. In a letter of February 9, 1840, he wrote to Botkin that "like a madman" he kept repeating Lermontov's famous "How weary! how mournful! . . ." This lyric plaint of the poet whom he was soon to recognize as the poet of the age, found a disquieting reverberation in Belinski's own life. With Belinski, life and theory continued to unroll together.

The rejection of Hegelianism, which the articles on Lermontov first clearly announced, was not achieved without turmoil and anguish. The correspondence of the early forties is frequently broken by outbursts of despair: "I am weary, cold, and empty. I have no hope of any personal happiness. Woe! Woe! Life is exposed." [2] Reality could not for long be justified as rational and necessary by a sensitive intelligence in painful contact with hardship and loneliness. The circumstances of Belinski's life kept him too close to bitter realities to allow him to remain in serene and harmonious aloofness. Neither could he remain content to see reality as chaotic, accidental, and unjustified. And he had already progressed too far in the rejection of the old nobility of spirit of his former "desert island" existence, as he now called it, to find refuge in inward withdrawal. Inwardness might indeed be only egotism in an attractive disguise: "The spirit of darkness and evil is nothing else than egotism. . . Egotism becomes more fearful when it naively considers itself to be self-denial and inner life." [3] Experience had forced him to see that withdrawal into idealist fantasies was empty egotism; whereas the justification of the world that lay without had become less and less tenable. Having moved through thesis and antithesis, he struggled to establish a synthesis which should include both the moral freedom of the individual and the reality of the objective world.

By the time of the essays on Lermontov, the first step forward was already being taken. The motto "reconciliation with reality" was giving place to a new motto: "struggle against the actual." The god of reality was in process of being overthrown by the god of "negation": "Sorrow, heavy sorrow overcomes me at the sight of barefoot boys playing knucklebones in the street, of ragged beggars and a drunken coachman, of a soldier coming from a parade, of a bureaucrat hurrying by with a briefcase under his arm, of a conceited officer and a haughty aristocrat. . . And this is society, existing on rational principles, the manifestation of reality! . . . And after this does a *man* have the right to forget himself in art, in science! . . . Negation is my god." [4] The nature of his negation is clear: he rejected any grandiose philosophical effort to justify an external reality which existed in such obvious disorder right before his eyes. It is in this sense that Lermontov is for him "the poet of negation"; that is, the negation of every easy acceptance of the world as it is.

But such negation risks a desperate loss of philosophical refuge. Having failed, even with Hegel's help, to rationalize the world, he cannot now turn to cultivate his own garden in private serenity. He has been too recently disillusioned, too rudely jolted into an awareness of his fellow-men, to take refuge even in the life of the mind: "What is it to me that *I* understand ideas, that to me there is opened a world of ideas in art, in religion, in history, when I cannot share this with all who should be my brothers. . . but who are alien and hostile to me because of their ignorance?" [5]

It is in this context of concern for the enlightenment of the individual that the new slogan is announced: "Sociality, sociality — or death! That is my device. What is it to me that the universal exists when the individual suffers?" [6] Out of this unusual combination of statements an important hint is to be taken. It is clear that "sociality" * here does not connote the superiority of society over the individual, that Belinski is not preaching the subservience of the individual to a social regime. For almost in the same breath he asserts the right of the individual against the universal. And protest against the philosophic universal (*obshchee*) implies, in-

* By its very awkwardness this Anglicized equivalent of Belinski's term *sotsialnost* may serve to suggest the novelty of Belinski's own word, in its turn an awkward Russian equivalent of the French *socialité*.

deed, a protest against society (*obshchestvo*). In effect, "social-ity" as Belinski means it here might be approximately interpreted as a principle of humanitarian concern for the welfare (Belinski would have said the enlightenment) of one's fellow-men. The principles of "negation" and "sociality" are thus joined, since sociality means the negation of the *status quo* in favor of superior human rights. From the individualism of Schiller's "abstract heroism," as Belinski called it, once condemned as noble but in-effectual, he had moved through an acceptance of reality into a new individualism, which recognized actuality while denying its rationality. The individual is now seen as locked within a con-text of objective reality — but locked in struggle.

But the individual whom Belinski thus resurrected had acquired a special significance: he had become the bearer of a rational reality of which the actual world is only an appearance. The individual had become the voice of a universal humanity whose evolution is a progress through all the accidental catastrophes of history. Belinski saw this progress as "the living bond passing like a live nerve through the living organism of the history of hu-manity." [7] Actuality may be far from rational, but this evolving human ideal is rational because it is the moral purpose which moves through the universe. The individual is the bearer of that ideal humanity, and by that fact the individual bears the obligation to assert the rights of humanity against the irrationality of actual existence. Since it is the individual human person who alone is the agent of humanity, he alone is creative. Only by the moral leadership of the creative individual are societies and peoples guided and enlightened. For "where and when did a people ever emancipate itself? Everything has always been ac-complished by the individual person. . . Russia has need of a new Peter the Great. . . " [8] By such diagnosis, what may have once seemed an egocentric morality is vindicated: Fichte and Schiller, whose subjective individualism had once been spurned, become "those prophets of humanity, those heralds of the kingdom of God on earth, those priests of eternal love and eternal truth not in bookish knowledge and Brahmanic contemplation only, but in living and rational *That* [*Ger.*, deed]." [9]

The more vociferously Belinski proclaimed moral man as the

bearer of the progress of humanity, the more radical became his negation of the immoral society against which man is called to protest: "In the words *God* and *religion* I see obscurity, darkness, the chain and the knout; and I now like those first two words equally as well as the last four." [10] The protest becomes at times almost a scream: "The human personality has become a point on which I fear to go out of my mind. I begin to love humanity in the fashion of Marat: in order to make happy the least part of it I believe I could eradicate the rest with fire and sword." [11]

One conspicuous focus of Belinski's concern for individual self-assertion continued to be the problem of the emancipation of women. Partly in reaction against the Stankevich circle mentality whereby women were regarded as creatures of a special purity, Belinski now condemns the romantic idealization of women as the mark of their servitude and argues for their equality with men, ridicules the duplicity of sexual morality, and questions the special sanctity of legal marriage. Such argument is clearly the corollary of a larger doctrine: that the shackles of ignominious custom have held the human person, the supreme apostle of true morality, in crippling bondage.

Yet the rejection of the restraints of custom does not carry with it a rejection of all tradition: "I do not repudiate the past, I do not repudiate history. I see in it a necessary and rational develop-ment of idea. I desire a golden age, yet not some former golden age of unconscious animal existence, but one prepared for by social life, by legislation, by marriage — in a word, by all that was necessary in its day but which is now stupid and sordid." [12] It is not history but actuality which is rejected, for it is through the circumstances of history that the individual works toward the progress of humanity. It is in this sense that "the idea of *socialism* . . . the idea of ideas . . . the alpha and omega of belief and knowledge . . . has absorbed history, religion, and philosophy." [13]

The rejection both of idealistic withdrawal and of philosophi-cal justification of actuality carried with it the rejection of Ger-man speculative abstraction in favor of French *socialité*. The French, formerly disparaged, now become "that energetic, noble people," who, to be sure, "do not understand the Absolute"; whereas "Germany is the nation of the Absolute, yet its govern-

ment is shameful." [14] Following his repudiation of Hegelianism
Belinski was, indeed, not long in moving to a "repugnance" for
the Germans which soon advanced "to the point of morbidity," [15]
as the result of his "unhappy years of tramping about in German
philosophy." [16]

The exchange of German for French models was, to be sure,
more than a symbolic act in a private philosophic drama played
by Belinski. His cultivation of a new respect for the French
coincided with the very years at the opening of the decade of the
forties when French social thought was becoming a dominant
vogue in Russian intellectual life. In these years, Schelling and
Hegel were being replaced by Proudhon, Fourier, Cabet, Louis
Blanc, as the prophets of the young intelligentsia. George Sand as
the literary spokesman of humanitarian socialism was to win a
devoted audience of enthusiastic readers in Russia. French writers
and thinkers like Pierre Leroux who preached a religion of humanity to bourgeois French society found a special appeal among
their Russian hearers, who themselves happened to be busy continuing a native tradition of protest against the injustices and
hypocrisies of their own national life. How stimulating the young
Russian reader found French radical social thought at this time
is suggested, for example, by Saltykov-Shchedrin: "From France
— of course, not from the France of Louis Philippe and Guizot,
but from the France of Saint-Simon, Cabet, Fourier, Louis Blanc,
and especially George Sand — there flowed into us a *belief in
humanity*, from which there shone forth for us a conviction that
the golden age was not behind us but before us." [17] In its young
intelligentsia Russia offered for the publicists of French utopianism an audience which was perhaps even more ready with sympathy and applause than was the intellectual class of bourgeois
France. Perhaps, also, the very fact of distance from France
allowed a cultivation of French theories in Russia in an atmosphere which could not have been created in France: perhaps
Annenkov is correct in concluding that the object of admiration
among the Russian intelligentsia of the forties was not contemporary France but an ideal France of the past Age of Enlightenment
and of the future.[18]

No Russian reader of French socialist works was likely to have

felt or expressed more enthusiasm than Belinski. By the end of
1842, George Sand had become for him "decidedly the Joan of
Arc of our times, the star of salvation and the prophetess of a
great future." [19] Her story, "Melchior," published at the end of
1842 in the *National Notes*, was for him "a divine creation,"
which "shook me like a revelation, like a stroke of lightning," by
her power to portray "love. . . [which is] not exalted or unbounded in feeling and hollow in content, the romantic love of
the German. . . ; her love is the reality and fullness of all love." [20]
Presumably for other reasons, *Le Compagnon du Tour de France*
likewise appealed to Belinski as "a divine creation." [21]

Belinski had at the same time become an avid reader of French
writings on the Revolution and on utopian social theory. Works
such as Thiers' *Histoire de la Révolution* and Cabet's *Le Peuple*
became favorites: "I am reading Thiers. . . A new world has
opened before me. I always thought that I understood the Revolution. Nonsense; I am only beginning to understand it. A greater
thing will never be done. The French are a great people." [22] During the winter of 1841 he met regularly with Panaev on Saturdays
to talk over the latter's readings in French history — while he
regretted that an earlier acquaintance with this world of social
thought had not saved him from his disgraceful past. Upon his
reunion with Belinski in 1843, Annenkov was greeted almost from
the first word by an outburst of praise for Louis Blanc's *Histoire
de dix ans*.[23]

Belinski's turn from German to French teachers was, however,
more an amalgamation than a new departure. He had not simply
dropped an old philosophic garment and donned a new one.
Above all, he had not unburdened himself of Hegel by a simple
sharp order of dismissal. His formal rejection of Hegel only succeeded, in fact, in making him into a better Hegelian than he had
ever been. In his vociferous defense of the concrete individual as
the sole effective bearer of the universal in history, he supposed
that he was repudiating Hegel; in reality, he had only just
achieved a valid comprehension of Hegel. By his negation of the
world of actuality in favor of a rational reality which exists behind
the world of appearance and which unfolds itself through the
history of humanity, he had finally come to grasp the major theme

of the Hegelian philosophy of history. By combining an original Schilleresque idealism with a subsequent realization of social and historical actuality, Belinski arrived at a position which Hegel might have been the first to certify: a dynamic conception of the concrete individual as the incarnation of the universal.

Even Belinski's "socialism" can be taken as a formulation of an essentially Hegelian position. Just as Hegel's conception of universality (*Allgemeinheit*) was grounded on the premise that the concrete individual has his existence only by reason of his relationship with other individuals, so Belinski's theory of socialism was grounded upon the notion that the individual's moral existence requires a humanitarian assertion of the universal human rights of all his fellows. Belinski fashioned a moral principle out of a conception which Hegel had originally formulated as an axiom of his epistemology.

That Hegelian thought could itself be given a radical as well as a conservative interpretation is clear from German intellectual history. In particular, the German Hegelians of the Left showed how Hegelianism could be employed to attack conservatism in the name of philosophical rationalism and political liberalism. Their journal, the *Hallesche Jahrbücher*, established in 1837 by E. T. Echtermeyer and Arnold Ruge, was known to Belinski. On at least one occasion, in the early part of 1841, his friend Botkin sent him an excerpt from the *Jahrbücher*, which, Belinski wrote, "I enjoyed very much and which even, as it were, resuscitated and fortified me for a moment. . . " [24]

German avant-garde theological thought, especially with Strauss and Feuerbach, similarly moved within a Hegelian context toward a conception of man as the object of his own worship. Ludwig Feuerbach's considerable vogue in Russia stemmed particularly from the effectiveness with which he used a Hegelian insight as the basis of a radical theological doctrine: if God is man's discovery of himself, then the real object of man's worship is man himself. Feuerbach's position was radical both in the sense that it implied the destruction of God, and also in the sense that it joined the main current of radical and socialist thought by offering a theological foundation for the religion of humanity.

In short, the radical wing of the Hegelian school offers abundant historical evidence that Hegelianism can by no means be simply equated with conservatism. As Belinski moved into his own phase of radicalism in the forties, he began by repudiating Hegel, whom he had interpreted as the teacher of an extreme conservatism. But Belinski's repudiation of Hegel, for all its vehemence, is superficial; he never really cast off his Hegelian convictions.

The major lessons which Belinski learned from his experience in Hegelianism became, indeed, the foundation of his final position: that the "idea" evolves within a context of historical reality in time and place and is not floating abroad in the cloudland of the Schellingesque Absolute; and that the individual has his significance from his particularization of the idea of humanity. A pseudo-Hegelian reconciliation with reality was thus abandoned by Belinski in favor of a more truly Hegelian doctrine of struggle with actuality.

Finally, there is another way in which Belinski's thought in the forties would have pleased Hegel. By then the history of his mind had become a living illustration of the Hegelian dialectic. For it requires no effort to see his thought in the forties as a synthesis of two preceding stages: his early subjective idealism, and its antithesis in "reconciliation with reality." In this sense also he had become Hegel's man — and he had done so in the very process of disowning Hegel.

Belinski's conception of the role of the literary artist in society constituted an obvious corollary of his final ideological position. The artist becomes the voice of the human protest which every individual is obliged to raise against the imperfect state of things as they are. The truly national poet is the poet who brings the enlightenment of a universal humanity to the particular people or nation among whom he lives. True national character in art becomes thereby the national expression of a humanity which is universal and which progresses "through the living organism of the history of humanity." [25] Such a conception of the national in art stands at the opposite pole from reproduction of superficial features of the national life. True art is not a work of aimless representation but a conscious enlightenment. The artist thus becomes a co-worker with Peter the Great, whose greatness as a Russian consisted precisely in his attack upon Russian national traditions in the name of a larger human ideal. "For me," Belinski once declared, "Peter is my philosophy, my religion, my revelation in all that concerns Russia." [26] The artist, like the reformer, becomes truly national to the measure of his power to raise his own national community to a fresh realization of its participation in the life of humanity. Just as every people must struggle to achieve its true nationality, so the work of art is the expression of a moral self-assertion against the restraints of particular time and place.

Seen in the context of his total ideological position, Belinski's philosophy of art is clearly tied to propositions of such generality that it is hardly likely to lend itself to simple formulation. In this circumstance lies perhaps the main reason why throughout the forties Belinski seems to speak of literature and the literary artist in such a wide variety of ways, sometimes even contradictory. The function that Belinski assigns to the artist is so large that at times he seems to expect the artist to be all things to all men, a glorified factotum, expert in all the devices for advancing the cause of human enlightenment. If at one place he seems to be arguing that the writer should be an advocate and a propagandist, at another place he insists that only by remaining an objective artist can the writer truly perform his function of enlightenment. In effect, Belinski deliberately weakened the distinction between artist and advocate because he had come to the conviction that art is itself an advocacy. Art is a weapon in the same way that truth itself is a weapon. The artist is an exponent of Reason; he is thus teacher and poet at the same time.

This compound definition of the literary artist and his function led Belinski to make statements on this subject throughout the forties which often seem to contradict each other; it also led Belinski's followers and later critics to find in him almost whatever it was they sought. This fundamental ambiguity in his final position has no doubt helped to perpetuate Belinski's name in the history of criticism, since he has, so to speak, a word for everybody. Thus even Soviet critics, working by a literary policy which Belinski would have found intolerable, can still claim him for their own and still manage to find something in his writings to support their case.

At least this much is clear: all the ambiguities in Belinski's final critical doctrine have their origin in his conception of literature as playing a part in the general progress of humanity, in his conception of the artist as a warrior against whatever impedes the historical march of Reason. As Belinski himself was well aware, such a doctrine requires a precarious balance to be maintained between the urgent protest which he was concerned with making and the human truth in whose name the protest was to be made. The artist could be the spokesman of humanity only by being a faithful witness to human truth. Such an ideological requirement could never be met unless the integrity of the artist was maintained; yet at the same time it imposed upon the artist a militant conception of himself.

For such a philosophy of struggle, Belinski's own personal life during the forties provided an appropriate background. The familiar personal hardships remained largely what they had always been — problems of personal health, of finances, of professional work; but they continued to increase in gravity. The external frustrations of a censorship which prevented him from dealing freely in print with the subjects which concerned him most, were matched by the inner frustrations of a mind which moved from one mood and conviction to another without finding rest anywhere. Thus by November 7, 1842, after the momentous changes of the early forties had taken place, Belinski was able to write to Bakunin's younger brother, Nicholas:

A while ago a great change occurred in me. I had already broken with romanticism, mysticism, and all other isms; but that was only negation, and nothing new had replaced the old which was destroyed. And I cannot live without beliefs, warm and fanatical, as a fish cannot live without water or a tree grow without rain. That is the reason why during the past year you saw me in so uncertain a state. . . Now I am again different. It is curious: Michael and I sought God by different roads and met in the same temple. I know . . . that he belongs to the left wing of Hegelianism . . . and sees through that pitiful, half-dead romanticism of Schelling. . . Moreover the road on which he has now set out is sure to bring him to all sorts of renewal. . .

Life has become easier for me. . . If I suffer, my suffering has become nobler and more elevated, for its causes are outside and not within me. In my soul I have that without which I cannot live: I have faith, which gives me the answer to all questions. Yet it is not really faith and not really knowledge, but *religious knowledge* and *conscious religion.*

Yet after two months he wrote to Botkin, in a letter dated December 9, 1842: "Life becomes harder and harder to bear. . . The walls of my quarters are hateful to me. I return to them with despair and repugnance in my soul, like a prisoner returning to jail."

This personal battle which Belinski continued to wage, while he lived, against the situation in which he was required to work found its theoretical expression in the critical doctrine that he continued to elaborate. While his private life was being occupied by an increasingly bitter struggle with the unhappiness of daily life, he became more and more vociferous in crying that art should communicate the protest of the individual against an imperfect world.

"The Division of Poetry into Genus and Species" and "The Idea of Art" (1841)

That the new theme of aggressive individualism had its roots in a philosophic context already established is strikingly demonstrated by Belinski's first essay following the rejection of Hegel: namely, "The Division of Poetry into Genus and Species" ("Razdelenie poezii na rody i vidy"), published in the *National Notes* early in 1841, just after the article on Lermontov's poetry. Here Belinski began the elaboration of an "anti-Hegelian" protest by the medium of a discussion inspired directly by Hegel. Belinski's essay is, in effect, a restatement of Hegel's chapter, "Die Gattungsunterschiede der Poesie," under which heading Hegel had divided poetry into epic, lyric, and dramatic.[27] In a letter of March 1, 1841, to Botkin, Belinski admitted that he had inserted whole portions from the notebooks of Katkov, who had been Belinski's teacher in Hegelian aesthetics, and that he had copied word for word from the section on lyrical poetry.

As with Hegel, so with Belinski — epic poetry represents a unity of inner and outer reality within an event; lyric poetry, the expression of the idea which precedes the event; and dramatic poetry, the synthesis of the two, by which objective event is used to portray subjective idea. In epic poetry, event is central; in dramatic poetry, man is central. In epic poetry, man is controlled by fate; in dramatic poetry, man controls the event. Already by this preliminary and abstract analysis, it is man, in his relation both to his society and, even more important, to the total human situation, who emerges as the hero of modern art.

Another essay of a similarly abstract nature written at this time is "The Idea of Art" ("Ideia iskusstva"). Composed during the first half of 1841 as part of a projected course on Russian literature which Belinski never completed, this essay remained unpublished during his lifetime. The purpose for which he originally intended to use his article no doubt worked to exclude from it ideas that he was likely to consider novel or still unsettled in his mind. Perhaps it is partly for this reason that the ideas put forth in the article seem to lag far behind his latest thought. In this crucial year of 1841 Belinski's reader might have expected major revisions and redefinitions. Perhaps the inadequacy of the essay to reflect Belinski's current movements of thought kept him from using it for journal copy — a commodity that was never in excess supply with him.

The major thesis of "The Idea of Art" is that "art is the *immediate* contemplation of truth, or thought in *images*." The first striking feature of this definition, Belinski comments, is that art is a form of thought. It is true that art has traditionally been set over against philosophy, as for example by Plato. And common opinion ascribes to poets a passionate and flighty nature and "a restless fancy, which is always carrying them from the actual to the ideal and which in their eyes removes any value from actual everyday happiness, to which they prefer some beautiful and unrealizable dream." To philosophers, on the other hand, common opinion ascribes a serious pursuit of wisdom and an inflexible will. Although the poet is considered a lovable child, the philosopher is held to be a stern servant of eternal truth. The difference between the two is thus taken to be almost the difference between fire and water or heat and cold; although it is true that both are felt to be engaged in similarly striving toward a higher form of life. As a matter of fact, Belinski continues, there is some validity in these popular notions. For although in different manners and in a different spirit, both the artist and the philosopher pursue a common end and work in a common stuff, which is idea.

"All that exists, all that is, all that we call matter and spirit, nature, life, humanity, history, the world, the universe — all is *thought* thinking itself. All existence, all the infinite variety of the facts and phenomena of the world's life, is nothing other than the facts and forms of thought. Hence thought alone exists; and outside of thought, nothing exists.

" . . . Thought consists in dialectical movement, or the development of idea out of itself. Movement or development is the life and essence of thought. . .

"The point of departure, the starting point of thought, is divine, absolute idea. The movement of thought consists in the development of this idea out of itself, according to the laws of ultimate (transcendental) logic or metaphysics. . . " This development is an immanent development, like the unfolding of an oak from an acorn.

Although spirit is the source of all existence, it requires the material world for its manifestation. But the material world itself develops by a gradual evolution, in which "the law of all development is that every subsequent stage is higher than the preceding. . . Everything has its place and time, and every subsequent phenomenon is, as it were, the necessary result of the preceding." Thus "every important event among humanity is perfected in *its time* and not before or after. Every great man perfects the work of his time, resolves the questions which are contemporary to him, and reveals by his activity the spirit of the time in which he was born and bred." In this way everything takes part in a universal evolution, "a single ladder from earth to heaven. . . Both in nature and in history there predominates not blind accident but strict and immutable inner necessity, through which all phenomena are bound together by inherent ties, by which harmonious order appears in the midst of disorder, and unity appears in variety, and by reason of which science is possible." This inner necessity is thought thinking itself. Man as a thinking being is the highest form of creation, and the whole of human life is idea in some form. Thus religion is "the immediate representation of truth," art, as the second form of thought, is "the immediate contemplation of truth," while the third and highest form is pure thought. Thus all phenomena are particularizations of the universal, and "the universal is idea." Thus "the whole ladder of creation is nothing but the particularization of the universal. . ."

Belinski seems to have forgotten for the moment that he ever quarreled with Hegel, who might well have written "The Idea of Art" himself — who in effect *did* write it. Was Belinski's hand going through familiar motions in the writing of this essay, while his mind groped toward new positions? Or did his aesthetic doctrine lag behind in a tardy continuance with Hegel, who had already been dismissed as chief on the ideological front? Or was he apathetically recopying old notes? In the absence of any sure answer to such questions, one can only conclude that at least this essay shows, as does the preceding "Division of Poetry," a continuing occupation with Hegelian formulae, in the midst of which Belinski's new emphasis upon man as individual and particular is gradually asserted.

"The Pedant" (1842)

That Belinski was ready to move from the relatively passive and uncontroversial writing of these abstract articles even to direct personal attack was abruptly demonstrated at the beginning of 1842 by an article called "The Pedant: A Literary Type" ("Pedant: literaturny tip"). Because of its personal reference, this sketch of only several pages made a considerable public impression. Its historical importance lies rather in the significant quarrel it heralded, a quarrel which soon broadened out into the momentous controversy between Westerners and Slavophiles which split the intelligentsia into major factions, divided upon an issue which Russian intellectual life has not yet resolved.

Stepan Petrovich Shevyrev, a professor of literature at the University of Moscow, had joined with his colleague, the historian Pogodin, to bring out a journal in 1840 called *The Muscovite* (*Moskvitianin*). It soon appeared that here was the organ of a whole school of thought about Russian culture, soon to become famous as the Slavophiles. In a word, the latter held that Russia should follow the direction indicated by native cultural traditions

rather than look to Europe for cultural guidance, as the Westerners advocated. During the forties especially, Belinski stands as
one of the leaders of the Westerners; so that his present quarrel
with Shevyrev, although at the moment mainly personal in nature,
constitutes a preliminary skirmish in a long war.

On several occasions during 1841, Shevyrev used the pages of
his new journal (which Belinski had been one of the first to
welcome) to attack Belinski — as a "nameless critic" (since his
columns in the *National Notes* appeared unsigned) who, "half
tipsy from German aesthetics, which he himself, by reason of his
ignorance of the German language, has never read but has only
heard about, and then in a distorted form, at third hand . . . has
the audacity, while lounging despondently in his critic's chair
and brandishing his speedy pen, to hold forth publicly on poetry
and morality." Except for a passing retort, Belinski managed for
the moment to swallow his indignation.

During a visit at the end of 1841 and the beginning of 1842
to Moscow, where he stayed with his friend Botkin, Belinski was
greeted with a further attack from Shevyrev, which appeared in
The Muscovite for January of 1842. In the course of an article
entitled "A View of the Current Trend of Russian Literature,"
Shevyrev referred to the "nameless knight" who carried on his
shield for device the word Conviction written in crooked letters,
and whom "one could still respect if this conviction were something constant and dependable. But when you see how often it
changes and how it sometimes attaches to completely unworthy
objects, that the knight says one thing today and tomorrow something else and fends off all contradictions by this one and the
same shield, then you finally turn away in disgust from such pre-
tence."

Belinski's rejoinder is one of his first pieces for the year 1842.
He tried hard to be witty and subtle, but his parody of Shevyrev
is clearly too heavy to rise above mere personal invective. Belinski ironically offers his sketch of "The Pedant" as a contribution
to a collection, popular at the time, of pictures showing the various trades and professions in Russia. His model for the pedant is,
of course, Shevyrev. The latter is not presented by name, to be
sure, but Belinski's public, especially in Moscow, could identify

"Liudor Ippolitovich Kartoffelin," and Shevyrev was reported to have stayed close to home for a while after the appearance of Belinski's satire.

This document of a private feud long since forgotten serves at least to mark the degree to which factional disputes quickly became personal, and also to show Belinski's growing readiness to move to the attack against hostile contemporaries as well as uncongenial ideas. At the end of March he wrote to Botkin: "Thanks for your news on the effect of 'The Pedant,' by reason of which I can breathe more easily for a while. I've come to the certain and strong feeling that I was born for literary controversy, and that my vocation, life, happiness, atmosphere, nourishment is *polemics*."

Gogol's Dead Souls *(1842)*

The interlude which followed the long 1841 essay on Lermontov's poetry, and which was largely filled by fruitless wrestling with both Hegelian abstractions and personal antagonists, was happily broken by the critical study of Gogol's *Dead Souls*, to which Belinski devoted several articles during 1842.

Throughout his life Belinski talked and wrote of a plan to analyze at length the whole work of Gogol. One can only guess at the reasons why the plan was never fulfilled. But it is clear from his various writings on the subject of Gogol, including the famous 1847 letter to Gogol, that his critical opinions of the novelist were in continual evolution. Beneath this reason may lie a deeper reason: for all his critical perception of Gogol's worth, especially notable in the essay of 1835 when Gogol's career had only begun, Belinski's basic orientations, not only literary but also intellectual and moral and spiritual, were of a quite different character from Gogol's. It is, in fact, a strange accident of literary history that Belinski should be known as Gogol's critic. Not only did a wide chasm separate their literary personalities, but the chasm widened swiftly as the years passed. Of course this very circumstance adds credit to Belinski for his ability to give critical recognition to an author who remained perhaps even more alien to him than he knew.

The origin for Belinski's present essay on Gogol was the appearance of the first part of *Dead Souls*. During his visit to Moscow at the beginning of 1842 he met Gogol, and the latter there gave him the manuscript of this first volume for presentation to the government censors in St. Petersburg. In a letter to Gogol dated April 20, 1842, Belinski wrote from St. Petersburg: "I await impatiently the appearance of your *Dead Souls*. . . When *Dead Souls* comes out I intend to write several articles on your works in general. . . On the whole I have a certain anxiety about how I should write about your works. I am impetuous and capable of getting caught in wild absurdities. But thank heaven I have at the same time a capacity for moving forward and for calling my own blunders and stupidities by their proper name, with just as much candor as I do the sins of others. For this reason I feel that I have changed a great deal since I last babbled on the subject of your stories and about *The Inspector*."

Some of the ways in which Belinski had changed appear in the course of his essay on *Dead Souls*. Of one point on which he had not changed he is proud to remind his readers at the outset: there has been no change in his high estimate of Gogol. "Of all the journals now in existence," he triumphantly states, "the *National Notes* was the *first* and *only* one to say — and to continue to say, from the day of his first appearance up to this moment — what place Gogol occupies in Russian literature. Various would-be critics, compilers, and literary hacks have pointed to our opinion of Gogol as proof of the utter stupidity of our journal. . . [Whereas] Gogol is an artist of great talent, a poet of genius, and the *foremost* writer in present-day Russia. . .

. . . No doubt Gogol will soon be praised by those very people who scorned us for praising him and who now, given the lie by the unprecedented success of *Dead Souls*, are like drowning men clutching at straws. . .

Meanwhile we still feel sure that everybody knows *who* was the first person in Russia to evaluate Gogol. . . Now everybody has become wise, even people who were born stupid, and they will all be able to make the egg stand on the table. After the appearance of *Dead Souls* there will be many literary Columbuses who will find it easy to discover a great new talent in Russian literature, a great new Russian writer: Gogol.

But it was not so easy to discover him when he was still really

new. To be sure, from his first appearance Gogol found ardent cham-
pions of his talent; but their number was too small. On the whole no
Russian poet has had so strange a fate as Gogol: even people who knew
his works by heart did not come forth to call him a great writer. No
one was indifferent to his talent; people either loved him madly or
hated him. And there is a profound reason for this, and one which
shows the vitality rather than the morbidity of our society. Gogol was
the first to look boldly and directly upon Russian reality; and if to
this is added his profound humor, his unlimited irony, it becomes clear
why for a long time he was not understood and why it was easier to
love him than to understand him. . . We shall soon have occasion to
speak in detail about Gogol's entire poetic work as a whole and to
examine all his works in their gradual evolution. But now we shall
limit ourselves to a general expression of our opinion of the worth
of *Dead Souls* — that great creation.

Our literature, in consequence of its artificial beginning and un-
natural development, has been condemned to become a spectacle of
fragmentary and most contradictory phenomena. We have already
said more than once that we do not believe there exists a Russian literature in the sense of a written expression of a historically evolving
national consciousness. But we see here a wonderful beginning of a
great future, a series of disconnected flashes, which are as brilliant as
lightning and as broad and sweeping as the Russian soul, but still only
flashes. All the rest which constitutes our day-to-day literary activity
has little or no relation to these flashes except perhaps the relation of
shade to light and dark to shine. Gogol began his career while Pushkin
was still alive, and when the latter died he fell silent, it seemed for
good. After *The Inspector* he published nothing until the middle of
the present year. During this interval of his silence, which so saddened
the friends of Russian literature and so gladdened the literary hacks,
there dawned and then died out on the horizon of Russian poetry the
bright star of the talent of Lermontov. After *A Hero of Our Time*
there appeared in the journals (the reader knows which ones) . . . a
few more or less noteworthy stories, but . . . nothing which constitutes a permanent literary achievement. . . And suddenly, in the
midst of this triumph of mediocrity . . . there appears a purely Russian, a national creation, drawn from the secret places of the life of
the people . . . a creation incomparably artistic in conception and
execution, in the personalities of its characters and in the details of
Russian life — and at the same time profound in its meaning. . . In
Dead Souls the author has taken such a huge step that everything
which he has written up to now seems weak and pale in comparison.
We consider the author's greatest success and greatest step forward
to be that everywhere in *Dead Souls* one feels and, as it were, touches
his subjectivity. Here we do not mean that subjectivity which by its
narrowness or limitation disfigures the objective reality of what the

author portrays; but that profound, vast, and human subjectivity which reveals in the artist a man with an ardent heart, a sympathetic soul, and an independent spiritual personality — that subjectivity which does not allow him to remain in apathetic indifference aloof from the world which he depicts, but forces him to experience in his *living soul* the manifestations of the external world, and thereby to breathe a *living soul* into them. . . This pathos * of subjectivity in the poet appears not only in . . . highly lyrical digressions; it appears continually, even in the midst of recounting the most prosaic subjects. . .

An equally important step forward in Gogol's talent is seen by us in the fact that in *Dead Souls* he has completely abandoned the Ukrainian element and has become a national Russian poet to the full extent of that word. At every word of his poem the reader can say:

Here is the Russian spirit, this smells Russian!

This Russian spirit is felt in the humor, in the irony, in the author's expressions, in the broad sweep of emotion, in the lyricism of the digressions, in the pathos of the whole poem, and in the personalities of the characters, from Chichikov to Selifan . . . in the policeman who, by the light of the lantern, half asleep, kills a bug between his fingernails and then goes back to sleep. We know that the prudery of many readers will be offended at seeing in print what is so close to them in their personal lives and will call obscene such tricks as the bug crushed on a fingernail; but that means they do not understand the poem, which is based on the pathos of reality as it exists. . .

Dead Souls will be read by everybody but will no doubt not please everybody. Among the many reasons why, is the fact that *Dead Souls* does not fit the popular conception of a novel as a story in which the main characters fall in love, separate, and then get married and live rich and happy. . . Moreover . . . *Dead Souls* demands study. In this regard it should again be repeated that humor is understandable only to a person of some depth and maturity. The popular mind doesn't understand or like it. . . The majority of our people understand "humor" and "the comic" as buffoonery, as caricature, and we are convinced that many will seriously . . . say and write that Gogol was joking when he called his novel a poem. . .

. . . It was not in fun that Gogol called his novel a "poem," [nor]

---

* The special sense in which Belinski used this favorite word is defined, in the course of Article Five on the works of Pushkin, as the condition in which "the poet appears in love with an idea as with a beautiful living creature . . . and he contemplates it not with his understanding, not with his intellect, not with feeling, but with the fullness of his moral being."

The word was apparently borrowed from Hegel, who introduced it in his *Aesthetics* as a term to signify the moral passion which motivates human action and "bildet . . . die ächte Domaine der Kunst" (*Sämtliche Werke*; Stuttgart, 1927; XII, 313-314).

did he mean by that a comic poem. Not the author but his book has told us so. We find nothing farcical or funny in it; by no word of the author's have we noted any intention to amuse the reader: everything here is serious, quiet, true, and profound. . . There can be no greater error or grosser misunderstanding than to look upon *Dead Souls* as a satire. [Despite Gogol's powerful lyrical passage on the troika of Russia, some] will see in *Dead Souls* a spiteful satire, resulting from coldness and indifference to what is native, to what is national. . . As for us, we on the contrary would accuse the author of too much emotion uncontrolled by calm and reasonable reflection . . . rather than of a lack of love and warmth for the native and the national. We speak of several places — fortunately few and unfortunately glaring — in which the author makes hasty judgments of the nationality of foreign races and without much reserve gives himself over to dreams about the superiority of the Slavic race over others. We think that it is better to leave to each his own and, while realizing one's own worth, to be capable of respecting the worth of others also.

Even in such brief indications it is possible to find evidence of the change in Belinski's thought which followed his repudiation of reality as rational. Above all, he now sees Gogol as a realistic painter of "reality as it exists." His mood in treating *Dead Souls* is almost grim: "by no word of the author's have we noted any intention to amuse the reader: everything here is serious, quiet, true, and profound." Nor is *Dead Souls* a satire. Gogol has painted the Russian world as it really is, and only prudery will find even the most vulgar touches in his work obscene. It is clear that such an assessment of *Dead Souls* fits with the present stage of Belinski's thought. Having abandoned the effort to rationalize reality, he now sees the Russian world in all its vulgarity and formlessness; and Gogol has simply depicted it as it is. Gogol's voice is the voice of the artist, in his "pathos of subjectivity," raised against the moral disorder of an actuality which he portrays through his power to feel the "pathos of reality."

This is quite different from what Belinski in 1840 had said of Gogol as the author of *The Inspector*. The contrast is especially striking since *Dead Souls* is fundamentally an extension into novel form of the theme of *The Inspector*. But for Belinski in 1840, the world of *The Inspector* was a world of shadows, and the play was for him a true comedy because it depicts conflict within the sphere of the illusory, "the continual conflict of the world of

appearance with the laws of rational reality." Although Belinski
had found comedy in the world of Khlestakov, he now finds nothing comic — and, indeed, not even satirical — in the very similar
world of Chichikov. In the meantime, it is clear, Belinski had lost
his sense of humor about Russian reality.

Thus Gogol, while remaining "the *foremost* writer in present-
day Russia," is now changed for Belinski in the character of his
appeal. Formerly the master of the world of illusion, the shadow
world of nonreality, where people like the Old-World Landowners merely eat and drink and then die, Gogol has now become
the master of the world of reality, which he depicts not with
humor but with a "pathos of subjectivity which does not allow
him to remain . . . aloof." Meanwhile it is not Gogol's world
which has changed; what has changed is Belinski's conception of
that world.

So firmly, indeed, did Belinski hold to his present view of
Gogol as the poet of contemporary Russian reality that when
Constantine Aksakov came forth to praise *Dead Souls* as a modern
epic, Belinski followed quickly with an emphatic rebuttal entitled
"A Few Words about Gogol's Poem: *The Adventures of Chichikov, or Dead Souls*." Perhaps the vehemence of Belinski's reply
was due largely to the personal drama taking place off-stage: the
final break with Aksakov, his former Moscow friend. But the
nature of Belinski's objection belongs to the character of his
thought at this time.

Prompted thus partly by personal hostility, Belinski declared
that for anyone to see in Gogol " 'the authentic ancient epic view,
the same as in Homer,' " as Aksakov had written, "shows that
he has completely misunderstood the pathos of *Dead Souls*," a
"poem" which is "diametrically opposed to the *Iliad*. In the *Iliad*,
life is exalted into apotheosis; in *Dead Souls* it is dissected and
negated. The pathos of the *Iliad* is a blissful rapture inspired by
the contemplation of a divine spectacle; the pathos of *Dead
Souls* is a humorous contemplation of life 'through laughter which
the world can see and tears which it neither sees nor knows.' "

Belinski disliked Aksakov's interpretation thus mainly because
it suggested a view of life quite alien to what Belinski preferred
to see in Gogol. Gogol had become for Belinski a passionate critic

of the contemporary Russian scene; in universalizing the appeal of *Dead Souls* by calling it an epic, Aksakov seemed to Belinski to be detracting from its contemporary significance. As a matter of fact, Belinski insisted, "only for Russia and in Russia can it have infinitely great significance. . . The higher the worth of Gogol as a poet, the more important is his meaning for Russian society and the less able is he to have any significance outside of Russia."

"Speech on Criticism" (1842)

That Belinski's insistence upon seeing Gogol as a critic of the Russian scene had its real roots in Belinski's current ideological position, is corroborated by an essay in the form of three articles which appeared soon after the discussion of *Dead Souls*. The point of departure of the essay was a speech on the subject of criticism delivered on March 25, 1842, as a special lecture at the University of St. Petersburg, by one Professor Nikitenko. In his elaboration of his own critical ideas Belinski, characteristically, soon left the professor and his speech far behind.

Belinski's thesis here is that both art and criticism, in so far as they remain valid expressions of the contemporary mind, are engaged in the analysis of contemporary reality. For "the spirit of analysis and investigation is the spirit of our time." Criticism itself is subject to criticism, since nothing is taken on authority. For the time is past when "abstract idealism constituted the happiness of the life [of humanity]. The world has grown up: it requires not the colored kaleidoscope of imagination but the microscope and telescope of reason. . . Reality — that is the motto and the last word of the contemporary world! Reality in facts, in knowledge, in the convictions of feeling and the conclusions of intellect — in all and everywhere reality is the first and last word of our age. . .

"To criticize is to search for and to find in the particular phenomenon the general laws of reason, and to define the degree of vital, organic correspondence between the particular phenomenon and its ideal. . . Thus criticism is not limited to art alone." Luther, for example, was a critic of the papacy; Voltaire was a critic of feudal Europe.

Indeed, the difference between criticism and art is mainly a difference of form, for both are concerned with expressing the same "consciousness of reality." The art of the present is itself a species of criticism, and "for our time an artistic work is dead if it portrays life only in order to portray life, without any strong subjective motivation which has its origin in the dominant thought of the age; if it is not a wail of pain or a dithyramb of exultation; if it is not a question or the answer to a question." Since criticism in Russia is still only the criticism of art and literature, "it is no exaggeration to say that only in art and literature, and consequently in aesthetic and literary criticism, does the intellectual consciousness of our society find expression."

Hence to limit art to an expression of the beautiful is to misjudge the art of the present. Art must have moral and intellectual content. "Our age . . . decisively rejects art for art's sake, beauty for the sake of beauty." The representative artists of the contemporary world, the Scotts, Byrons, Schillers, and Goethes, are "philosophers and critics in poetic form." Even the greatest artist will lose his appeal if he creates a world of his own out of touch with the "historical and philosophical reality of the age." The history of French literature shows that Hugo, Balzac, Dumas, Sue, Vigny — those artists who wrote for the sake of writing, as birds sing — have already been forgotten in favor of George Sand, who by the power of her convictions has become "the foremost poetic glory of the contemporary world." Her appeal endures. All such talents are moral, "demanding sympathy for humanity, love for truth." As for the others, "they are happy if they can sing; they are superior to humanity, superior to their struggling brothers, who vainly turn toward them eyes full of supplication and hope, while they live for themselves and find joy and consolation in their own souls. And they call this poeticized egotism life in the Absolute and the Eternal, removed from the vulgar affairs of the contemporary world," whereas "art is subject, as is everything living and absolute, to a process of historical development, and . . . the art of our time is an expression, a realization in artistic form, of the contemporary conscience, of contemporary thought concerning the end and the meaning of life, the ways of humanity, the eternal truths of existence."

How can the poet freely follow his inspiration and at the same time serve his society? Because by his upbringing in his society he has become a part of it. Then how can he fail to express his age and society? Only by being trained in outmoded traditions, a training which has often led even the noblest persons to seek isolation from their society, to take refuge within themselves, and to look out upon the world in despair. Such persons even have been known to succeed in finding philosophical support, particularly in the German philosophy of art, "in which there is really a great deal of profundity, truth, and illumination, but in which there is also a great deal that is . . . philistine, ascetic, and antisocial."

Whereas "freedom of creation agrees easily with service to contemporary society: it is not necessary to force oneself to write to order, to suppress the fancy; all that is required is to be a citizen, a son of one's society and era . . . ; all that is needed . . . is a wholesome practical feeling for the truth which does not separate . . . creative works from life."

How far Belinski has come from his declaration of just a few short years ago when he argued in the 1840 essay on Menzel, "Let [art and society] each go its own way without hindering the other." Now his major insistence is that the artist must prepare himself to become the enlightener of his society by being first its full-fledged member. In his present view, art reaches its maturity only when it succeeds in becoming the expression of a particular age, and the artist likewise fulfills his function only by being a citizen of his society. The progress of Russian literary history, indeed, is its movement in this direction.

Such is the theme of "A Historical View of Russian Criticism," presented as a second article in the discussion of the "Speech on Criticism." Here Belinski reviews some opinions which he had expressed more than once before, and he now proceeds to marshal them in support of his present argument. He repeats, for example, the contention that Russian literature arose not from a need in Russian society but out of a spirit of blind imitation of foreign literatures. To this familiar point he now adds a new comment: "But at the same time our literature has had upon society a great and beneficial influence as the vital source of humanistic and humane education."

Russian literature began in the same way as Russian civilization — "by imitation, by a blind adoption of forms. As with civilization, its movement and development consisted in a strain toward independence and nationality, and its every success was a step toward that goal. Russian poetry first shone forth in the fables of Krylov, the form of which was borrowed and imitative, but in which the Russian language and the practical Russian mind nonetheless found a means for their unfolding which was broad, free, and unforced. But the fable is only one variety of poetry, created, moreover, by the eighteenth century. . . Russian poetry began properly with Pushkin. In asserting this we do not at all intend to disparage the poets of brilliant gifts who preceded our poetic Proteus. Without them he would not have existed, or at least he would have been far different from what he was. Each of these gifted poets was a step forward for our literature; and the incompleteness of their success was determined not by any deficiency in their ability but by the immaturity of a society unable to provide content for an independent poetry. Pushkin was the first Russian poet, if by poet is meant artist. The native poetic power of Derzhavin was superior to the poetic power, for example, of Batiushkov; but *as an artist* Batiushkov is incomparably superior to Derzhavin. Derzhavin, that *bogatyr* of Russian poetry, was bound by the spirit of his time, which understood poetry only as a *triumphal ode* for all occasions — for a military victory or simply for a festival — and which was convinced that poetry is 'sweet and pleasant like tasty lemonade in the summertime.'" As Derzhavin, although limited by his time, brought his contribution to Russian poetry, so did his successors. Thus Zhukovski introduced dreamy melancholy and fantasy from German and English romantic poetry; while Batiushkov brought something of the artistry of the classical world.

It was on the shoulders of these predecessors that Pushkin arose to become the first distinctively *Russian* poet, by combining the gifts of others with an originality which none of the others possessed.

That is why we begin Russian poetry with him and call him the first Russian poet. That does not at all mean that there were no poets before him, or even none worthy of attention, respect, love, reputation, and praise; it means only that they expressed the gradual efforts of Russian poetry, beginning with Kantemir and Lomonosov, to turn from being artificial and imitative and to become national and independent, from being bookish to being alive, social, in touch with life and society; whereas Pushkin expressed the victory and triumph of these efforts and exertions. Pushkin is an artist in the full meaning of the word; that is his predominant significance, his highest worth, and perhaps his inadequacy, in that the more he became an artist, the more he moved away from contemporary life and its interests and took an ascetic direction, at the end causing his society to cool towards him, whereas until then it had unconditionally idolized him. It seems that in his nature there was not a drop of prosaic blood but all was a pure fire of poetry. He turned all that he touched, even the most prosaic objects, into poetic images full of life and magic. His verse is sculpture, painting, and music, all in one. To him could be applied without reservation his own verses on Ovid:

> He had the magic gift of song,
> A voice like sounds of flowing water.

No one has been so bound historically with the traditions of Russian literature as was Pushkin. He studied ancient authors whom no one reads today. . . Art as art, poetry as poetry, in Russia, is the work of Pushkin. Without him we would have had no poetry — and that is so because he was so much a poet and an artist, perhaps too much so, to the detriment of his greatness in other ways. And that is why — we repeat — we begin Russian poetry with him and call him the first Russian poet, first even in time.

This is our thought on the development of Russian poetry and Russian literature: its history, in our opinion, is the history of its efforts to pass from artificiality and imitativeness to naturalness and independence, from being bookish to being alive and social. This is still going on today. . . And soon the time will come when this problem will be solved and this work will be completed. Already at the present time there is noticeable a new demand upon art — a demand for rational content which shall correspond to the historical spirit of the current age. And once already there appeared in Russia a great new poet, whose first works, even his early and immature ones, showed a fullness and richness of profound content along with an artistry of form worthy of his predecessor, Pushkin. But an untimely death abruptly dashed all hopes, hopes which were endless and immeasurable.

Belinski's essay goes on, and is later followed by a third part; but the main argument has been made. What, in substance, has he said? What is the significance of the apparent ambivalence toward Pushkin, who is praised in one sentence as an artist who first gave independent expression to his age, and regarded in the next sentence as "perhaps too much a poet," who remained so pure an artist that he drew away from his society? Why the passing reference to the "great new poet," Lermontov, in this connection?

It is in its suggestion of such questions that the essays on the "Speech on Criticism" can be seen to anticipate the series of essays on Pushkin. It is the latter essays which give Belinski's answers to the former questions. In essence his answer will be: only with Pushkin was a real beginning made toward an independent Russian literature, a literature determined by Russian literary history and by Russian society. Precisely by standing on the shoulders of his predecessors Pushkin showed himself a creature of native tradition. By this dependence upon Russian history and society Pushkin became the epitome of the true artist, who is always marked by the fact that he expresses his age. Thus Pushkin emerges as the great Russian artist of the past. But the age of Pushkin, having brought for the first time into clear realization the principle that society molds the artist, has been superseded by a new age, whose principle is that the artist molds his society. This new principle is best demonstrated by the work of Lermontov, who engaged in waging war upon his society rather than in merely painting its portraits. Pushkin, just by being the perfect model of the artist, cannot satisfy the new age which followed him.

Fame and Despair

The year 1842, marked especially by the criticism of *Dead Souls* and the dissertation on criticism, may serve to date the beginning of a final stage in Belinski's thought: the consolidation of a position which he had been gradually coming to adopt since his recognition of Lermontov and repudiation of Hegel.

The doctrine that the enlightened individual, and above all the artist, is and must be the voice of a human protest, continued to shape Belinski's thought throughout the forties. By this doctrine, the earlier effort to accept reality as it exists as inherently rational, was abandoned in favor of a conviction that man in history can fashion an increasingly rational reality. As Belinski becomes more and more conscious of history and more and more sure of the advance of human reason through time, he also becomes increasingly strident in calling for struggle against the existing historical situation: more aware of the historical evolution of society, and less inclined to rationalize the existing phase.

In this ideological context, literature has a special place prepared for it: at its best, it is the self-expression of the light-bearers in society. The assurance with which Belinski was willing by this time to entrust the art of literature to an embattled minority, a small band of enlightened spirits on the march through history, is nowhere more openly declared than in an article written at the end of 1843: "View of the Chief Facts of Russian Literature for 1843" ("Vzgliad na glavneishie iavleniia russkoi literatury v 1843 g.").

Here Belinski is first concerned to make clear that literature as he means it is only a select part of that great mass of material which goes by the name. His division is fourfold: 1) "Kopeck literature," to be distinguished from 2) "trade literature" mainly by the amount of money its producers hope to make — for both are interested only in engaging public attention with anything that will sell; 3) "graybeard literature," cultivated by literary Old Believers who "look on things with the eyes of the good old days" and "anathematize all that is new and best," still following the spirit of Derzhavin and Karamzin even after the age of Pushkin and Lermontov; and finally 4) genuine literature. The last is only emerging; it can hardly claim more than a dozen advocates; but it is more fertile and more promising than any of the others. It travels "a thorny and difficult road leading to the attainment of sacred and eternal truth, to the realization of the ideal upon earth; and slowly, but surely and independently, it marches along its way, invisibly advancing the enlightenment of society. . . Answering to the voice of universal and genuinely Russian learning, nobly sympathizing with all that is edifying, it deals with the main questions of existence, destroys old rooted prejudices, and indignantly raises its voice against the dark side of contemporary life, evoking reality in all its fearful nakedness. . . This literature does not ascribe to us virtues which we do not possess; does not hide our failings from us; but tries, so far as possible, to uncover and to expose them. . . Wherefore so many denunciations and so many reproaches for lack of patriotism are suffered by this disinterested literature at the hands of narrow-minded . . . pedants."

Literature in its true sense, Belinski continues, has thus not attained a brilliant position in Russian life; but there is no reason to despair of its future. Although the past year has not been rich in works, at least it gives evidence of progress from childhood to maturity. For in spite of backward forces, Russian literature is going forward. "The voice of its few genuine advocates, strong in truth and unity, drowns out the discordant cries of a numerous crowd . . . motivated by personal interest."

Belinski's militant conception of literature may seem almost an oddity to a modern reader. But the energy with which he sought to bind the fate of Russian literature to the progress of Russia's national enlightenment probably determined the extent of the intellectual influence which he came to wield. Like every leader, he led because he so well expressed the will of his following; and in his day, to have hope in the future of Russian literature meant also to have hope in the future of Russia herself. Not that many persons shared such serious convictions; but within the small circle of those who did, Belinski's utterances found considerable resonance.

Not only did Belinski acquire by the forties a substantial personal reputation, but the *National Notes*, the journal which he served for more than six years as chief critic, became, largely through his efforts, the most influential journal of its day. Already at the beginning of 1840 Botkin urged Belinski to persuade Kraevski to print his signature with his articles, instead of leaving them unsigned, since his name was now famous. Belinski, in his answer to Botkin, agrees with Botkin's proposal; but he shows how little deference Kraevski paid to his prestige when he refuses to argue the point with his publisher, whom he has found "in some of his convictions stubborn as the devil." Yet it was primarily Belinski who brought the journal its highest honors, among which might be counted the accusations of socialist radicalism made in 1844 by S. S. Uvarov, Minister of Public Instruction.

Belinski's fame as a writer was by now founded on more than his polemical position: he could claim to be the chief discoverer and interpreter of both Gogol and Lermontov, and before the forties had advanced very far, he emerged as the chief interpreter of Pushkin. Before his death he was to give the first critical support to the early work of Turgenev, Goncharov, and Dostoevski. And these are only the most eminent of the literary reputations which Belinski helped to form; yet they alone span the entire "golden age" of modern Russian literature.

Belinski's public fame was not matched by personal good fortune. In almost every respect his private life was ill-starred. The very work of journalism which brought him intellectual prestige brought also private misery. His curses on his job and his employers fill his letters, especially during the decade of his greatest fame. On February 6, 1843, he wrote to Botkin: "Work on the journal has come to disgust me to the point of morbidity," since he is held to the job only by necessity and must continually turn out his stint in great haste. "Hunger, hunger alone teaches to write quickly and much." By January 2, 1846, he wrote to Herzen that he had decided to leave Kraevski and his *National Notes*, since "working against a deadline for a journal sucks the living strength out of me, as a vampire sucks blood. . . It dulls my brain, ruins my health, and perverts my character." Kraevski, who when he first engaged Belinski in 1839 seemed to the latter a "good, warm, interesting person," now seems "a vampire, ever ready to suck the blood and soul out of a person and then to throw him out the window like a squeezed lemon."

Meanwhile Belinski's literary chores in these years were heavily burdened by the constant deterioration of his health. This is so familiar a theme throughout his active years that his complaints during the forties are distinguished mainly by a crescendo of despair, ranging from a letter of February 6, 1843, to Botkin: "I begin to realize with fear and horror that I won't last long," to a letter of January 14, 1846, written to Herzen: "It is a terrible thing to leave wife and daughter without a crust of bread."

As for Belinski's marriage, information is of course insufficient for any real knowledge of it; but the few pointed indications which are given are not promising. In November of 1843 he married the young Orlov woman whom he had first met in Moscow during the preceding summer, at the time of a long visit to old friends there. Just a month before their marriage he confessed bluntly to his fiancée that there was "nothing fiery, nothing ardent" in his love for her;[28] and of the marriage itself he "expressed the opinion unreservedly and before everyone, loudly and often," that it lacked any "poetic quality."[29] One can only guess what lay behind the reproach made to his wife, in a letter sent on his way to the Crimea in 1846, that "nothing, neither living together nor separating, will teach you to understand my character."[30] To the irritations of married life, the death of a small son in 1847 added its burden.

Yet it is in an intermediate area lying somewhere between private life and public activity that Belinski's chief dissatisfactions must be located. A few sympathetic friends, even the Petersburg circle which gradually organized around him, was not enough to give him the support he needed. The more extreme his convictions, the less he felt them shared. The more radical his ideology, the more restless he became with having to limit himself to mere literature. As early as February 6, 1843, he wrote to Botkin: "I read no poetry (but keep reading through Lermontov, more and more steeping myself in the fathomless ocean of his poetry); and when I happen to run across the poems of Fet or Ogarev I say: 'It's all right, but isn't it shameful to waste time and ink on such nonsense?' " A letter of March 8, 1843, to Tatiana Bakunin, sister of Michael, reveals the central frustration: his failure to find in his world an answering reality, the anxiety of not being in gear with the only actuality he could ever hope to know, the calamity of having to live "in a society in which everything human appears to have no bond with a reality which is savage, sordid, and meaningless — yet which for a long time to come will be maintained by the law of force. . . Give such a man [Belinski's reference, although not explicit, is to himself] an atmosphere proper to his capacities for action, and he will be resurrected. But that atmosphere . . . yes, you understand that it is nowhere to be found. No such atmosphere exists for me now, and none ever will; but it

has been a big step for me to have realized and understood that."
This concluding statement offers a consolation which Belinski
often appropriated for himself. But it is easy to find him admitting
that he remains inconsolable in his loss of all "illusions" about
himself. His new "realism" has been bought at heavy cost, leaving
him, as he confessed to Botkin in 1843, "no hopes for life, since
fancy no longer consoles and reality is profoundly understood." [31]
His hard-won disillusionment with all that he considers idealistic
brings him no joy; happiness continues to be equated with the
capacity to remain an idealist. So he writes on March 8, 1843, to
Tatiana Bakunin: "My nature is not alien to the act of negation,
and I have passed through several phases of it; but to give up the
desire for happiness, the impossibility of which is so mathemati-
cally clear to me — I still have no power."

Belinski's career throughout his life during the forties was thus
founded on the unstable union of rising public prestige and continuing private discontent. It can even be said that it was the
depth of his discontent, often his despair, with the world in which
he lived that determined the extent of his public reputation. By
the zeal of his attack upon Russian life as he knew it, he won the
devotion of the young Russian intelligentsia, whom he would
doubtless have attracted less if he had been a happier person.

Essays on the Works of Pushkin (1843–1846)

Belinski's series of essays on the writings of Alexander Pushkin
is his major critical work in several senses: it is the most interesting work he published during the four years, 1843 to 1846,
which comprise the central years of his mature period; and it is
his one full-length study of a major contemporary figure, carried
through on a scale on which he only promised to treat those other
eminent contemporaries, Gogol and Lermontov.

In the context of Belinski's intellectual development, the striking
fact about the Pushkin articles is that he should have written them
at all, during these years. Pushkin would seem to be — and, indeed, Belinski so presents him — the prime example of the literary
artist who eludes the tendentiousness which Belinski now appears
to be urging. It is, in fact, in the course of these essays on Pushkin,

particularly in Article Five, that Belinski first makes public a growing impatience with the "pure" poet.

Why did Belinski just at this time select Pushkin to write about at such length? There is, of course, no simple answer. Partly his choice shows a continuing readiness to give due place to literary events regardless of his ideological preferences: the victory of the literary critic over the ideologue. Partly his work is the account of a plan which he had long considered, to write at length on the first Russian poet; perhaps, as historian of Russian literature, he was merely proceeding chronologically — at least there is evidence that he intended to go on to similar studies of Gogol and Lermontov.

That there were intellectual hindrances in the way of a full study of Pushkin, Belinski himself admits on the opening pages of the First Article (1843):

> For a long time we have promised a complete review of the works of Pushkin. The present article is a beginning in the fulfillment of our promise, delayed for reasons which it would not be superfluous to explain here. Everyone knows that the eight volumes of Pushkin's works were published after his death in a manner that was very slipshod in all respects, both typographically . . . and editorially. . . But the worst thing of all about this edition was its incompleteness. . .
>
> But in addition to all this there was still another, more important and, so to speak, more internal reason for our delay. The year of Pushkin's untimely death moves, as the days go by, farther and farther from the present and, without noticing it, we become used to looking upon Pushkin's poetic career not as interrupted but as completely finished. This powerful poetic spirit took many creative secrets along with him into his early grave — but not the secret of his moral development, which had attained its apogee and therefore promised only a series of artistically great works but could not promise a new literary age, such as is always signalized not only by new works but by a new spirit. . . A new generation, arising on the foundation of a new social awareness, formed by influences from the poetry of Gogol and Lermontov, while placing a high value on Pushkin, at the same time makes a calm and dispassionate appraisal of him. This means that society is moving forward, that it is advancing by its eternal process of the renewal of the generations, and that a later generation has already succeeded Pushkin. In Russia everything grows not by years but by hours, and five years is for her almost a century. But a new opinion about such a great fact as Pushkin cannot be formed suddenly or appear in a completely finished state; but like everything living,

it has to develop out of the very life of society. Every new day, every new fact in life and literature is bound to change opinion about Pushkin.

From the very beginning of his career Pushkin aroused the most contradictory judgments. Thus *Ruslan and Liudmila* immediately became the center of a Russian variant of the European battle between classicism and romanticism. As Pushkin attracted ardent followers, so he also called forth bitter antagonists; moreover, as he matured, certain elements among his following began to cool toward him. His unexpected death brought a further change in his reputation: shocked and saddened by his passing, some critics began to eulogize him as not only the greatest Russian poet but as the greatest poet of all time.

Meanwhile time moved on, and life with it. . . Russian society . . . turned its glances toward a new poet who had boldly and proudly revealed to it new aspects of life and art. Whether Lermontov was equal or superior in talent to Pushkin is not the question. What is clear is that, even without being superior to Pushkin, Lermontov was called to express and to satisfy by means of his poetry an age which was incomparably higher, in its requirements and in its character, than the age to which Pushkin's poetry had provided expression. . . [And then] another poet [i.e., Gogol], who had entered upon a literary career during Pushkin's lifetime, and had been hailed by him as the great hope of the future . . . finally impressed the public by a crea- tive work which was to constitute a whole age both in the annals of literature and in the annals of the evolution of social consciousness. . . Discussion of Pushkin finally ceased, but not because questions con- cerning him ceased to interest the public, but because the public no longer wanted to hear the repetition of old, one-sided opinions. . . We repeat: an opinion could be developed only with time and in time; and without any false shame we can say that one of the chief reasons why we could not fulfill sooner our promise to our readers of a review of the works of Pushkin, was an awareness of the lack of clarity and certainty in our own understanding of the poet's signif- icance. . .

Moreover . . . the more we thought about Pushkin the deeper we saw into his living bond with past and present Russian literature, and we were convinced that to write about Pushkin meant to write about all of Russian literature: for as earlier Russian writers explain Pushkin, so Pushkin explains those writers who followed after him. This thought is both valid and consoling: it shows that, regardless of the poverty of our literature, it has vital movement and organic develop- ment, and consequently a history. . .

. . . Following these articles on Pushkin we will soon undertake a review (also long promised) of the works of Gogol and Lermontov. And although our journal has spoken often and at length of these writers, still the promised articles will in no wise be a repetition of what we have already said.

Belinski's discussion, as it moves on into the first articles of the Pushkin series, proceeds to show how Pushkin first revealed the organic historical development of Russian literature: that is, by standing upon the shoulders of creative leaders like Karamzin, who "first in Russia replaced the dead language of books with the living language of social life," and Zhukovski, who, by introducing the romantic cult of the life of the heart (with its cult of fantasy, soon repudiated), brought Russian poetry into touch with human life in society. Indeed, Pushkin was able to become the first poet to express an independent, self-conscious national life mainly because such life had not existed for his predecessors. Only in the post-Napoleonic age was Russian intellectual life aroused to independent self-scrutiny, partly by the ardor of a new romanticism, whereby the constraints of an old pedantry in literature were broken. This newness of independent cultural life had to come before Pushkin could make his declaration of Russian literary independence; a society had to be awakened before it could find its voice in art.

Thus sustained by a new vitality of cultural life, Pushkin was enabled to emerge as Russia's first "artist in poetry." Before Pushkin, Russian poetry was a beautiful face put on a didactic message; the meaning of the poem was not in the poetic creation itself but in its morally useful content. "But in order to be an expression of life, poetry must first of all be poetry." Otherwise a work is "like a woman with a great soul but an ugly face: it is possible to be impressed by her, but not to love her. . . " Pushkin's dominant "pathos," on the other hand, was his passion for creation which is exclusively artistic in intention. An "artistic beauty of human feeling" dominates his work.

As objective artist, Pushkin accepts the world. His muse may suffer from the discords of life but looks on them with a certain resignation, "not carrying in her soul any ideal of a better reality or any belief in the possibility of its realization."

"In his outlook Pushkin belongs to that school of art whose day has already completely passed in Europe and which for us cannot create a single great poet. The spirit of analysis, the indomitable pursuit of investigation, thought filled with love and hate, have now become the life of all true poetry. In this respect the present age has passed beyond the poetry of Pushkin and has rendered the bulk of his work void of that excited interest which is possible only to a satisfactory answer to the troubled, painful questions of the day."

Belinski thus halts, approximately at midpoint in his eleven-chapter study of Pushkin, in an abrupt transition from the realization of Pushkin as the spokesman of his society to the identification of Pushkin with an era that has passed. With Pushkin, Russian literature first achieved a mature artistic expression of Russian life; but in the age following Pushkin a new demand is made upon the artist: he must do more than express his society; he must enlighten it. The work of Pushkin showed Russian society as the creator of Russian literature; the work of the present age must show Russian literature as the creator of Russian society.

As a model of the poet-virtuoso, Pushkin the man is dominated by Pushkin the artist. "The more perfect Pushkin became as an artist, the more his personality was hidden and disappeared behind the marvelous, luxuriant world of his poetic meditations." Whereas for contemporary man, life supersedes art, pathos supersedes idea, person supersedes artist. The writer who hides in objective artistry is soon lost to his public, who seek answers and fail to find them in his work. And "every intelligent person has the right to demand either that a poet by his poetry give him answers to the questions of the age or that it at least be troubled by those grave problems which it leaves unsolved. He who remains a poet by and for himself, contemptuous of the crowd, risks being the only reader of his works." Pushkin's poem "The Poet" is an excellent expression of the idea that the poet's greatness appears only in the spell of inspiration; "but this idea is now completely false . . . Our age bends the knee only before the artist whose life is the best commentary on his works."

Belinski's growing preference of life to art, of man to artist, tended to create a theoretical dichotomy between "pure" poetry and the literature whose primary service is the work of human enlightenment. That dichotomy he never succeeded either in formulating or in resolving satisfactorily. The willingness to recognize Pushkin as a great artist which the first articles on Pushkin show is joined in Article Five by the assertion of Pushkin's inadequacy to fulfill the needs of Belinski's own day. Should the conclusion be drawn that art is inadequate for Belinski's time, or does he mean to argue that his age requires a redefinition of art? The problem is never clearly resolved. Here as elsewhere, Hegel had predicted Belinski, by a dual conception of romantic art in which content transcends form and, at the same time, of a progressive transcendence of art itself.[32]

That Belinski failed to harmonize his theoretical defense of the integrity of art with his insistence that art perform a service of enlightenment, is apparent throughout the criticism of his later years. Nowhere is it more apparent than in the criticism of Pushkin, where Belinski the man persists in superseding Belinski the critic. For all his theoretical recognition of Pushkin as the "poet-artist," it is precisely Pushkin's masterly achievement of artistic ambiguity that Belinski is least willing to respect.

Belinski's original effort is to preserve the "purity" of genuine art while he moves toward a personal concern with literature "as a living source of humanistic, human education," as he had written in the discussion of Nikitenko. There he had also said that in no case should the writer become a hireling: "freedom of creation agrees easily with service to contemporary society, for it is not necessary to force oneself to write to order, to suppress the fancy; all that is required is to be a citizen, a son of one's society and era . . . ; all that is needed is . . . a wholesome practical feeling for truth which does not separate . . . creative works from life." Just as art for art's sake is an extreme position, so also is art for a moral's sake. In the idea of "pure art, which is an end in itself . . . there is a basis, but its exaggeration is obvious at the first glance. This idea is of pure German extraction; it could appear only among a contemplative people. . . Essentially this is the dangerous extreme of another dangerous extreme: namely, the notion of art as didactic, educative, cold, dry, dead, creating works which are nothing but rhetorical exercises on assigned themes. There is no question that art must above all remain art, while at the same time expressing the spirit and direction of society at a particular period."

This insistence that art should remain art, that "it is impossible to violate the laws of art with impunity," remained at the base of Belinski's critical theory to the end of his career. But by varying methods he proceeded to set "pure" art off in a special enclosure. In the process he moved all the way from the claim that such art, as for example the art of Pushkin, belongs to an age that is past, to the claim that "pure, isolated, unconditioned — or, as the philosophers say, absolute — art never existed anywhere." From a readiness to relegate Pushkin to a "school of art whose day has . . . passed," Belinski gravitated toward a refusal to respect the purity of pure art. His insistence that art remain art was continually asserted; but the assertion was made questionable by an equal insistence that art serve the cause of enlightenment. The equivocal character of Belinski's final position is apparent throughout his critical judgments.

Just as he had formerly criticized Lermontov for not bringing Pechorin around to sharing Belinski's own conviction of the rationality of reality, so he now accuses Pushkin of failure to do full justice to his own present dogma: the theme of human dignity. Such, according to Belinski, is the failure, for example, of "The Gypsies" ("Tsygany"). "Pushkin himself did not intend to say what he actually said"; he failed to remain true to his original design because "the spontaneously creative element in Pushkin was incomparably stronger than the element of conscious thought." Pushkin had consciously set out to show Aleko as a man breaking through the restraints of civilized society. "Wishing and intending to create out of the poem the apotheosis of Aleko as a defender of the rights of human dignity, the poet instead created a fearful satire of him and of men like him. . . Everyone, even at the first superficial glance, will see that in Aleko Pushkin intended to show the figure of an individual so penetrated by the consciousness of human dignity that in the social structure he sees only the degradation and disgrace of that dignity; hence, cursing society and indifferent to his own life, Aleko seeks in savage gypsy freedom that which civilized society, fettered by prej-

udices and proprieties . . . was unable to give him." In his answer
to Zemphira's question whether he regrets the life he left behind,
Aleko stands forth as "a creature endowed with a luminous intellect, an ardent love for truth, and a profound sorrow over the
degradation of humanity. . . You see in him a hero of conviction,
a martyr to ultimate revelations inaccessible to the crowd. . .
How high he stands above that despised crowd, which he so
mercilessly strikes with the thunder of his noble indignation!"

But Aleko as the defender of human dignity turns out a sorry
failure, whom Pushkin allowed to be ruined by the curse of
jealousy, itself a form of violation of human dignity. As a moral
man, Aleko should have blessed Zemphira's new love, hiding his
suffering from the world and especially from his loved one. The
old dramatic notion of vengeance is out of date. Having set out
to make Aleko his hero, Pushkin, "perhaps unconsciously obeying
the mysterious inner logic of spontaneous creativity," has made
his real hero out of the old gypsy. Having made this unexpected
change of theme, Pushkin might at least have ended on that note,
by repeating in the epilogue the gypsy's protest to Aleko: "You
want freedom only for yourself." Instead Pushkin allows the
poem to end in an emphasis upon the subsidiary fact of sorrow
in the gypsy camp.

Beginning with a clear moral theme, Pushkin allowed his
meaning to change character completely, by making the uncultivated gypsy, rather than the civilized Aleko, the moral hero of
the poem. But by such a moral philosophy, "the development of
humanity through civilization would have no meaning." Whereas
civilized man is in fact morally superior to the savage, and "the
life of the spontaneously natural man can in no wise enrich
humanity with any great lesson." Indeed, the old gypsy here is
not the hero of the poem but rather an observer, in the tradition
of the Greek chorus; and Aleko remains the central figure, although he weakens the poem by the "melodramatic" quality of
his character and behavior.

Even in phrasing Pushkin is guilty of "ultra-romantic" touches,
as when he calls the "fugitive" bear "the shaggy guest of the
tent" — whereas it is obvious that the bear is a captive and not a
fugitive, and a prisoner more than a guest. When Belinski thus

comes forth in defense of the outraged dignity of bears, one wonders how much further ideological bias can carry him.

Belinski's eagerness to look for a defense of his own principles in the work of art is, to be sure, only sometimes expressed, and sometimes held in check. But even fair critical appreciation may be motivated by unobjective sympathies. Perhaps Belinski's appreciation of the character of Onegin, the "suffering egotist," whose very apathy is a form of death-in-life which "the dull rabble" cannot know — perhaps even here Belinski is being partly swayed by ulterior considerations, such as his identification of himself with Onegin, who for all his faults is real, "able to be happy or unhappy only in and through reality." Lenski, on the other hand, " a romantic and nothing more," is willingly sacrificed by Belinski, who in violation of Pushkin's own ambiguity of attitude in Chapter Six of the poem, prefers to accept only one of Pushkin's evaluations of the potentialities of the dead Lenski, whom he condemns as one of "the enemies of all progress."

Thus in the review of *Eugene Onegin*, Belinski proceeds to pass moral judgment upon the personages rather than aesthetic judgment upon the characters which Pushkin had created. It is in such a spirit of moral judgment that Belinski's chief comments upon Tatiana are made. The dignity of the person, whether man or woman, provides him with the credo by which the character of Tatiana is judged. Tatiana's strength is that she is not the mere plaything of her society, that she is not concerned, like most girls, only with opportunities for marriage, however accidental; but "deep and strong," forced by her rough contact with the sardonic Onegin to keep the life of her heart within herself. It is this moral superiority which gives the greater force to Tatiana as the depiction of woman's shameful lot, when at the end of the poem she remains true to her unloved husband.

"Thus in the characters of Onegin, Lenski, and Tatiana, Pushkin depicted Russian society in one phase of its formation. . . " In the author of the poem himself, "you everywhere see the Russian landowner."

If by such critical emphasis the artistic integrity of *Eugene Onegin* is given only partial recognition, at least it is not seriously attacked. The outcome is quite different when Belinski's idolization of Peter the Great causes him to see in "The Bronze Horseman" ("Medny Vsadnik") "an apotheosis of Peter the Great," in which "we recognize the triumph of the universal over the individual, though not refusing our sympathy to the suffering of the individual," since we realize that "the bronze giant cannot perfect the destinies of individuals while safeguarding the destiny of the people and the state." At such points of weakness Belinski gives concrete evidence of the damage which his ideology can inflict upon his criticism, although that ideology may in itself seem broad and inclusive enough. But perhaps even in the diffuse generality a danger can be seen, as when Belinski singles out as a special quality of Pushkin's genius "a capacity to develop in men . . . a feeling of *humanism*, if that word is taken to mean an unlimited regard for the worth of the person as a person."

It is quite possible, however, to argue that Belinski's credo of art as the expression of a protest in favor of a "universal humanity" need not of itself attack the integrity of the work of art. Belinski himself continued, off and on, to argue that only as art remains art can it perform its true service of enlightenment, that "in order to be an expression of life, poetry must first of all be poetry." For only true art can give a full, objective, many-sided portrayal of the human scene. In theory, Belinski remained more or less faithful to that ideal of art. But the vulnerability of that ideal became more and more apparent under the pressure of a contention that art is valuable only in the measure of the value which inheres in the human service it performs. As the ideal of human integrity became more vivid to Belinski, the ideal of artistic integrity lost its first rank of importance. Art might remain art and at the same time suffer a weakening of its power to command respect. The instability of Belinski's final critical position depended not upon a disparagement of art but upon a devotion to a human ideal by which art was superseded.

"Thoughts and Notes on Russian Literature" (1846)

The articles on Pushkin constitute a major elaboration of the principle that the function of the literary artist is and should be the expression of his age and his society. In so far as Pushkin was a great Russian artist, he gave expression to the Russian life of his time; in so far as he withdrew from the life of his time into "pure" art, his significance declined.

The counterproposition of Belinski's doctrine, that literature should guide and enlighten the life of society, was given its major statement in the same year which brought the Pushkin essays to a conclusion. "The powerful and beneficent effect of our literature upon society" is the theme of "Thoughts and Notes on Russian Literature" ("Mysli i zametki o russkoi literature"), published in Nekrasov's *Petersburg Miscellany* (*Peterburgski Sbornik*) of 1846. Here Belinski not only repeats his familiar claim for literature in Russia, that "in it, in it alone, is all our intellectual life and all the poetry of our life"; but he proceeds to enumerate specific ways in which this is so. In reading over Belinski's arguments in the course of this article, one may well wonder when a national literature has ever been so honored and so burdened by national obligations.

The first claim to be made for literature in Russia is that "only in its sphere do we cease to be Ivans and Peters and become simply persons associating with other persons and having relations with them." In other words, literature is able to join separate persons in a common humanity, by which they are both humanized and socialized.

More specifically, Russian society, so notoriously broken by historical division and class difference, is unified by the common bond of Russian literature: "The beginning of a rapprochement among social classes, which is the beginning of a cultured society . . . is merged with the beginning of our literature. . . Social enlightenment and culture at first flowed among us in a tiny stream, hardly noticeable, but nevertheless a stream flowing from the highest and noblest source: from the very source of learning and literature."

In this way "literature in our country serves as a meeting point for people who are *inwardly* separated in all other respects. . . The first Russian journals, the very names of which are now forgotten, were published by circles of young men who were brought together by their common passion for literature. Education has a leveling effect. Even in our time the friendly circle is not at all rare in which can be found a titled lord, a commoner, a merchant, a tradesman — a circle whose members have completely forgotten the external differences which separate them and mutually respect each other simply as persons. Here is the true beginning of cultivated social life, a beginning made for us by literature. . . Financial interests, commerce, trading on the stock exchange, balls, meetings, dances also provide a bond, but one which is purely external and hence not living, not organic, although necessary and useful. People are joined together inwardly by common moral concerns, by similarity of ideas, by equality of education, and, along with all this, by a mutual respect for each other's human worth. But all our moral concerns, all our spiritual life has been focussed up to now, and for a long time to come will continue to be focussed, exclusively upon literature. It is the living source from which all human feelings and ideas filter through into society."

Indeed, to speak of the progress of our culture is to speak of the progress of our literature, for our culture shows the immediate effect of our literature upon the concepts and mores of our society. "Our literature has created the morals of our society, has already educated several quite distinct generations, has laid the foundation for an internal meeting of social classes, has formed a kind of public opinion." This moral force which literature exercises is especially important for the youth of Russia, for "the impressions of youth are strong, and youth accepts as indubitable truth what first of all impressed the feeling, the imagination, and the mind." Such a moral function is particularly served by a literature which is devoted to holding the faults of contemporary social life up to ridicule.

So effective a social agent does Belinski now find in literature that it becomes for him the basis upon which is built that community of minds which is the central focus of Russian intellectual life: namely, the intelligentsia. The name was to come later, and Belinski here passes over the fact itself with a certain understandable haste; but the reference is clear: "Our literature . . . has created a kind of special class within society, differing from the usual *middle class* in that it is made up not only of merchant and tradesman elements but consists of persons of all classes brought together by cultural interests, which with us are focussed exclusively upon a love of literature."

Russian literature was slow in achieving its influential place in Russian society because it was slow in achieving its own independent existence. From Kantemir and Lomonosov until the time of Pushkin, Russian literature remained an imitation of the foreign. Then, feeling its power, it became a master instead of a student; but while copying from foreign themes it attempted to recreate both European and Russian life. But its success in portraying native Russian life was not conspicuous until the appearance of Gogol. Only with Gogol did Russian literature finally turn to Russian life. Even Pushkin and Lermontov, who express the Russian mind so well for Russians, do not express the distinctive character of Russian life with sufficient fullness so that a foreigner can learn about Russia from reading their works. Whereas among European writers even the second-rate, as well as the first-rate, do a good job of depicting the characteristic life of their society. If it is a virtue to lose one's cultural identity so easily, it is a virtue more valuable for the future than for the present.

The fact is that Russian culture has not yet provided Russian literary artists with a rich enough content to allow them to equal the work of the major European artists. In purely formal excellence the best Russian poets may equal them, but the Russians still call their poets Shakespeares and Byrons, thus paying deference to the latter. And we still feel a need to know them which they do not feel to know us. The present promise of Russian literature is such that in time there will exist a distinctively Russian literature equal to any of the literatures of Europe. But such a literature does not exist at present.

To a new emphasis upon the social function of literature in Russia, Belinski thus added an argument familiar since the "Literary Reveries," from which he once threw the challenge: "We have no literature!" The "Thoughts and Notes" suggest that since that time the critic's respect for Russian literature had considerably increased, to the point where he could write a whole article about "the powerful and beneficent effect of our literature upon society." Russian literature had at least advanced to the point of performing a major social function. And it is its potential performance in the future that inspires his hope in it. But he continues to insist that both Russian literature and Russian society have a long way to go in their pursuit of national identity. The important — and encouraging — point, however, is that they are sure to advance together, mutually sustaining one another; and that they are both moving and will continue to move in the same direction: that is to say, toward increasing national enlightenment.

Last Years

An ironical discrepancy exists between the optimism of Belinski's public pronouncements regarding Russian cultural life and the deepening sadness of his private life and thought. At least a partial explanation can be given. As the "realism" of his last years left him exposed to the formlessness of Russian life, his hope for a new day in Russia was forced to rise; and at the same time he more and more urgently insisted that literature, the one great medium of social and cultural enlightenment, must serve the major cause: the cause of national progress. In this way the unhappy fortunes of his life, and of the ideological system which evolved with it, conspired to enforce the radicalism of his views. Indeed, the several important articles of these last years, conveying a confidence in the future of Russian life and letters which he hardly matched elsewhere, were written by a dying man. His "View of Russian Literature for 1847" was, in fact, dictated from his deathbed.

Much of 1846 and 1847 Belinski spent traveling, ostensibly for his health, the condition of which is certainly not unrelated to a general restlessness which seems now to invade his whole existence. His literary hack work, which he had so often bewailed, now seems intolerable. Kraevski, his employer, has now become in his mind "not a man but a devil." Finally, on February 7, 1846, Belinski submitted his formal resignation from the journal which he had made famous, and in which his articles, including the last of the Pushkin articles, continued to appear for several months. Meanwhile he had been collecting a number of pieces which he intended to publish on his own, in an almanac to be entitled *The Leviathan*. Along with old friends such as Botkin, Herzen, and Panaev, he had drawn upon such new literary friends as Dostoevski, Nekrasov, and Goncharov.

Soon after his break with the *National Notes*, he began to plan a trip to the South, together with the famous actor, Shchepkin. On May 16, 1846, the pair of travelers left Moscow, and by mid-June Belinski was settled in Odessa, where a stay of several weeks seemed to improve his failing health. By mid-October he returned to St. Petersburg. It soon appeared that the trip had not performed a cure: within a month after his return, Botkin noted that his friend's health was worse and even wrote on November 20 to Annenkov: "It is apparent that his death is approaching."

By the end of the year 1846 Belinski had moved to his last job, on the journal which Pushkin had founded and once made famous: *The Contemporary (Sovremennik)*. In December Belinski submitted his "View of Russian Literature for 1846." During the preceding October he had turned over to *The Contemporary* all the material gathered for his projected almanac. These new professional ties soon felt to Belinski as irksome as the old. Panaev as co-editor seemed "poor" and "empty"; whereas Panaev's colleague, the poet Nekrasov, appeared to Belinski "as a manager, one of the worst; perhaps only Panaev is worse." On February 6, 1847, he wrote to Botkin: "My repugnance for literature and journalism *as a trade* grows from day to day, and I don't know what will finally come of it. It is more difficult to fight repugnance than need; it is a disease."

Financially each year promised less hope than the last. Already by February of 1847 Belinski had collected from Nekrasov and Panaev 1400 of the 2000 rubles due him for that year's labors on *The Contemporary*. That this was no new or unusual situation for Belinski, however, is clear from many references, such as the note written near the end of 1845 by the historian Granovski: "Belinski is dying of hunger and does his work on a piece of bread. The doctors advise him to relax, but how could he live? Herzen has no money, and I have nothing but debts; hence we are in no position to help him." [33]

On April 3, 1847, Botkin wrote to Kraevski: "Belinski is going to take the waters. I'm glad that I was able to get around 2000 together for him for this trip. For at least a half a year he should get away from both literature and his wife. He is low in spirits, and as for his physical state, the less said the better." [34] On May 5, the ailing Belinski left by boat for Western Europe. Passing through Stettin, he went on to Berlin, where Turgenev met him and then accompanied him to Dresden and to Salzbrunn, famous for its spa. It was in Salzbrunn that Paul Annenkov met him and remarked, in a letter of May 29, that he had hardly recognized this "old man" dressed in a long coat and carrying a heavy cane. It was also in Salzbrunn that Belinski received, on July 13, a long letter from Gogol, which he answered within several days by his famous Letter to Gogol.

Before long the traveler moved on to Frankfurt-am-Main, Mainz, Cologne, then to Brussels, and finally to Paris. Here he spent two months, from mid-July to mid-September, continuing medical treatments and spending all his free time among his friends the Herzens, Turgenev and Mme. Viardot, and Michael Bakunin. Whether through the ministrations of good medical care or of such good company, the invalid seemed to improve in health. It also helped that he liked Paris, of which he wrote that it "from the very first sight surpassed all my expectations, all my dreams" — although his traveling-companions usually remarked a certain absent-mindedness in him, as did Turgenev on one occasion when he showed Belinski the Place de la Concorde. "Isn't that surely one of the most beautiful squares in the world?" exclaimed Belinski, and then turned to talk of Gogol. Such behavior prompted Turgenev to say of him that "he pined away in a foreign country, so drawn was he back to Russia. . . He was very much a Russian, and outside of Russia he died away, like a fish in air." [35] Perhaps Belinski was thinking of his life in Russia and of all that the word "German" had meant to him there, when he described Germany, in a letter of September 29 sent to Annenkov from Berlin, as "honorable and stupid."

In this same letter to Annenkov Belinski had written that his health now seemed improved. But hardly had he sent the letter off when he suddenly came down with a cold, the first in a series of discomforts which tormented him all the way back to St.

Petersburg. After a few days among the winter snows of the capital, he soon lost all the advances in health which his vacation abroad might have accomplished. The weeks which followed his return he managed to fill with considerable literary activity, including a number of long letters. But by December 7 he had written his last letter by his own hand.

As the new year wore on, it became clear that Belinski's health was failing. He coughed constantly. But he continued his literary labors at least long enough to write, in two installments, a literary review of considerable interest, entitled "A View of Russian Literature for 1847" (the second part of which he was obliged to dictate), as well as a few lesser pieces. But with that his literary career was ended, even before he reached the age of thirty-seven.

One last letter, dictated to Annenkov on February 15, has survived to show that Belinski's last thoughts only reinforce the main direction of the preceding years. The letter is filled chiefly with two concerns: the latest works of Russian literature, and mounting enthusiasm for the spirit of the French Enlightenment. Turgenev, Druzhinin, and Dostoevski all come in for criticism — and, oddly enough, it is Druzhinin's latest story which receives the highest praise. With Turgenev's latest chapters from the famous *Sportsman's Sketches* (*Zapiski Okhotnika*) the critic appears less fully satisfied. As for Dostoevski's latest work, "The Landlady" ("Khoziaika"), he finds it "dreadful rubbish." To these last literary judgments is added a significant outburst in favor of the great personality as opposed to the common people. "Where and when did the people ever obtain freedom for themselves? Everything has always been done through the individual . . . Russia now needs a new Peter the Great." In this final note his gospel of the enlightened individual finds a new herald: "the noble personality of Voltaire! What warm sympathy for all that is human and rational, for the misery of the common people! What he has done for humanity!"

This final philosophy of rationalistic and humanistic enlightenment received, during these last months, the one public tribute which the Russia of Nicholas I was prepared to offer: the suspicion of the police. The rulers of official Russia had never been his admirers, not even when his thought became for a while conciliatory and reactionary; now that he openly admitted his radicalism, their sudden solicitude, especially in the anxious year 1848, was seriously disquieting. Their suspicions were not fully allayed even by his death, on May 26: strange visitors attended even his modest funeral.

The poverty in which Belinski left his family at his death, and the official obscurity to which even his name was consigned until almost a decade had passed, are only final details in the picture of his destiny in the Russia of his day. This situation in which he lived and worked cannot be omitted from the formative background of his thought. Under happier circumstances, his intellectual development would have been different. For he articulated a historical period which is distinguished by the degree to which its major intellectual concern was identified with the urgent and unhappy problems of the day. The latest book, the latest issue of a leading journal, was welcomed first of all by anxious expectations of a new resolution for the largest problems of national destiny. The circumstances of contemporary life in Russia not only shaped and influenced the thought of the intelligentsia to which Belinski belonged: they provided the fundamental terms of every problem, philosophical or aesthetic or political, which seriously occupied the attention of this most serious generation.

Last Literary Judgments

That Belinski kept alive, during the last years of his life, both vigorous ideological convictions and an enthusiastic interest in the latest literary events is proved by his judgments of contemporary authors. As always with him, ideology was liable to lay a heavy hand upon his criticism; but nevertheless he managed to extend a critic's greeting to a whole new generation of writers who would some day richly justify his praise. With what serious concern he took the measure of every literary work according to the scale of his doctrine is most dramatically shown in his last encounter with an old literary idol: Nicholas Gogol.

At the beginning of 1847, there appeared from the pen of Gogol a strange book which was destined to bring its author far more pain than profit: a book entitled *Selected Passages from*

Correspondence with Friends (*Vybrannye mesta iz perepiski s druziami*). It contained a heterogeneous but coherent collection of serious writings, in the form of essays and letters, upon a variety of topics. What bound the assortment together and made the book news was the author's theme: in a word, a critique of Russian life grounded upon Gogol's own philosophy of religious conservatism. In many respects he approached a Slavophile position; but the mixture of private belief and political conservatism was his own. Gogol's spiritual tragedy was still to be played out, and both his book and his own later reflections upon it show that he was far from having clarified his own thought at this time. No doubt the excesses of the book were largely those of a mind intent upon consolidating its position, the central tenet of which was that every Russian who hoped to save Russia should turn first of all to the salvation of his own soul. In this effort, Gogol was deeply engaged in working out his own spiritual freedom; in the meantime he was willing to set himself up as advisor on other people's problems.

Even these few words about a state of mind and spirit which often seems too tangled for an observer to unravel at all, can suffice to anticipate the reception Gogol could expect from a reader like Belinski. It is hardly necessary even to attempt an analysis of the argument between these two men: they simply stood at opposite poles in every relevant respect. It is abundantly clear that neither understood what the other was talking about.

Nevertheless Belinski undertook to review Gogol's work, in an article which appeared in *The Contemporary* for January, 1847. Belinski's presentation successfully reduced the book to nonsense. He showed no patience with Gogol's "letters," which in his mind were "not letters but rather the strict and frightening exhortations of a teacher to his students," handed out by someone who "considers himself to be something on the order of a *curé de village*," willing to adjudicate subjects ranging all the way from the historicity of Homer (Gogol thought Wolf's theory "stupid") to the causes of malfeasance in office (Gogol held that the greed of their wives drove Russian officials to crime).

What Belinski found to be the "most curious part of this book" was a series of four letters on the subject of *Dead Souls*. Here the outraged critic enumerated the author's main positions; they all seemed perversely intended to give comfort to the enemy and mortal injury to the very critics who had been hailing Gogol as a great writer. Belinski argued: Gogol's dissatisfaction with his own work could only prove his detractors right; his recognition of his chief talent as an ability to portray human sordidness could only convince his enemies of how low and disreputable were his literary intentions; his claim that he was born not to initiate a new age in literature but to save his own soul could only serve to discountenance his friendliest critic, whom he had further embarrassed by admitting the justice of the criticism of his enemies. How dire was Gogol's predicament in Belinski's opinion is clear from the closing lines of the review: "Woe to the man whom nature herself created an artist, woe to him if, dissatisfied with his road, he rushes off onto a strange path! On that new path he is bound to stumble, and afterwards it is not always possible to find the old road again."

Such words from Belinski had their effect on Gogol, although for Gogol's own reasons. Above all, he saw a single cause for Belinski's attack: namely, the critic's chagrin at feeling rejected by a favorite author, whose defense had become for Belinski a sensitive point of pride. Gogol now regretted this outcome, "because this man spoke on my behalf over a period of ten years" and "despite excesses and enthusiasms, nevertheless justly pointed out many characteristics of my works which went unnoticed by others who considered themselves his intellectual superiors." [36] He cautioned Belinski not to take the *Selected Passages* as a personal affront, for the book was not so meant. Indeed, Gogol wrote, it was hard to see why the book created such an uproar, why "Easterners, Westerners, and neutrals, all were offended. . . You looked upon my book with the eyes of a wrathful person and consequently almost everyone has seen it in a different light." [37] This is the letter which Belinski received at Salzbrunn in the course of his 1847 trip abroad for his health, and which he immediately answered, in mid-July, with the now famous Letter to Gogol.

Although Belinski's original review would seem to have given Gogol legitimate cause for his diagnosis of Belinski's reaction,

Belinski, in his letter from Salzbrunn, was above all concerned with showing Gogol that a great deal more was involved than merely a personal affront. In this Belinski was, of course, nearer the truth than Gogol. Gogol's little understanding of Belinski at this time is, in fact, clearly shown in his superficial interpretation of the cause of Belinski's anger. Belinski's whole life's philosophy was implicated. In his effort to make this clear, he proceeded to declare his whole philosophy. It is this fact which made the resulting letter famous; it said so much, and said it with such fire and eloquence.

Belinski had, of course, another reason for his animation: Gogol was still his literary idol, even though the great master had ceased to function. Gogol's book had been to Belinski a blow to all he held dear, and a blow delivered by Russia's first artist, who should have been her first light-bearer. Throughout his famous letter Belinski repeats the sad thought: "If your name were not printed on this book, who would have thought that this pompous and sordid clatter of words and phrases was the work of the author of *The Inspector* and *Dead Souls?*"

Belinski's long cry for "civilization, enlightenment, and humanity" in mortal struggle against "Russian autocracy, Orthodoxy, and nationalism," made his letter a manifesto for Russian radicals. Not long after Belinski's death the young Dostoevski almost went to his doom for the crime of reading it.

Yet Belinski had hardly joined issues with Gogol, whose sad resignation before a misunderstanding too vast for argument slowly becomes evident. He answered Belinski's letter twice, in a long letter and in a short one, and then showed how futile he considered lengthy explanation by sending only the short one. In both he soon put argument aside in favor of considering Belinski's own spiritual state. Thus in the longer, unposted letter he returned Belinski's earlier accusation: "How far you have wandered from the right path! . . . Why did you leave the peaceful road which you had once chosen? What could be finer than to explain to a reader the beautiful things to be found in the works of our writers. . . That road would have led you to reconciliation with life. . . But now your mouth breathes bitterness and hatred." [38] In the letter which he sent to Belinski he closed with the words: "Just as I have much to learn concerning what you know and I do not, so you should learn at least a part of what I know and you unjustly hold in scorn. But meanwhile think above all of your health; forget current problems for a while. Then you will return to them with great freshness and so with greater profit both for them and for yourself. With all my heart I wish you peace of soul, the primary good, without which it is impossible to work and act reasonably in any career whatever." [39]

Far from giving Belinski pause, however, his quarrel with Gogol only fortified his militant convictions. One of these remained, in spite of all that had passed, a supreme regard for Gogol's achievement as a writer. In the "View of Russian Literature for 1847," the last article he wrote, he presented Gogol as the great champion of the "Natural School," which first succeeded in turning Russian literature to the realities of Russian life. Since, by the argument of this and more than one other article, the whole progress of Russian literature is its progress toward reality, Gogol becomes the most crucial figure in modern Russian literature. "All of Gogol's works are devoted exclusively to depicting the world of Russian life, and he has no rival in the art of reproducing it in all its truth." Russian literature, which had been imitative and rhetorical, now "strove to become natural, naturalistic. This effort . . . constitutes the meaning and the soul of the history of our literature"; and "in no other Russian writer was this striving so successful as it was in Gogol."

The paradoxical consequence of such praise was that through it, far more than by any attack, Belinski did his greatest critical injustice to Gogol. For it was his glorification of Gogol's "naturalism" that persuaded whole future generations to narrow their insight into Gogol's deep and tragic vision. By his exaltation of Gogol, fully as much as by his strictures, Belinski made known his increasing willingness in these last years to impose his doctrine. And the fact that the imposition was made with so much righteous conviction only helped to give to Belinski's tendentiousness a greater capacity for doing harm.

That Gogol continued, however, during Belinski's last years to serve him as a model of what the contemporary Russian writer should be, is clear not only from his repeated claims for the Natural School, which he considered Gogol to have established, but also from his estimate of a new important writer, the young Fedor Dostoevski. The story of Belinski's excitement over Dostoevski's first work, *Poor Folk* (*Bednye Liudi*), is now famous. The critique of that work which Belinski included in his review of Nekrasov's *Petersburg Miscellany* of 1846 opens with a discussion of Gogol and his new literary school, contemptuously dubbed "natural" by its enemies for its violation of the traditional "*pruderie*" of Russian letters. It is to membership in this school that Belinski proceeds to recruit Dostoevski. Dostoevski's first two stories, *Poor Folk* and *The Double* (*Dvoinik*), both indicate that Gogol is Dostoevski's "literary father." The son, while "living his own life . . . nevertheless owes his existence to his father. However rich and marvelous Dostoevski's talent may come to be in the future, Gogol will always remain the Columbus of that immeasurable and inexhaustible domain of creativity in which Dostoevski is to find his vocation."

With both *Poor Folk* and *The Double* at hand, Belinski was understandably slow to decide precisely wherein the genius of the youthful Dostoevski lay. But that this young writer would occupy a major place among Russian authors, Belinski was fully convinced; and he made his conviction clear not only through more than one amazingly prophetic pronouncement, but also by a significant comparison between the literary debut of Dostoevski and that of the great and beloved Lermontov.

Throughout his brief critical comments upon Dostoevski's first stories, Belinski shows a perception and a sympathy which soon transcend the bounds of ideological requirement. One might perhaps have expected a display of impatience at *The Double* — at least a preference for the simpler and clearer human story of *Poor Folk*. Instead, the critic finds that "it is obvious at first glance that in *The Double* there is even more creative talent and depth of thought than in *Poor Folk*." And if, as Dostoevski's critics complain, he is guilty of "prolixity" in this story, it is, Belinski replies, a prolixity which comes not from "poverty of talent" but from "that richness which is especially characteristic of a young and unmatured talent," and should rather be called "exces-

sive fertility." Indeed, "if the author of *The Double* were to put
a pen in our hand along with the unconditional right of excising
from the manuscript of his *Double* all that might seem to us
prolix and superfluous, we would not raise our hand to a single
passage, for every single passage in this novel is beyond perfection." In fact, what has been called the prolixity of *The Double*,
and to a lesser extent of *Poor Folk*, is the result of there being
too great an accumulation of "perfect passages," an embarrass-
ment of riches.

The climax of Belinski's praise is reached in his concluding
words: "As for the opinions of the majority, that *The Double*
is a poor story, that the talk about its author's unusual talent is
exaggerated, etc., Mr. Dostoevski need not worry. His talent belongs with those which are not immediately achieved and recognized. In the course of his career many talents will appear to com-
pete with his, but they will end by being forgotten at the very
time when he will be reaching the height of his reputation. . .
Now . . . we wish to confine ourselves to advising Mr. Dostoevski to print all the criticisms [of his enemies] in a future edition
of his works, as did Pushkin, who appended to the second or
third edition of *Ruslan and Liudmila* all the critiques and reviews
in which his poem had been attacked."

Belinski's early recognition of the size of Dostoevski's talent,
at a time when the novelist's main achievement was still many
years away, must count among his triumphs as a critic — one who
could at times lay the most fervent ideological conviction aside in
deference to the appearance of literary genius. And his subsequent
disapproval of Dostoevski's later work, his readiness to find in
Mr. Prokharchin a "disagreeable surprise" and in *The Landlady*
(*Khoziaika*) a "monstrosity," far from impugning Belinski's critical power, only gives further evidence of both the independence
and the perspicacity of his judgment.

To the generation of Dostoevski belongs another great novelist
who helped to make Belinski famous as a critic: Ivan Turgenev.
Even more than Dostoevski, Turgenev by his early work was
likely to mislead a critic. Yet already in his 1843 review of Turgenev's "tale in verse," *Parasha*, Belinski detected an "unusual
poetic talent," skillfully employed in telling a story which could

not fail to excite Belinski's interest: a story of the victory of mediocrity over idealism, of the "laugh of Satan" at a young person's naïve faith in life.

Between this praise of Turgenev's first work and his last critical review, Belinski continued to discuss, for the most part with lively approval, all of Turgenev's writings as they appeared. It was inevitable that the critic of the new "realism" would find in Turgenev's first distinctive prose work, the early tales from *A Sportsman's Sketches* (*Zapiski Okhotnika*), many admirable qualities: "accurate observation; deep thought, called up from the secret places of Russian life; a fine and elegant irony, beneath which so much feeling is concealed — all this shows that the author, besides having a creative gift, is a son of our time, who bears in his breast all its sorrows and questions."

If in his last article, "A View of Russian Literature for 1847," Belinski described Turgenev as a writer who "does not possess a talent for pure creation, [who] cannot create characters and place them in such relations to one another as to form thereby novels and stories," who "would hardly be successful in faithfully creating a character the like of whom he had not met in actuality" — if in this the critic seems less than prophetic about the future creator of Bazarov, the basis of his judgment must have pleased even Turgenev: "He must always stand upon the ground of reality."

The breadth of Belinski's literary interests and critical views is nowhere more apparent than in his assessment of the varied display of literary works produced during the latter forties. In diverse ways these works, written by young authors of great promise, gave explicit form to the human protest which Belinski continued to declare. The frustrations of the emotional life in Herzen's *Who Is to Blame?* (*Kto vinovat?*) (1845); the indictment of romantic love and romantic revery in Druzhinin's *Polinka Saks* (1847); the defense of womanhood in Herzen's *Thieving Magpie* (*Soroka-Vorovka*) (1846); the sympathetic portrayal of peasant life and sorrow in Grigorovich's *The Village* (*Derevnia*) (1846) and *Poor Anton* (*Anton Goremyka*) (1847), and in Turgenev's *Khor and Kalinych* (1847); the obscure drama of humanity among the insulted and injured in Dostoevski's *Poor Folk*

(1845) — all were sure to excite Belinski's enthusiastic approval.
But his reviews of Russian literature for 1846 and for 1847 show
that he was not correspondingly quick to elevate these works to
first artistic rank merely as a reward for the vividness with which
they illustrated his own ideological positions. Thus it is not
enough that Dostoevski's *Poor Folk* gives convincing expression
to the humanity of the downtrodden; the structure of the work of
art is still of primary importance; and here the author should have
cut his work by a tenth and cleared out his unnecessary repeti-
tions of the same words and phrases. Similarly Grigorovich's tale,
The Village, for all its faithful description of peasant life, belongs
to notable creations of the year 1846 in "light literature"; and the
author would have done better to work in scattered sketches than
to have attempted a story. Mere realism is not enough to make a
work of art: Dostoevski's *Mr. Prokharchin* is impressive more as
the account of an actual mystifying experience than as a work of
art, in which it is the artist's duty to create and illuminate an
organic unity which can be observed simultaneously from many
angles. Fidelity to reality is not enough to make an artist; and not
every disciple of the Natural School can hope to equal the genius
of its master, Gogol. Nor is the "negative direction" of the
Natural School more than a road to a greater destination: namely,
the habit of truth in art, which when the time comes will also
know how to paint "positive manifestations of life."

In these last essays, Belinski gave his Hail and Farewell to more
than one new literary talent arising from the generation which
was to succeed him. Of these an eminent name, as the succeeding
years would make it, was that of Ivan Goncharov, whose first
novel, *A Common Story* (*Obyknovennaia istoriia*), appeared in
1847. It is Belinski's critique of this famous novel which best shows
that, for all his frequent exhibitions of critical tolerance and acumen, he was still the creature of his own doctrine.

It might have been predicted that Belinski would seize upon
Goncharov's novel as a depiction of his own moral evolution.
The defeat of empty idealism in young Alexander Aduev, the
triumph over him of the world of "reality," was certain to call
forth Belinski's vigorous approval. So insistent is he, indeed, that
this is the whole theme of the book, that he simply refuses

to credit the weighty qualifications introduced by the author of the novel. It is true that Goncharov, with doubtful artistic wisdom, confined his major qualifications to a brief Epilogue. But the events of the Epilogue shape the entire meaning of the novel. For in it the author's model of the new "realistic" man of the forties, Peter Aduev, is observed heading into moral bankruptcy. Belinski blandly recognizes here "a lesson for persons of sober character," that "evidently passions too are necessary for human nature to be complete"; but his interpretation is fundamentally unchanged by the crucial breakdown in the life of the hard-driving, worldly-wise Peter Aduev.

An objective reading of *A Common Story*, supplemented by the remarks about the book which the author included in an 1879 essay entitled *Better Late than Never* (*Luchshe pozdno, chem nikogda*), suggests that Goncharov intended to write a *Fathers and Sons* of the thirties and forties, a tragedy of the generations. Mainly by reason of a fundamental structural incongruity, that intention was realized with only partial success. But it must still be conceded that in the story of Alexander and Peter, each shares equally in the final tragedy; not only Alexander's dreams and ideals have come to ruin, but Peter's selfish practicality likewise. It is this ambiguity of meaning (however inadequately achieved) that Belinski refused to respect because his private moral system found its equilibrium elsewhere. He preferred to cry about the book to Botkin, saying, "What a fearful blow it is to romanticism, revery, sentimentalism, provincialism!" [40] rather than to listen to the much less categorical voice of its author speaking through his work.

Belinski's movement, in his last appraisals of individual authors and individual works, between critical objectivity and doctrinaire opinion, reflects a similar movement in his critical theory during the last years of his life. His theoretical effort, especially as reflected in his final "View of Russian Literature for 1847," was to reconcile a recognition of the integrity of the work of art with an increasing insistence that art perform a social function. It was perhaps inevitable that whatever balance he might succeed in striking for a while was sure to rest on a precarious foundation. From time to time his personal correspondence seems even to confess that in his private mind the balance does not seem worth maintaining. As early as 1843 he wrote, in a complaint against the censorship, "About art you can gabble as you please, but about the real thing — i.e., about morals and morality — there's no use wasting time and energy." [41] By December of 1847 he had advanced to the point of announcing: "I no longer require any more poetry and artistry than is necessary to keep a story true; that is, to keep it from degenerating into allegory or taking on the character of a dissertation. . . The chief thing is that it should call forth questions, that it should have a moral effect upon society. If it achieves that goal even entirely without poetry and artistry, for me it is *none the less* interesting, and I do not read it but devour it. . . Of course, if a story raises issues and has a moral effect on society along with a high order of artistry, it is thereby all the better in my opinion. Nevertheless the important thing with me is the substance and not the decoration. Let a story be ever so artistic, if it has nothing to say . . . *je m'en fous.* I know that I take a one-sided position, but I do not wish to change it and I feel sorrow and pity for those who do not share my opinion." [42]

His public statements are much less blunt. Much of the theoretical discussion contained in "A View of Russian Literature for 1847" is devoted to showing that the surest road for Russian literature lies between the extremes of art-for-art's-sake and pure didacticism. The former "is essentially the dangerous extreme of another dangerous extreme: namely, of art as didactic, educative, cold, dry, dead, the productions of which are nothing but rhetorical exercises on assigned themes. Without any doubt art must above all remain art, while being at the same time the expression of the spirit and direction of society at a particular period. With whatever beautiful ideas a poem is filled and however effectively it deals with contemporary problems, if there is no poetry in it, it can contain neither beautiful ideas nor any problems, and all that can be noted in it is perhaps a good intention badly carried out. . . It is impossible to violate the laws of art with impunity."

That Belinski was not always as willing as such formal statements suggest to respect the work of art as an end in itself was primarily a result of his redefinition of the function of art. "In

our age art and literature, more than ever before, have become
the expression of social questions, because in our time these questions have become more familiar, more accessible to all, clearer,
a common concern of the first order, at the head of all other
questions." Increasingly, in Belinski's thought, art had become
a means to an end: a means either to the *expression* of society or
to its *enlightenment*. For all his occasional praise of the literary
artist and the effective literary work, his major enthusiasms were
more and more attracted to the cause of moral protest which he
demanded that art declare. By the very urgency of the public
mission which he assigned to art, he threatened the precarious
integrity of the artist. He thereby revealed his growing doubt in
the capacity of spontaneous and objective art to advance and to
celebrate the cause of human dignity to which he had so fervently
dedicated himself.

B*elinski* was so placed in time and circumstance that he took for his own the major questions and the major conflicts of a generation. And so central did the figure of Belinski come to be and so influential was his activity as a critic that the fate of these contemporary concerns came to depend heavily upon the outcome of his personal ideological drama.

A primary intellectual concern of Belinski's generation was with the problems of a native culture in Russia and of a native literature in which that culture might find its expression and its celebration. Belinski's first articles only added one more statement of a realization commonly shared: that Russian culture and Russian literature both suffered from a brokenness of native traditions, which left Russian intellectual life open to the dangers of uncreative imitation of the West, at one extreme, and of an unenlightened nationalism, at the other extreme. The problem for Russian literature was to become an expression of native life while at the same time avoiding a narrow provincialism.

Meanwhile the main intellectual tradition to which the young Russian intelligentsia of the twenties and thirties turned for direction was a German romantic conception of art and society which offered both advantages and disadvantages for a Russian philosophy of national self-expression. The chief value of that tradition was that it carried a conception of the particular national culture as the individualization of a universal life of nature and of humanity. Belinski for one was quick to assimilate that thought, which runs through all his critical writing from the "Literary Reveries" of 1834 to the "View of Russian Literature for 1847." The major disadvantage of German romantic idealism was that it provided no help in the justification of the Russian reality which Russian literature was obliged to portray. On the contrary, as Belinski's early career and later recapitulations show, the tradition of philosophic idealism, mediated mainly through Schelling, only helped to isolate the Russian intellectual from the Russian actuality against which he was already all too eager to turn his back.

It is this need for taking a systematic attitude toward the reality of Russian life that can be seen at the center of each of Belinski's major ideological positions. Under the guidance of Schelling and Fichte, his hope was to transcend that reality; under Hegel, to rationalize it; by the device of "sociality" and "negation," to attack it. At each stage a tension is maintained between the ideal and the real, between art and life. At no point is Belinski tempted to allow an uncritical acceptance of Russian life as it exists before his eyes, in his own world of daily hardship. By virtue of some ideological scheme, reality must be conceptualized, accounted for, justified; and the function of literature must be defined within the context of that justification. If the reality of social and cultural life is only the mundane manifestation of a transcendent "eternal idea," then the artist can rise above the disharmony of the visible world and make of art a creation of the Absolute. If the national life is only one facet of an all-embracing rational reality, then it does not require the ordering service of art, and art and society can each go its separate road in the assurance that all cultural activity is rational. If, however, the only rational reality is the universal progress of humanity which evolves behind the appearance of the visible world, then the work of the artist is to bring into national life the enlightenment of a universal humanity whereby the national life may be judged and elevated.

No justification of reality can be stable if reality itself is consistently felt to be unacceptable. Hence the history of recurring collapse in Belinski's intellectual pilgrimage, at least until his arrival at an ideological position which, far from requiring acquiescence, found its basis in a belligerent critique of the world of things as they are. Even this final conceptualization is, of course, a form of idealism — of a kind which, instead of looking upward to a transcendent Absolute, looks ahead in time. Belinski never succeeded in reconciling himself to the reality of Russian life. Even his so-called "reconciliation" was in effect an ideological superstructure raised over existence as he knew it — and not very solidly built, as witness its early and disastrous disintegration. In the battle with reality which continued throughout his career, Belinski's major move was from the effort to make Russian life acceptable toward the conviction that acceptance would be treason to the cause of humanity.

Meanwhile Belinski's criticism of literary works constituted a kind of running illustration of his ideological positions. This should not be taken to mean that he put a subordinate value upon the work of literary art. Rather it shows how firm was the connection he forged between art and ideology and how crucial was the function which he assigned the artist to perform in Russian society. If his private philosophizing, such as the private correspondence reveals, had found no issue in the judgments which his professional work required him to pass upon the achievements of Russian literature, then there would be reason to conclude that he had put literature in a subordinate place. Belinski's avid concern for the function of literature in society is proved by the fact that his writing, both private and professional, is all of a piece: what he experienced in his most intimate moods and reflections ultimately made its public appearance in his published criticism.

That Belinski's ideological development worked to shape his critical theory is an obvious conclusion to be drawn from the foregoing discussion. He emerges at the end of a personal ideological evolution with a theory of art in many ways antithetical to the theory with which he began. In 1835 he took as the chief question of all critical judgment: "Is this work really artistic? Is this author really a poet?" Whereas in 1844 he saw the "poet-artist" Pushkin as the member of "a school of art whose day has . . . passed." This dramatic shift in emphasis from an initial to a final position is made understandable only by the progress of a personal idealism which filled the intervening years.

It must also be remembered, however, that one important influence in the shaping of Belinski's ideological positions was the evolving literature itself. The bond which tied literary criticism to ideology also tied ideology to literature. In this regard a remarkable fact is apparent: that each of Belinski's three major "periods" is intruded upon by a major artist who could be fitted only with difficulty into the critic's current scheme. In the period of Schellingesque idealism, it was the "realist" Gogol who arrived to be announced; of Hegelian reconciliation with reality, Lermontov; of "negation," Pushkin. These three, the principal literary figures of Belinski's day, agreed least easily with his philosophy. That fact alone gives reason to suspect that they helped to disintegrate his philosophical positions; for he was too perceptive a critic to let their significance go unexplained. At the worst, he distorted his aesthetic critique of their work in order to preserve his system.

This willingness to impose his philosophy upon the work of literary art resulted, as has been said, not from indifference to art but, on the contrary, from an unfailing respect for the function of art. That respect was the heritage of a tradition carried already in Belinski's day by other members of the young intelligentsia: a tradition, mainly drawn from German sources, which carried an uncommonly high regard for the literary work, particularly as an expression of cultural self-consciousness. Always for Belinski, the work of literary art is more than a merely enjoyable or even merely utilitarian act. He constantly expresses contempt for those who would turn literature "into a trade, a form of relaxation, an innocent pastime, in a class with card games and dancing." For him, as for his generation, the success of the work of literary art was of critical importance. From the beginning Belinski's earnest question was: Have we a literature? For the successful emergence of a coherent literature registered the success of the whole cultural endeavor to which the intelligentsia of the twenties and thirties were dedicated: the cultural autonomy, the moral justification, the intellectual enlightenment of Russian national life. Literature was taken seriously because it articulated the most serious concerns of national destiny.

Belinski's progress, furthermore, is not from a greater to a lesser respect for literature; perhaps his respect even increases.

Literature came to be even more than the articulation of a national cultural life: to it was assigned the active function of molding the national culture. The artist as the conscience of his time and of his society "does not imitate life but competes with it." Literature as the expression of universal humanity does much more than paint pictures of national life; it brings a human criticism and a human enlightenment to the national life. "Only in its sphere do we cease to be Ivans and Peters and become simply persons." By fortifying the bond of human solidarity, literature performs a service within the national economy, of unifying the separated factions and classes that have lost their ties with each other. Thus harmony in social life can be promoted by the good services of literature. Indeed, "in speaking of progress in the cultivation of our society, we are speaking of the success of our literature, for our culture is the immediate effect of our literature upon the understanding and the morals of society."

Such a directive function in society can be performed, to be sure, by a literature which consists in nothing else than the portrayal of life as it is. Belinski knew the moral meaning of the unmoralistic work of art. At one time he agreed that "morality in a work should consist in the complete absence of any claim on the part of the author to a moral or immoral purpose. Facts speak louder than words; a true portrayal of moral disorder is more powerful than any sallies against it. Yet do not forget that such portrayals are true only when they are devoid of conscious purpose." But he proved the vulnerability of that doctrine of objectivity by laying less and less emphasis upon its importance, until at last he seemed almost to be denying it. By the increasing pressure of the conviction that art has a historical mission to perform, that it must deal with the questions of the day, that it is properly defined as "thought in the form of images" — by this the morality of objectivity came to be suppressed in favor of a more explicit assignment of moral and social obligation to the artist.

If the moral function in society which Belinski finally required the writer to assume tended to discourage the spontaneity of true art, at least he could still claim to have preserved a deep conviction of the significance of art. In a period when the demand for an independent literature threatened to turn Russian literature into a work of narrow provincialism, decked out in an artificial display of local color, Belinski was wise enough to call literature to a larger task, which at length became that of the representation of humanity. At no time did he lose sight of a supranational understanding of "national character" in literature. Even his Westernism was always balanced by a demand that only the humanity of the West was useful to Russia, who should repudiate all borrowings, whether from Europe or from Asia, which did not advance the progress of a universal humanity.

There was never any danger that Belinski's critical theory would fail to ascribe a large enough purpose to the activity of art. The danger was rather that he should become altogether too ambitious, too earnest, too explicit in the moral demands which he laid upon the artist. By the very dignity of the purpose which he called upon art to serve, he sobered and disheartened the unpredictable, exultant nonchalance of the creative passion.

In the history of criticism in modern Russia, it was left to Belinski's more intransigent successors to draw extreme "utilitarian" conclusions about the proper function of Russian literature. Not Belinski but the increasing urgency of national problems is responsible for this evolution. Yet it is true that he stands as the original spokesman of a critical doctrine whereby every cultural activity, and mainly that of literature, is ultimately judged by its service to a common good. By the very success of his effort to give meaning to an emerging modern literature, he helped to impose an encumbering moral constraint upon it. Precisely that one good service which he devoted his life to performing has worked, by the paradox of history, toward the occasional furthering of unfortunate consequences.

Notes

Chapter I: Introductory

1. Marc Ickowicz, *La Littérature à la lumière du matérialisme historique* (Paris, 1929), p. 23.
2. *Ibid.*, p. 208.
3. J.-M. Guyau, *L'Art au point de vue sociologique*, 2nd ed. (Paris, 1889), p. 21.
4. Georgi V. Plekhanov, *Iskusstvo i obshchestvennaia zhizn* (Moscow, 1922), p. 28.
5. Leon Trotski, *Literature and Revolution* (New York, 1925). Trotski's argument is a classic example of the contention that art should remain more or less free in order to be socially more serviceable.
6. *Ibid.*, pp. 218–228.
7. Mikhail Lifshitz, *The Philosophy of Art of Karl Marx* (New York, 1938), p. 60.
8. Karl Marx, *Das Kapital*, 3rd ed. (Hamburg, 1883), p. 4; *Theorien über den Mehrwert* (Berlin, 1923), I, 381–382.
9. Lifshitz, p. 74.
10. Karl Marx, "Einleitung," *Zur Kritik der politischen Oekonomie*, 4th ed. (Stuttgart, 1919), p. xlix.
11. *Ibid.*, pp. xlix–l.
12. Lifshitz, p. 44.
13. Ivan I. Ivanov, *Istoriia russkoi kritiki* (St. Petersburg, 1900), IV, 396–397.
14. Pavel V. Annenkov, "Zamechatelnoe desiatiletie (1838–1848)," *Literaturnye vospominaniia* (Leningrad, 1928), pp. 315–316.
15. Vissarion G. Belinski, "Nikitenko, Rech o kritike; statia I" (1842), *Polnoe sobranie sochineni Belinskogo*, ed S. A. Vengerov, 11 vols. (St. Petersburg, 1900–1917), VII, 294. (In succeeding references this edition will be referred to as *Works*.)
16. Ivan S. Turgenev, "Vospominaniia o Belinskom" (1868), *Polnoe sobranie sochineni* (St. Petersburg, 1898), XII, 25; N. G. Chernyshevski, "Ocherki Gogolevskogo perioda russkoi literatury," *Polnoe sobranie sochineni* (St. Petersburg, 1906), II, 1–276.
17. Iuli Aikhenvald, "Belinski," *Siluety russkikh pisatelei*, 3rd ed. (Moscow, 1917), III, 1–15.

Chapter II: Russian Reality and German Idealism

1. Prince P. A. Viazemski, "Zamechaniia na kratkoe obozrenie russkoi literatury 1822-go goda"(1823), *Polnoe sobranie sochineni*, ed., Count S. D. Sheremetev (St. Petersburg, 1878), I, 103.
2. From Peter I. Chaadaev, "Lettre première" (1829) of the "Lettres sur la philosophie de l'histoire," in *Sochineniia i Pisma*, ed. M. Gershenzon (Moscow, 1913–1914), I, 74–93.
3. See Mme de Staël, *De l'Allemagne* (1810).
4. Ivan V. Kireevski, "Obozrenie russkoi slovesnosti za 1829 god" (1830), *Polnoe sobranie sochineni*, ed. M. Gershenzon (Moscow, 1911), II, 27.

5. Dmitri Venevitinov, "Neskolko myslei v plan zhurnala" (ca. 1827), *Polnoe sobranie sochineni*, ed B. V. Smirenski (Moscow–Leningrad, 1934), p. 217.

6. *Ibid.*, p. 220.

7. Kondrati F. Ryleev, "Neskolko myslei o poezii" (1825), *Sochineniia i Perepiska*, ed. P. A. Efremov, 2nd ed. (St. Petersburg, 1874), pp. 197–202.

8. Vissarion G. Belinski, "Literaturnye mechtaniia," *Works*, I, 383.

9. Nikolai I. Nadezhdin, "O nastoiashchem zloupotreblenii i iskazhenii Romanticheskoi Poezii," in *Works* of Belinski, I, 524.

10. Kireevski, "Obozrenie," 38.

11. Ivan V. Kireevski, "Nechto o kharaktere poezii Pushkina" (1828), *Polnoe sobranie sochineni*, ed. M. Gershenzon (Moscow, 1911), II, 13.

12. Prince Vladimir F. Odoevski, "Predislovie" to *Russkie Nochi*, ed. S. A. Tsvetkov (Moscow, 1913), p. 8.

13. This point is suggested by Dmitry I. Cizevsky — in his *Gegel v Rossii* (Paris, 1939), p. 239 — who enumerates the new fields of interest toward which leading figures were turning by the forties.

14. The argument of Venevitinov's article cited in Note 5 above.

15. Friedrich Karl von Moser, "Von dem deutschen Nationalgeist" (1765), in Paul Kluckhohn, *Die Idee des Volkes* (Berlin, 1934), p. 2.

16. Johann Gottlieb Fichte, "Achte Rede: 'Was ein Volk sei, in der höhern Bedeutung des Worts, und was Vaterlandsliebe,'" *Reden an die deutsche Nation* (1808), *Werke; Auswahl in sechs Bänden*, ed. F. Medicus (Leipzig, 1911), V, 492, 495.

17. Friedrich Wilhelm Joseph Schelling, *Ueber das Verhältniss der bildenden Künste zu der Natur, Sämmtliche Werke* (1. Abtheilung; Stuttgart and Augsburg, 1856–1861), VII, 301.

18. Alexander Herzen, *Byloe i Dumy* (Leningrad, 1946), p. 215.

19. A. I. Koshelev, *Zapiski* (n.p., n.d.), p. 32.

Chapter III: Belinski — Arrival (1811–1834)

1. These traits are listed by D. S. Mirsky, *History of Russian Literature*, ed. F. J. Whitfield (New York, 1949), p. 322.

2. From D. P. Ivanov, "Vospominaniia o Belinskom," *Moskovskie Vedomosti*, 1861, no. 135; cited in A. N. Pypin, *Belinski, ego zhizn i perepiska*, 2nd ed. (St. Petersburg, 1908), p. 6, note 2.

3. As quoted in Pypin, p. 13.

4. Beginning of review of the poetry of A. Koptev, Petersburg, 1834; in *Sobranie sochineni V. G. Belinskogo*, K. Soldatenkov and N. Shchepkin, eds., 12 vols. (Moscow, 1859–1867), I, 436–437.

5. Alexander Herzen, *The Memoirs of Alexander Herzen*, parts I and II, tr. J. D. Duff (New Haven, 1923), p. 122.

6. K. F. Bachmann, *Die Kunstwissenschaft in ihrem allgemeinen Umrisse dargestellt* (Jena, 1811). Chistiakov, a co-founder and secretary of the "literary evenings," was at this time making a translation of Bachmann which Nadezhdin later reviewed in 1832 in *The Telescope* (review reproduced in Belinski's *Works*, I, 531 ff.).

7. Belinski's "Introduction" to the play. *Works*, I, 35–36.

8. Ivanov-Razumnik, "Vissarion Grigorevich Belinski: kritiko-biograficheski ocherk," *Sobranie sochineni Belinskogo*, 3 vols. (St. Petersburg, 1911), I, xxi.

9. I. I. Panaev, *Literaturnye vospominaniia*, 3rd ed. (St. Petersburg, 1888), p. 255.
10. Pypin, p. 395.
11. Panaev, p. 197.
12. Letter to Mikhail Bakunin, March 8, 1843. Pypin, p. 437.
13. Letter to Stankevich, October 2, 1839. *Belinski: Pisma*, ed. E. A. Liatski, 3 vols. (St. Petersburg, 1914), I, 347. (In succeeding references, this work will be listed as *Letters*.)
14. Letter to Botkin, April 8, 1842. Pypin, pp. 408–409.
15. A. L. Volynski, "V. G. Belinski," *Russkie kritiki* (St. Petersburg, 1896), p. 41.
16. Paul Miliukov, *Le Mouvement intellectuel russe* (Paris, 1918), p. 124.
17. *Ibid.*, p. 126.
18. *Ibid.*, p. 130.
19. Letter from Stankevich to Mikhail Bakunin, January 9, 1838. Miliukov, p. 132.
20. Annenkov, pp. 212–214.
21. An incident recounted by Panaev, p. 260.
22. Letter to Nikolai Bakunin, December 9, 1841. Pypin, p. 391.
23. Letter of September 20, 1833. *Letters*, I, 56–57.
24. *V. G. Belinski: Sbornik statei* (Moscow & Petrograd, 1923), pp. 42–43.
25. Letter to Botkin, September 8, 1841. Pypin, p. 381.
26. First article on Pushkin (1843).
27. Said by Belinski to Goncharov. Ivan Goncharov, "Zametki o lichnosti Belinskogo," in M. K. Kleman and N. K. Piksanov, *V. G. Belinski v vospominaniiakh sovremennikov* (Leningrad, 1929), pp. 311–312.
28. Letter to Botkin, January 16, 1841. Pypin, p. 353.
29. Letter of February 6, 1843. *Ibid.*, p. 430.
30. Goncharov, p. 306.
31. Cizevsky, p. 133.
32. Letter to Botkin, April 13, 1842. *Letters*, II, 297.
33. J. Billig, *Der Zusammenbruch des Idealismus bei den russischen Romantikern* (Berlin, 1930), p. 3.
34. Letter to Panaev, August 10, 1838. Pypin, p. 222.
35. Letter to Botkin, February 28, 1847. *Ibid.*, p. 520.

Chapter IV: The Argument of The Telescope

1. Letter of May 21, 1833. Pypin, p. 69.
2. Page 115.
3. Letter to Belinski, November 26, 1834. Pypin, p. 100, note 1.
4. Pypin, p. 77.
5. P. Prozorov, "Belinski i Moskovski universitet v ego vremia," in Kleman and Piksanov, p. 90.
6. Johann Gottfried von Herder, German philosopher, poet, and critic (1744–1803). Belinski's access to Herder is difficult to document, but it is established that both Stankevich and Nadezhdin were familiar with Herder. Stankevich's private correspondence contains numerous references to him (W. Setschkareff, *Schellings Einfluss in der russischen Literatur der 20er und 30er Jahre des XIX. Jahrhunderts*, Leipzig, 1939, p. 4); and in at least one review of recent German philosophy Nadezhdin gives a short account

of Herder's *Kalligone*—which ends, however, with the remark that "[Herder's] voice had no influence upon the history of *aesthetics*" (review of Chistiakov's translation of Bachmann's *Teoriia iziashchnikh iskusstv*, in Belinski's *Works*, I, 534).

Chapter V: The Rationalization of Reality

1. Quoted from Pavel Annenkov, *Biografiia Stankevicha* (Moscow, 1857), p. 134; in Pypin, p. 141.
2. Fichte, *Werke*, I, 217–274.
3. Letter to Mikhail Bakunin, August 16, 1837. *Letters*, I, 121.
4. Panaev, p. 157.
5. Letter to Mikhail Bakunin, August 14, 1838. *Letters*, I, 219.
6. Letter to Mikhail Bakunin, August 16, 1837. *Letters*, I, 121–122.
7. Letter to Mikhail Bakunin, November 1, 1837. Pypin, p. 163.
8. Letter to Mikhail Bakunin, August 16, 1837. *Letters*, I, 122–123.
9. Letter to Mikhail Bakunin, June 20, 1838. *Letters*, I, 193.
10. Letter to Mikhail Bakunin, October 12–24, 1838. *Letters*, I, 259–306.
11. *Ibid.*, p. 276.
12. Letter to Mikhail Bakunin, written between November 15 and 21, 1837. *Letters*, I, 167–168.
13. Quoted in letter from Koltsov to Belinski, February 21, 1838. N. K. Piksanov, *Letopis zhizni Belinskogo* (Moscow, 1924), pp. 68–69.
14. Letter to Mikhail Bakunin, November 1, 1837. Pypin, p. 170.
15. Letter to Mikhail Bakunin, August 16, 1837, Pypin, p. 179.
16. Letter to Mikhail Bakunin, June 20, 1838. Pypin, pp. 190–191.
17. Letter from Belinski to Stankevich, April 19, 1839. *Letters*, I, 318.
18. Letter from Belinski to Stankevich, September 29–October 8, 1839. *Letters*, I, 347.
19. Cizevsky, pp. 119, 128.
20. Aikhenvald, p. 5.
21. Belinski, review of Fonvizin and Zagoskin, *Works*, IV, 8.
22. Annenkov, pp. 221–223.
23. Panaev, pp. 196–197.
24. Annenkov, p. 236.
25. Belinski, review of Fonvizin and Zagoskin, *Works*, IV, 11.
26. *Ibid.*, p. 8.
27. Panaev, p. 198.
28. I. I. Ivanov, IV, 549.
29. Letter to Botkin, September 5, 1840. *Letters*, II, 159.
30. *Ibid.*, p. 158.
31. Letter to Botkin, June 13, 1840. *Letters*, II, 129.
32. Letter to Botkin, February 9, 1840. *Letters*, II, 33.
33. Letter to Botkin, April 16, 1840. *Letters*, II, 110.
34. Letter to Botkin, February 24, 1840. *Letters*, II, 60–61.
35. Letter to Botkin, February 9, 1840. *Letters*, II, 32.
36. Letter to Botkin, December 16, 1839. *Letters*, II, 15–16.
37. Letter to Botkin, October 4, 1840. *Letters*, II, 163–165.
38. Letter to Botkin, October 25, 1840. *Letters*, II, 172.
39. Letter to Botkin, March 1, 1841. *Letters*, II, 212–214.

Chapter VI: The Human Protest (*1841–1848*)

1. Quoted in A. I. Herzen, *Polnoe sobranie sochineni i pisem*, ed. M. K. Lemke (St. Petersburg, 1919), XIII, 246–247.
2. Letter to Botkin, April 20, 1842. *Letters*, II, 307.
3. Letter to the Bakunin sisters, March 8, 1843. *Letters*, II, 350.
4. Letter to Botkin, September 8, 1841. *Letters*, II, 266–267.
5. *Ibid.*, p. 266.
6. *Ibid.*
7. Letter to Botkin, February 17, 1847. *Letters*, III, 174.
8. Letter to Annenkov, February 15, 1848. *Letters*, III, 338–339.
9. Letter to N. A. Bakunin, April 6, 1841. *Letters*, II, 232.
10. Letter to Herzen, January 26, 1845. *Letters*, III, 87.
11. Letter to Botkin, June 28, 1841. *Letters*, II, 247.
12. Letter to Botkin, September 8, 1841. *Letters*, II, 268.
13. *Ibid.*, p. 262.
14. Letter to Botkin, December 11, 1840. *Letters*, II, 186.
15. Letter to Botkin, February 6, 1843. *Letters*, II, 334.
16. Belinski as quoted in Annenkov, p. 436.
17. From *Za rubezhem*; quoted in Vengerov, p. 281.
18. Annenkov, p. 291.
19. Letter to N. A. Bakunin, November 7, 1842. *Letters*, II, 318.
20. *Ibid.*, pp. 327–328.
21. Letter to N. A. Bakunin, August 24, 1843. *Letters*, II, 378.
22. Letter to Botkin, September 8, 1841. *Letters*, II, 269.
23. Annenkov, p. 304.
24. Letter to Botkin, March 1, 1841. *Letters*, II, 212.
25. Letter to Botkin, February 17, 1847. *Letters*, III, 174.
26. Letter to K. D. Kavelin, November 22, 1847. *Letters*, III, 300.
27. Hegel, *Aesthetik*, in *Sämtliche Werke*, XIV, 319–581.
28. Letter to M. V. Orlova, October 13, 1843. *Letters*, III, 57.
29. Annenkov, p. 585.
30. Letter from Belinski in Nikolaev to his wife, July 30, 1846. *Letters*, III, 146.
31. Letter of February 6, 1843. Pypin, p. 432.
32. See Hegel, "Die romantische Kunstform," in *Aesthetik*, pp. 120–240; especially "Das Ende der romantischen Kunstform," pp. 228–240.
33. Letter to Frolov, October 17, 1845. Kleman and Piksanov, p. 197.
34. *Bumagi A. A. Kraevskogo*, ed. I. A. Bychkov (St. Petersburg, 1893), p. 138.
35. Pypin, p. 537.
36. Letter of June 20, 1847, written from Frankfurt, Germany, to N. I. Prokopovich. *Pisma N. V. Gogolia*, ed. V. I. Shenrok (St. Petersburg, n.d.), III, 496.
37. Letter written ca. June 20, 1847, from Frankfurt, Germany. *Pisma*, III, 491–492.
38. Letter written not much before August 10, 1847. *Pisma*, IV, 33.
39. Letter dated from Ostend, August 10, 1847. *Pisma*, IV, 46.
40. Letter to Botkin, March 17, 1847. *Letters*, III, 199.
41. Letter to Botkin, February 6, 1843. *Letters*, II, 331.
42. Letter to Botkin, December, 1847. *Letters*, III, 324.

Index